PEREGRINE BOOKS

THE NECESSITY OF ART

A MARXIST APPROACH

On the first appearance in English of what is probably one of the most influential books on art to be published since the war, Kenneth Tynan wrote:

'In this challenging new Pelican Ernst Fischer, the Austrian poet and critic, surveys the whole history of artistic achievement through Marxist eyes.

'People have always needed art: but why have they needed it? And what shaped the forms whereby they satisfied their need? Fischer's answers to these questions should be as voraciously studied and debated here as they have been on the Continent.

'The book abounds in signs that Fischer is an empirical rather than a doctrinaire Marxist; you never feel he is tailoring his reactions to fit a thesis. "A new art," he says, "does not come out of doctrines but out of works. Aristotle did not precede . . . Homer, Hesiod, Aeschylus and Sophocles; he derived his aesthetic theories from them."

'Marxism has long needed an Aristotle; and in Ernst Fischer I suspect it has found its man.'

Ernst Fischer was born in Austria in 1899 and joined the Communist Party in 1934. He founded and was chief editor of *Neues Osterreich*, but from 1959 until his death in 1972 he confined himself to the literary field. His publications include *Art Against Ideology*, *Marx in His Own Words* and *Lenin in His Own Words*, the latter two in collaboration with Franz Marek.

ERNST FISCHER

THE NECESSITY OF ART
A Marxist Approach

TRANSLATED BY
ANNA BOSTOCK

Penguin Books

Penguin Books Ltd, Harmondsworth, Middlesex, England
Penguin Books, 625 Madison Avenue, New York, New York 10022, U.S.A.
Penguin Books Australia Ltd, Ringwood, Victoria, Australia
Penguin Books Canada Ltd, 2801 John Street, Markham, Ontario, Canada L3R 1B4
Penguin Books (N.Z.) Ltd, 182–190 Wairau Road, Auckland 10, New Zealand

—

Von der Notwendigkeit der Kunst first published by
Verlag der Kunst, Dresden, 1959
This translation first published in Pelican Books 1963
Reprinted 1964, 1970, 1971
Reissued in Peregrine Books 1978

—

Copyright © Ernst Fischer, 1959
Translation copyright © Anna Bostock, 1963
All rights reserved

—

Made and printed in Great Britain
by Cox & Wyman Ltd,
London, Reading and Fakenham
Set in Monotype Garamond

CONTENTS

CHAPTER ONE

THE FUNCTION OF ART

'POETRY is indispensable – if I only knew what for.' With this charmingly paradoxical epigram Jean Cocteau has summed up the necessity of art – as well as its questionable role in the late bourgeois world.

The painter Mondrian spoke of the possible 'disappearance' of art. Reality would, he believed, increasingly displace the work of art, which was essentially a substitute for an equilibrium that reality lacked at present. 'Art will disappear as life gains more equilibrium.'

Art as a 'life substitute', art as a means of putting man in a state of equilibrium with the surrounding world – the idea contains a partial recognition of the nature of art and its necessity. And since a perpetual equilibrium between man and the surrounding world cannot be expected to exist even in the most highly developed society, the idea suggests, too, that art was not merely necessary in the past but will always remain so.

Yet is art really no more than a substitute? Does it not also express a deeper relationship between man and the world? Indeed, can the function of art be summed up at all in a single formula? Does it not have to satisfy many and various needs? And if, as we reflect upon the origins of art, we become aware of its initial function, has not that function also changed with the changing of society, and have not new functions come into being?

This book is an attempt to answer questions such as these, founded on the conviction that art has been, still is, and always will be necessary.

As a first step we must realize that we are inclined to take an astonishing phenomenon too much for granted. And it is certainly astonishing: countless millions read books, listen to music, watch the theatre, go to the cinema. Why? To say that they seek distraction, relaxation, entertainment, is to beg the question. Why is it distracting, relaxing, entertaining to sink oneself in someone else's life and problems, to identify oneself with a painting or a piece of music or with the characters in a novel, play, or film? Why do we respond to such 'unreality' as though it were reality intensified? What strange, mysterious entertainment is this? And if one answers that we want to escape from an unsatisfactory existence into a richer one, into experience without risk, then the next question arises: why is our own existence not enough? Why this desire to fulfil our unfulfilled lives through other figures, other forms, to gaze from the darkness of an auditorium at a lighted stage where something that is only play can so utterly absorb us?

Evidently man wants to be more than just himself. He wants to be a *whole* man. He is not satisfied with being a separate individual; out of the partiality of his individual life he strives towards a 'fulness' that he senses and demands, towards a fulness of life of which individuality with all its limitations cheats him, towards a more comprehensible, a more just world, a world that *makes sense*. He rebels against having to consume himself within the confines of his own life, within the transient, chance limits of his own personality. He wants to refer to something that is more than 'I', something outside himself and yet essential to himself. He longs to absorb the surrounding world and make it his own; to extend his inquisitive, world-hungry 'I' in science and technology as far as the remotest constellations and as deep as the innermost secrets of the atom; to unite his limited 'I' in art with a communal existence; to make his individuality *social*.

If it were man's nature to be no more than an individual, this desire would be incomprehensible and senseless, for as an individual he would then *be* a whole: he would be all that he was capable of being. Man's desire to be increased and supplemented indicates that he is more than an individual. He feels that he can attain wholeness only if he takes possession of the experiences of others that might potentially be his own. Yet what a man apprehends as his potential includes everything that humanity as a whole is capable of. Art is the indispensable means for this merging of the individual with the whole. It reflects his infinite capacity for association, for sharing experiences and ideas.

And yet: is this definition of art as the means of becoming one with the whole of reality, as the individual's way to the world at large, as the expression of his desire to identify himself with what he is not, perhaps too romantic? Is it not rash to conclude, on the basis of our own near-hysterical sense of identification with the hero of a film or a novel, that this is the universal and original function of art? Does art not also contain the opposite of this 'Dionysian' losing of oneself? Does it not also contain the 'Apollonian' element of entertainment and satisfaction which consists precisely in the fact that the onlooker does *not* identify himself with what is represented but *gains distance* from it, overcomes the direct power of reality through its deliberate representation, and finds, in art, that happy freedom of which the burdens of everyday life deprive him? And is not the same duality – on the one hand the absorption in reality, on the other the excitement of controlling it – also evident in the way the artist himself works? For make no mistake about it, work for an artist is a highly conscious, rational process at the end of which the work of art emerges as mastered reality – not at all a state of intoxicated inspiration.

In order to be an artist it is necessary to seize, hold, and transform experience into memory, memory into expression, material into form. Emotion for an artist is not everything; he must also know his trade and enjoy it, understand all the rules, skills, forms, and conventions whereby nature – the shrew – can be tamed and subjected to the contract of art. The passion that consumes the dilettante *serves* the true artist: the artist is not mauled by the beast, he tames it.

Tension and dialectical contradiction are inherent in art; not only must art derive from an intense experience of reality, it must also be *constructed*, it must gain form through objectivity. The free play of art is the result of mastery. Aristotle, so often misunderstood, held that the function of drama was to purify the emotions, to overcome terror and pity, so that the spectator identifying himself with Orestes or Oedipus was liberated from that identification and lifted above the blind workings of fate.

The ties of life are temporarily cast off, for art 'captivates' in a different way from reality, and this pleasant temporary captivity is precisely the nature of the 'entertainment', of that pleasure which is derived even from tragic works.

Bertolt Brecht said of this pleasure, this liberating quality of art:

> Our theatre must encourage the thrill of comprehension and train people in the pleasure of changing reality. Our audiences must not only hear how Prometheus was set free, but also train themselves in the pleasure of freeing him. They must be taught to feel, in our theatre, all the satisfaction and enjoyment felt by the inventor and the discoverer, all the triumph felt by the liberator.

Brecht points out that in a society of class struggle, the 'immediate' effect of a work of art demanded by the ruling aesthetic is to suppress the social distinctions within the audience and thus, while the work is being enjoyed, create a collective not divided into classes but 'universally human'. On the other hand, the function of 'non-Aristotelian drama' which Brecht advocated was precisely to divide the audience by removing the conflict between feeling and reason which has come about in the capitalist world.

> Both feeling and reason degenerated in the age of capitalism when that age was drawing towards its end, and entered into a bad, unproductive conflict with each other. But the rising new class and those who fight on its side are concerned with feeling and reason engaged in *productive* conflict. Our feelings impel us towards the maximum effort of reasoning, and our reason purifies our feelings.

In the alienated world in which we live, social reality must be presented in an arresting way, in a new light, through the 'alienation' of the subject and the characters. The work of art must grip the audience not through passive identification but through an appeal to reason which demands action and decision. The rules according to which human beings live together must be treated in the drama as 'temporary and imperfect' so as to make the spectator do something more productive than merely watch, stimulating him to think along with the play and finally to pass judgement: 'That's not the way to do it. This is very strange, almost unbelievable. This must stop.' And so the spectator, who is a working man or woman, will come to the theatre to

. . . enjoy, as entertainment, his own terrible and never-ending labours by which he is meant to support himself, and suffer the shock of his own incessant change. Here he may *produce himself* in the easiest fashion: for the easiest fashion of existence is in art.

Without claiming that Brecht's 'epic theatre' is the only possible kind of militant working-class drama, I quote Brecht's important theory as an illustration of the dialectic of art and of the way that the function of art changes in a changing world.

The *raison d'être* of art never stays entirely the same. The function of art in a class society at war within itself differs in many respects from its original function. But nevertheless, despite different social situations, there is something in art that expresses an unchanging truth. It is this that enables us, who live in the twentieth century, to be moved by prehistoric cave paintings or very ancient songs. Karl Marx described the epic as the art form of an undeveloped society,* and then added:

But the difficulty is not in grasping the idea that Greek art and epos are bound up with certain forms of social development. It rather lies in understanding why they still constitute with us a source of aesthetic enjoyment and in certain respects prevail as the standard and model beyond attainment.

He then offered the following answer:

Why should the social childhood of mankind, where it had obtained its most beautiful development, not exert an eternal charm as an age that will never return? There are ill-bred children and precocious children. Many of the ancient nations belong to the latter class. The Greeks were normal children. The charm their art has for us does not conflict with the primitive character of the social order from which it had sprung. It is rather the product of the latter, and is rather due to the fact that the unripe social conditions under which the art arose and under which alone it could appear can never return.

Today we may doubt whether, compared with other nations,

* *A Contribution to the Critique of Political Economy*, Kegan Paul, Trench Trübner, 1904.

the ancient Greeks were 'normal children'. Indeed, in another connexion Marx and Engels themselves drew attention to the problematic aspects of the Greek world with its contempt for work, its degradation of women, its eroticism reserved solely for courtesans and boys. And since then we have discovered a great deal more about the seamy side of Greek beauty, serenity, and harmony. Today our ideas of the ancient world coincide only in part with those of Winckelmann, Goethe, and Hegel. Archaeological, ethnological, and cultural discoveries no longer allow us to accept classical Greek art as belonging to our 'childhood'. On the contrary, we see in it something relatively late and mature, and in its perfection in the age of Pericles we detect hints of decadence and decline. Many works, once praised as 'classical', by the sculptors who followed the great Phidias, a large number of those heroes, athletes, discus throwers, and charioteers, strike us today as empty and meaningless compared with Egyptian or Mycenean works. But to go deeper into these matters would take us too far from the question Marx raised and the answer he supplied.

What matters is that Marx saw the time-conditioned art of an undeveloped social stage as a *moment of humanity*, and recognized that in this lay its power to act beyond the historical moment, to exercise an eternal fascination.

We may put it like this: all art is conditioned by time, and represents humanity in so far as it corresponds to the ideas and aspirations, the needs and hopes of a particular historical situation. But, at the same time, art goes beyond this limitation and, within the historical moment, also creates a moment of humanity, promising constant development. We should never underestimate the degree of continuity throughout the class struggle, despite periods of violent change and social upheaval. Like the world itself, the history of mankind is not only a contradictory discontinuum but also a continuum. Ancient, apparently long-forgotten things are preserved within us, continue to work upon us – often without our realizing it – and then, suddenly, they come to the surface and speak to us like the shadows in Hades whom Odysseus fed with his blood. In different periods, depending on the social situation and the

needs of rising or declining classes, different things which
have been latent or lost are brought again into the light of day,
awakened to new life. And just as it was no coincidence that
Lessing and Herder, in their revolt against the feudal and the
courtly and all the contemporary false posturings with wig and
alexandrine, discovered Shakespeare for the Germans, so it is
no coincidence that, today, Western Europe in its denial of
humanism and in the fetish-like character of its institutions
reaches back to the fetishes of pre-history and constructs false
myths to hide its real problems.

Different classes and social systems, while developing their
own ethos, have contributed to the forming of a universal
human ethos. The concept of freedom, though it always corresponds to the conditions and aims of a class or a social system,
nevertheless tends to grow into an all-embracing idea. In the
same way, constant features of mankind are captured even in
time-conditioned art. In so far as Homer, Aeschylus, and
Sophocles mirrored the simple conditions of a society based on
slavery, they are time-bound and out of date. But in so far as, in
that society, they discovered the greatness of man, gave artistic
form to his conflicts and passions, and hinted at his infinite
potentiality, they remain as modern as ever. Prometheus bringing fire to earth, Odysseus in his wanderings and his return,
the fate of Tantalus and his children, all this has preserved its
original power for us. Though we may regard the subject-
matter of *Antigone* – a struggle for the right to give honourable
burial to a blood relative – as archaic, though we may need
historical commentaries in order to understand it, the figure of
Antigone is as moving today as it ever was, and so long as there
are human beings in the world they will be moved by her
words: 'My nature is to join in love, not hate.' The more we
come to know of long-forgotten works of art, the clearer
become their common and continuous elements, despite their
variety. Fragment joins fragment to make humanity.

We may conclude from a constantly growing wealth of
evidence that art in its origins was *magic*, a magic aid towards
mastering a real but unexplored world. Religion, science, and
art were combined in a latent form – germinally as it were – in

magic. This magic role of art has progressively given way to the role of illuminating social relationships, of enlightening men in societies becoming opaque, of helping men to recognize and change social reality. A highly complex society with its multiple relationships and social contradictions can no longer be represented in the manner of a myth. In such a society, which demands literal recognition and all-embracing consciousness, there is bound to be an overwhelming need to break through the rigid forms of earlier ages where the magic element still operated, and to arrive at more open forms – at the freedom, say, of the novel. Either of the two elements of art may predominate at a particular time, depending on the stage of society reached – sometimes the magically suggestive, at other times the rational and enlightening; sometimes dreamlike intuition, at other times the desire to sharpen perception. But whether art soothes or awakens, casts shadows or brings light, it is never merely a clinical description of reality. Its function is always to move the *whole* man, to enable the 'I' to identify itself with another's life, to make its own what it is not and yet is capable of being. Even a great didactic artist like Brecht does not act purely through reason and argument, but also through feeling and suggestion. He not only confronts the audience with a work of art, he also lets them 'get inside' it. He himself was aware of this, and pointed out that it was not a problem of absolute contrasts but of shifting stresses. 'In this way the emotionally suggestive or the purely rationally persuasive may predominate as a means of communication.'

True as it is that the essential function of art for a class destined to change the world is not that of *making magic* but of *enlightening* and *stimulating action*, it is equally true that a magical residue in art cannot be entirely eliminated, for without that minute residue of its original nature, art ceases to be art.

In all the forms of its development, in dignity and fun, persuasion and exaggeration, sense and nonsense, fantasy and reality, art always has a little to do with magic.

Art is necessary in order that man should be able to recognize and change the world. But art is also necessary by virtue of the magic inherent in it.

CHAPTER TWO

THE ORIGINS OF ART

ART is almost as old as man. It is a form of work, and work is an activity peculiar to mankind. Marx defined work in these terms:

> The labour process is ... purposive activity ... for the fitting of natural substances to human wants; it is the general condition requisite for effecting an exchange of matter between man and nature; it is the condition perennially imposed by nature upon human life, and is therefore independent of the forms of social life – or, rather, it is common to all social forms.*

Man takes possession of the natural by transforming it. Work is transformation of the natural. Man also dreams of working magic upon nature, of being able to change objects and give them new form by magic means. This is the equivalent in the imagination of what work means in reality. Man is, from the outset, a magician.

Tools

Man became man through tools. He made, or produced, himself by making or producing tools. The question of which came first – man or tool – is therefore purely academic. There is no tool without man and no man without tool; they came into being simultaneously and are indissolubly linked to one another. A relatively highly developed living organism became man by working with natural objects. By being put to such use, the objects became tools. Here is another definition of Marx's:

> The instrument of labour is a thing, or a complex of things, which the worker interposes between himself and the subject-matter of his labour, and one which serves as the conductor of his activity. He makes use of the mechanical, physical, and chemical properties of things as means of exerting power over other things, and in order to

* *Capital*, Allen & Unwin, 1928.

make these other things subservient to his aims. Leaving out of consideration the gathering of ready-made means of subsistence, such as fruits, for which purpose man's own bodily organs suffice him as the instrument of labour, the object of which the worker takes direct control is not the subject-matter of labour but the instrument of labour. Thus nature becomes an instrument of his activities, an instrument with which he supplements his own bodily organs, adding a cubit and more to his stature, scripture notwithstanding.... The use and the fabrication of instruments of labour, though we find their first beginnings among certain other animal species, is specifically characteristic of the human labour process, and for that reason Benjamin Franklin defined man as a 'tool-making animal'.*

The pre-human being which developed into man was capable of such development because it had a special organ, the hand, with which it could grasp and hold objects. The hand is the essential organ of culture, the initiator of humanization. This does not mean that it was the hand alone that made man: nature, and particularly organic nature, does not allow of such simple and one-sided sequences of cause and effect. A system of complicated relationships – a new *quality* – always comes out of a set of diverse reciprocal effects. The passing of certain biological organisms into the tree stage, favouring as it did the development of vision at the expense of the sense of smell; the shrinking of the muzzle, facilitating a change in the position of the eyes; the urge of the creature now equipped with a more acute and more precise sense of vision to look in all directions, and the erect body posture conditioned by this; the release of the front limbs and the enlargement of the brain due to erect body posture; changes in food and various other circumstances acted together to create the conditions necessary for man to become man. But the directly decisive organ was the hand. Thomas Aquinas was already aware of the unique significance of the hand, that *organum organorum*, and expressed it in his definition of man: '*Habet homo rationem et manum!*' And it is true that the hand released human reason and produced human consciousness.

Gordon Childe points out in *The Story of Tools*:†

* ibid.

† V. Gordon Childe, *The Story of Tools*, Cobbett Publishing Co., 1944.

Men can make tools because their forefeet have turned into hands, because seeing the same object with both eyes they can judge distances very accurately and because a very delicate nervous system and complicated brain enables them to control the movements of hand and arm in precise agreement with and adjustment to what they see with both eyes. But men do not know by any inborn instinct how to make tools nor how to use them; that they must learn by experiment – by trial and error.

A system of completely new relationships between one species and the entire rest of the world came about through the use of tools. In the working process, the natural relationship of cause and effect was, as it were, reversed; the anticipated, foreseen effect became, as 'purpose', the legislator of the working process. That relationship between events which, as the problem of 'finality' or 'final cause', has driven many a philosopher to distraction, was developed as a specially human characteristic. But what is this problem? Let me quote once more one of Marx's clear definitions:

We have to consider labour in a form peculiar to the human species. A spider carries on operations resembling those of a weaver; and many a human architect is put to shame by the skill with which a bee constructs her cell. But what from the very first distinguishes the most incompetent architect from the best of bees, is that the architect has built a cell in his head before he constructs it in wax. The labour process ends in the creation of something which, when the process began, already existed in the worker's imagination, already existed in an ideal form. What happens is not merely that the worker brings about a change of form in natural objects; at the same time, in the nature that exists apart from himself, he realizes his own purposes, the purpose which gives the law to his activities, the purpose to which he has to subordinate his own will.

This is a definition of the nature of work by the time it has reached the wholly developed, wholly human stage. But a long distance had to be travelled before this final form of work, and therefore the final humanization of the pre-human being, was attained. Action determined by purpose – and from this the birth of the mind, the birth of consciousness as the prime creation of man – was the outcome of a long and laborious process. Conscious existence means conscious action. The original existence of man was that of a mammal. Man *is* a mammal, but he begins to *do* something different from all other mammals. The animal, too, acts from 'experience', that is to say from a system of conditioned reflexes; that is what we call the 'instinct' of an animal. The organism which developed into man acquired a new kind of experience leading to a unique turning-point, insignificant though it may have appeared at the outset: the experience that nature can be used as a means to achieve a man's purpose. Every biological organism is in a state of metabolism with the surrounding world – it continually gives and takes something to and from that world. But this taking is always done directly, without an intermediary. Only human work is *mediated metabolism*. The means has preceded the purpose; the purpose is revealed by the use of the means.

Biological organs are not replaceable. True, they were formed as a result of adaptation to the conditions of the outside world; but an animal must manage with the organs it has got and make the best of them. Yet the instrument of labour, which is outside the organism, *is* replaceable, and a primitive one can be discarded in favour of a more efficient one. With a natural organ, the question of efficiency does not arise: it is as it is, the animal must live as its organs will allow and adapt itself to the world in the manner in which its organs are adapted to it. But a being which uses a non-organic object as an instrument need not adapt its requirements to that instrument – on the contrary, it can adapt the instrument to the requirements. The question of efficiency cannot exist until this possibility arises.

Man's discovery that some instruments are more or less useful than others, and that one instrument can be replaced by another, led inevitably to the discovery that an imperfect, available instrument can be made more efficient: i.e., that an instrument need not be taken directly from nature but can be *produced*. The discovery of greater or lesser efficiency in itself requires a special observation of nature. Animals, too, observe nature, and natural causes and effects are reflected or reproduced in animal brains. But, for an animal, nature is a given fact, unchangeable by any effort of will, like its own organism. Only the use of non-organic, replaceable, and changeable means makes it possible to observe nature in a new context, to foresee, anticipate, and bring about events.

There is a fruit to be picked from a tree. The pre-human animal reaches for this fruit, but its arm is too short. It tries everything but cannot reach the fruit; and after repeated, frustrated attempts it is forced to give up and turn its attention elsewhere. But if the animal takes a stick, its arm is extended; and if the stick is too short, it can choose a second and a third one, until at last it has found one that will do the job. What is the novel element here? It is the discovery of varying possibilities and the ability to choose among them, hence the ability to compare one object with another and decide on its greater or lesser efficiency. With the use of tools, nothing is, in principle, any longer impossible. One only needs to find the right tool in order to reach – or accomplish – what was previously out of reach. A new power over nature has been gained, and this power is *potentially unlimited*. In this discovery lies one of the roots of magic and, therefore, of art.

In the brain of the higher mammal, an inherited reciprocal effect has been established between the centre which signals hunger – the organism's lack of necessary foodstuffs – and the centre which is stimulated by the sight or smell of a piece of food, say a fruit. Stimulation of one of the centres involves the other; the mechanism is delicately attuned: when the animal is hungry, it looks for a piece of food. Through the interposition of the stick – the instrument for fetching the fruit down from the tree – a new contact between the brain centres is established. This new cerebral process is then strengthened by being repeated countless times. At first the process takes place in one direction only: the stimulation of the 'hunger–fruit' complex is extended to include the centre which, putting it crudely, reacts to 'stick'. The animal sees the fruit it wants and looks for the stick which is associated with it. This can scarcely yet be called thinking: the element of purpose characteristic of the working process – which is the creator of thought – is still absent. So far it is not yet the purpose of the stick to fetch down the fruit: the stick is only the instrument for doing so. This one-sided process, this inter-dependent working of the brain centres, can, however, be reversed if the mechanism is refined by frequent repetition. In other words, it may then go like this: here is the stick; where is the fruit it can fetch down?

Thus the stick – the instrument – becomes the starting-point. The means now serves the end, which is to fetch down the fruit. The stick is not just a stick; something new has been magically added to it: a *function*, which now becomes its essential content. And so the instrument commands more and more interest; it is examined for its greater or lesser ability to fulfil its purpose; the question arises whether it might not be made more serviceable, more useful, more efficient, whether it cannot be changed so that it may better fulfil its purpose. Spontaneous experimentation – 'thinking with the hands', which precedes all thought as such – now begins gradually to be transmuted into purposeful reflection. This reversal of the cerebral process is the beginning of what we call work, conscious being, conscious doing, anticipation of the result by cerebral activity. All thought is nothing other than a shortened form of experimentation transferred from the hands to the brain, the innumerable preceding experiments having ceased to be 'memory' and having become 'experience'.

A different example may illustrate this idea more conveniently. Gordon Childe writes in *The Story of Tools*:

The oldest surviving or *eolithic* tools are made of stone – those used by Pekin man of quartz deliberately collected and carried to his cave. A tiny fraction only were artificially shaped, better to serve Sinanthropic needs. Even these lack any standardized form and might have served many purposes. One feels indeed that on each occasion when a tool was required, a handy piece of stone was adapted to meet the moment's need. So such might be called *occasional tools*. . . .

Standardized tools emerge. Among the great mass of miscellaneous occasional tools of very varied shapes of lower paleolithic times, two or three forms stand out that occur again and again with very little variation at a vast number of sites in Western Europe, Africa, and Southern Asia; their makers have obviously been trying to copy a recognized standard pattern.

This tells us something of extreme importance. Man, or the pre-human being, had originally discovered – while gathering objects – that, for instance, a sharp-edged stone can take the place of teeth and fingernails for tearing apart, cutting up, or crushing a prey. A stone that happens to be available becomes an *occasional tool* and is thrown away again when it has fulfilled its momentary function. Anthropomorphous apes also sometimes use such occasional tools. Through repeated use, a firm connexion is established in the brain between the stone and its usefulness; the creature about to become man begins to collect and preserve such useful stones, although no definite function or concrete purpose is as yet connected with each stone. The stones are all-purpose instruments to be experimented with from case to case and tested for their specific applications. Two things eventually emerge from these repeated and varied experiments, from this 'thinking with the hands': first, the discovery that stones of a particular shape are more useful than others, that it is possible to choose among the accidental offerings of nature, the reference to purpose thus becoming more and more dominant; secondly, the discovery that it is unnecessary to wait for these offerings, because nature can be corrected. Water, climate, the elements can shape a stone so that it becomes 'handy'. When once the almost-man took natural objects 'in hand' and began to use them as instruments, his active hands discovered that he could shape and alter a stone himself, and from this discovery they learned that there is inherent in a piece of flint the *potentiality* of becoming sharp-edged and, hence, a useful tool.

There is nothing in the least mysterious about this potentiality – it is not a 'power' with which the stone is endowed, nor did it, like Pallas Athene, spring from a creative consciousness. On the contrary, creative consciousness developed as a late result of the *manual* discovery that stones could be broken, split, sharpened, given this shape or that. The shape of the hand-axe, for instance, which nature produces from time to time, was useful for a number of activities: and so gradually man began to copy nature. In producing tools like this he was not obeying any 'creative idea' but only imitating; his models were stones he had found and whose usefulness he had experimentally tested. He produced on the basis of his experience of nature. And the thing that was in his mind in this early productive phase was not the end result of an idea; he was not carrying out a plan; what he saw before him was a very real hand-axe, and he tried to make another like it. He was not implementing an idea but imitating an object. Only very gradually did he depart from the natural model. By using the tool and constantly experimenting with it, he slowly began to make it more useful and more efficient. Efficiency is older than purpose; the hand, rather than the brain, has long been a discoverer. (One need only watch a child untying a knot: it does not 'think', it experiments; only gradually, out of the experience of its hands, comes the comprehension of how the knot is tied and how best to disentangle it.)

The anticipation of a result – the setting of a purpose to a working process – only comes after concentrated manual experience. It is the result of constantly referring back to the natural product and of many more or less successful tests. It is not looking ahead but looking back that produces the idea of purpose. Conscious doing and conscious being developed in work and along with work, and only at a later stage did a clearly recognized purpose emerge to give each tool a specific shape and character. It took man a long time to rise above nature and confront it as a creator.

When he did, the difference was this. His brain no longer reflected things merely literally: because of the experience of work, it could now also reflect natural laws and reckon with *causal* relationships. (It could recognize, for instance, that muscular energy can be transferred to a tool and thence to the working object, or that friction produces heat.) Man took the place of nature. He did not wait to see what nature would offer him: more and more he forced it to give him what he wanted. He made nature more and more his servant. And out of the increasing usefulness of his tools, out of their increasingly specific character, out of their increasingly successful adaptation to the human hand and the laws of nature, out of their increased *humanization*, objects were created which could not be found in nature. More and more the tool lost its resemblance to any natural object. The function of the tool displaced its original nature-likeness, and as a result of growing efficiency its purpose – the intellectual anticipation of what it could do – became more and more important. This transformation of the nature of work could only occur when work had reached a comparatively highly developed stage.

Language

The development towards work demanded a system of new means of expression and communication that would go far beyond the few primitive signs known to the animal world. But work did not only demand such a system of communication, it also encouraged it. Animals have little to communicate to each other. Their language is instinctive: a rudimentary system of signs for danger, mating, etc. Only in work and through work do living beings have much to say to one another. Language came into being together with tools.

In many theories of the origins of language, the important role played by work and tools is overlooked or underestimated. Even Herder, who uncovered factors of immense importance in his revolutionary studies and his brilliant argument against the 'divine origin' of language, failed to see the significance of work to the birth of language. Anticipating the results of later research, this is how he described his view of prehistoric man:

Man stepped into the world: what an ocean immediately raged around him! With how great an effort did he learn to distinguish! to recognize his various senses! to rely only on the senses he had recognized!

Herder foresaw what science was later to confirm: that prehistoric man saw the world as an indeterminate whole, and that he had to learn to separate, differentiate, select whatever was most essential to his own life among the world's many and complex features, so as to establish the necessary equilibrium between the world and himself, its inhabitant. Herder is right when he says:

Even as an animal, man already had language. All the wild and violent, all the painful sensations of his body as well as all the strong passions of his soul were expressed directly through screams, calls and wild, inarticulate sounds.

These animal means of expression are undoubtedly an element of language. 'Traces of these natural sounds can still be heard in all original languages.' Yet Herder understood that these natural sounds were 'not the actual roots' of language, 'but only the juices that nourished those roots'.

Language is not so much a means of expression as of communication. Man gradually became familiar with objects 'and gave them names taken from nature, imitating nature as far as possible by their sounds. . . . It was a pantomime in which body and gestures collaborated'. Original language was a unity of words, musical intonation, and imitative gesture. Herder says:

The first vocabulary was compiled from the world's sounds. The idea of the thing itself was still suspended between the action and its perfomer: the *tone* had to indicate the *thing*, just as the *thing* supplied the *tone*; and so *verba* became *nomina* and *nomina* became *verba*. . . .

Early man did not yet make a clear distinction between his activity and the object to which it was related; the two formed an indeterminate unity. Although the word became a *sign* (no longer a simple expression or imitation), a multitude of concepts were still included within this sign; pure *abstraction* was only gradually arrived at.

Sensory objects were sensorily described – and from how many sides, how many aspects they could be described! And so language was full of weird, undisciplined word inversions, full of irregularities and quirks. Images were reproduced as images wherever possible, and in this way a wealth of metaphors, idioms and sensory nouns was created.

Herder recalls that the Arabs had fifty words for a lion, two hundred for a snake, eighty for honey, and more than a thousand for a sword: in other words, sensory nouns had not yet been completely concentrated into abstractions. Ironically he asked those who believed in the 'divine origin' of language:

Why did God invent a superfluous vocabulary?

And again:

A primitive language is rich because it is poor – its inventors had no plan and so could not afford to economize. Is God, then, supposed to be the idle inventor of the most undeveloped languages?

And finally:

This was living language. The huge repertoire of gestures establish-ed, as it were, the rhythm and the limits which confined the spoken words, and the great wealth of definitions which lay in the actual vocabulary replaced the art of grammar.

The more man gathers experience, the more he comes to know different things from different aspects, the richer his language must become.

The more often his experiences and his new characteristics are repeated in his own mind, the firmer and more fluent his language. The more he distinguishes and classifies, the more ordered his language.

Alexander von Humboldt developed and refined Herder's revolutionary discoveries, although in some respects he gave Herder's materialist and dialectical ideas an idealistic, meta-physical twist. Humboldt declared that language was 'image and sign at the same time, not quite the product of the impres-sion created by objects nor yet quite the product of the speaker's arbitrary will'. He also noticed with equal clarity that thought was 'not only dependent on language in general, but also, to a certain extent, determined by each separate language'. This brings to mind a remark of Goethe's: 'Language makes people far more than people language.' Emphasizing the importance of articulation (without which there can be expression but never language), Humboldt arrived at an almost mystical conclusion:

In order that a man may truly understand even a single word – understand it not only as a sensory impulse but as an articulate sound defining a concept – the whole of language must already be present within his mind. Nothing is separate in language; each and every element declares itself as part of the whole. Natural as it is to assume that language was formed gradually, its actual invention can only have occurred in a single instant. Man is man through language alone – but in order to invent language he must have been man already.

We may agree with this view in so far as it anticipates the idea that prehistoric man saw the world as an indeterminate whole, out of which he created language bit by bit. But the dialectical solution of the problem – man becoming man together with work and language, so that neither man on the one hand nor work and language on the other came first – this is lacking in Humboldt. He merely hinted at a dialectical process and dressed it up in idealistic terms: 'The mutual dependence of thought and work makes it clear that languages are not really means of presenting an already known truth but, rather, of discovering a truth unknown until that moment.' Certainly it is a matter of progressive discovery; but what is discovered is reality rather than 'truth': reality created in work and through work, in language and through language.

Of the many linguistic theories that have been formulated since Humboldt's day, I should like to mention Mauthner's, for it is an exciting one. Mauthner stated that language grew out of 'reflex sounds'; but, he added, imitation was also an essential element in language. Not only human reflex sounds (of joy, pain, surprise, etc.) but also other natural sounds are imitated in language. At the same time language must not be regarded simply as imitation – it must also be articulate, i.e. it must become a sign bearing only remote 'conventional' resemblance to the object itself, even in cases where actual sounds are imitated. All onomatopoeia is, in reality, a matter of signs and metaphors. In these metaphors there is often a mysterious concordance with real things, so that one is *reminded* by them of lightning, thunder, death, and so forth. 'This, or something very like it, must have been the formative stage of language,' Mauthner wrote, 'not the legendary "roots of language" we hear about.'

The twofold nature of language as a means of communication and expression, as an image of reality and as a sign for it, as a 'sensory' grasping of the object and as an abstraction, has always been a special problem of poetry as distinct from every-day prose. The desire to go back to the source of language is inherent in poetry. Schiller wrote:

Language puts everything in terms of reason, but the poet is supposed to put everything in terms of the imagination; poetry calls for vision, language supplies only concepts. This means that the word robs the object it is meant to represent of its sensual and individual nature and thrusts a property of its own upon it, a generalness that is foreign to the original object; and so the object either fails to be represented freely or is not represented at all, but only described.

In every poet there is a longing for an original, 'magic' language.

In a completely different context from Mauthner, who believed 'reflex sounds' to be the origin of language, Pavlov defined language as a system of conditioned reflexes and signals. Mauthner's reflex sounds are elemental, inarticulate means of expressing joy, pain, etc. Pavlov's conditioned reflexes are events within living nervous systems corresponding to events occurring in regular sequence in the outside world (e.g. a dog salivates on hearing the sound of a gong which has become the signal for feeding time). Here a word is a signal and language is a most highly developed system of signals. When discussing the nature of hypnosis, Pavlov wrote:

For the human being the word as such is, of course, just as real a conditioned reflex as all the other conditioned stimuli man has in common with the animal world, but over and above that, the word is more significant and comprehensive than any other stimulus; indeed there are no stimuli at all in the animal world that can even remotely compare with the human word, quantitatively or qualitatively. . . . The wide range and rich content of the word explains why so many different activities can be suggested to a hypnotized person, activities which may involve both the external and the internal world of that person.

Without work – without his experience of using tools – man could never have developed language as an imitation of nature and as a system of signs to represent activities and objects, i.e.

as an *abstraction*. Man created articulate, differentiated words not only because he was a being capable of pain, joy and surprise, but also because he was a *working* being.

Language and gesture are very closely interconnected. Bücher deduced from this that speech evolved from reflex actions of the vocal organs incidental to the muscular efforts involved in the use of tools. As the hands became more finely articulated, so did the vocal organs, until the awakening consciousness seized on these reflex actions and elaborated them into a system of communication. This theory emphasizes the significance of the collective working process, without which systematic language could never have been formed out of the primitive signals, mating cries, and cries of fear that were the raw material of language. The animal's signal notifying some change in the surrounding world developed into a linguistic 'work reflex'. This was the turning-point from passive adaptation to nature to active changing of nature.

Among hundreds of 'occasional tools' of various kinds it is impossible to distinguish each by a specific sign; but if a few standard tools are evolved, then a specific sign – or name, or *noun* – becomes both possible and necessary. When a standard tool is imitated time and time again, something completely new happens. All the imitations, made to resemble each other, contain within them the same prototype; the prototype, in its function, its form, and its usefulness to man, recurs again and again. There are many hand-axes yet there is only one. Man can take any of the imitations instead of the original hand-axe because all of them serve the same purpose, produce the same effect, and are similar or identical in their function. It is always this tool that is meant, and none other; it does not matter which particular sample of the standard hand-axe happens to come to hand. Thus the first abstraction, the first conceptual form, was supplied by the tools themselves: prehistoric man 'abstracted' from many individual hand-axes the quality common to them all – that of being a hand-axe; in so doing, he formed the 'concept' of a hand-axe. He did not know he was doing it. But he was nevertheless creating a concept.

Making alike

Man made a second tool resemble the first and by so doing produced a new, equally useful and equally valuable tool. Thus 'making alike' grants man a *power over objects*. A stone which was previously useless acquires value because it can be made like a tool and so recruited into man's service. There is something magical in this process of 'making alike'. It brings mastery over nature. Other experiences confirm this strange discovery. If you imitate an animal, make yourself look and sound like that animal, you can attract it and stalk it more closely, and the prey falls more easily into your hands. Here again, resemblance is a weapon of power, of magic. The primeval instinct of the species adds still greater force to the discovery. This instinct makes all animals suspicious of those of their own species that deviate from the normal, the albinos, the freaks of every kind. They are instinctively seen as rebels against the tribe. They have to be killed or driven out of the natural collective. Thus similarity is universally significant, and prehistoric man – who had by now acquired practice in comparing, choosing, and copying tools – began to attach enormous significance to *all* similarity.

Advancing from one similarity to another, he arrived at an ever-increasing wealth of abstractions. He began to give a single name to whole groups of related objects. It is the nature of such abstractions that they often (though not always) express a real connexion or relationship. All tools of a particular kind, it will be remembered, came out of the first tool of which they were an imitation or copy. The same is true of many other abstractions: the wolf, the apple, etc. Nature is reflected in newly discovered connexions. The brain no longer reflects each tool as something unique; nor does it reflect every seashell in that way. A *sign* has been evolved to cover all tools, all seashells, all objects and living beings of the same kind. This process of concentration and classification in language makes it possible to communicate more and more freely concerning the outside world, which man shares with all other men.

The same is true of processes and, above all, of the social process of work. The emerging human collective repeated the same process many hundreds of times. Gradually it found a sign – a means of expression – for this collective activity. It may be assumed that this sign came out of the working process itself, reflecting some sort of rhythmic regularity. It indicated a specific activity and was so directly connected with it that its sound or sight immediately excited all the brain centres in which the activity was registered. Such signs were of immense importance to early man; they had an organizing function within the working group or collective, because they meant the same thing to all its members.

A collective working process requires a coordinating working rhythm. This working rhythm is supported by a more or less articulate unison chant. Such chants, be they the English 'Heave-o-ho!', the German '*Horuck*', or the Russian '*E-uch-nyem*', are essential to the rhythmic accomplishment of the work. In such refrains, which have a certain magic attaching to them, the individual preserves the collective even if he is working outside it. George Thomson (with whose splendid work *Studies in Ancient Greek Society: The Prehistoric Aegean** I was unfortunately not acquainted until this book was practically finished, so that I can only refer to it in passing) analyses the ancient work songs as a combination of refrain (collective unison chant) and individual improvisation. He quotes *inter alia* a chant recorded by the Swiss missionary Junod. A Thonga boy breaking stones at an African roadside for his European employers sang:

> '*Ba hi shani-sa, ehé!*
> *Ba ku hi hlupha, ehé!*
> *Ba nwa makhofi, ehé!*
> *Ba nga hi njiki, ehé!*'
>
> They treat us badly, *ehé!*
> They are hard on us, *ehé!*
> They drink their coffee, *ehé!*
> And give us none, *ehé!*

The first word-signs for working processes – chanted

* Lawrence & Wishart, London, 1949.

sounds providing a uniform rhythm for the collective – were probably, at the same time, command signals intended to arouse the collective to action (in the same way as a warning cry produces an immediate passive reaction, e.g. the flight of the herd). Thus there was *power* stored up in every linguistic means of expression – power over both man and nature.

It was not only a question of prehistoric man believing that words were a powerful tool – they actually did increase his control over reality. Language not only made it possible to coordinate human activity in an intelligent way and to describe and transmit experience and, therefore, to improve working efficiency: it also made it possible to single out objects by attaching particular words to them, thus snatching them out of the protective anonymity of nature and bringing them under man's control. If I make a notch in a tree growing in a forest, that tree is doomed. I can instruct someone else to go and cut down the tree I have marked; he will recognize it by the notch. A name given to an object has a similar effect: the object is *marked*, distinguished from other objects, and delivered into the hands of man. There is an unbroken line of development from the making of tools to the marking and taking possession of those tools (by a notch, say, or a series of notches or a primitive ornament) and thence to their naming, whereby they become recognizable and graspable to every member of the collective.

The standard tool was reproduced by imitation, which singled it out by a kind of magic from among other stones, hitherto subject to the power of nature alone. It may be assumed that the first linguistic means of expression, too, were nothing other than imitation. The word was regarded as largely identical with the object. It was the means of grasping, comprehending, mastering the object. We find that nearly all primitive races believed that by naming an object, a person, a demon, they would exercise some power over them (or else incur their magic hostility). This idea is preserved in innumerable folk tales: we need only remember the sly Rumpelstiltskin with his triumphant

> Glad I am that no one knows
> That Rumpelstiltskin I am styled.

A means of expression – a gesture, an image, a sound, or a word – was as much a tool as a hand-axe or a knife. It was only another way of establishing man's power over nature.

Thus a being evolved out of nature through the use of tools and through the collective working process. This being – man – was the first to confront the whole of nature as an active *subject*. But before man became his own subject, nature had become an *object* for him. A *thing* in nature becomes an object only through becoming the object, or the instrument, of work. A subject–object relationship occurs only through work.

The gradual separation of man from nature, whose creature he remains although he faces it more and more as a creator, gave rise to one of the most profound problems of human existence. It is perfectly reasonable to speak of man's 'double nature'. While still belonging to nature, he has created a 'counter-nature' or 'super-nature'. Through his work, he has made a new kind of reality: a reality which is sensory and supra-sensory at one and the same time.

Reality is never an accumulation of separate units existing side by side without connexion. Every material 'something' is interconnected with every other material 'something'; between objects there exists a vast variety of relationships. These relationships are as real as the material objects, and only in their relationships to each other do objects constitute reality. The richer and more complex these relationships become, the richer and more complex is the nature of reality. Let us take an object produced by work. What is it? In terms of mechanical reality it is nothing other than a 'mass' gravitating towards other 'masses' ('mass' itself also being the term for a relationship). In terms of physico-chemical reality it is a fragment of concrete matter composed in a certain way of certain atoms and molecules and subject to certain rules peculiar to those particles. In terms of human and social reality it is a tool, an object of utilitarian value, and, if it is exchanged, it gains an exchange value. Man's new relationships with nature and with his fellow-men have penetrated this fragment of matter and endowed it with a new content and quality which it previously did not possess. And so man, the working being, is the creator of a new reality, a super-nature, whose most extraordinary product is the mind. The working being elevates itself, by work, into a thinking being; thought – i e., mind – is the necessary result of man's mediated metabolism with nature.

By his work, man transforms the world like a magician: a piece of wood, a bone, a flint is fashioned to resemble a model and thereby transformed into that very model; material objects are transformed into signs, names, and concepts; man himself is transformed from an animal into a man.

This magic at the very root of human existence, creating a sense of powerlessness and at the same time a consciousness of power, a fear of nature together with the ability to control nature, is the very essence of all art. The first toolmaker, when he gave new form to a stone so that it might serve man, was the first artist. The first name-giver was also a great artist when he singled out an object from the vastness of nature, tamed it by means of a sign, and handed over this creature of language as an instrument of power to other men. The first organizer who synchronized the working process by means of a rhythmic chant and so increased the collective strength of man was a prophet in art. The first hunter who disguised himself as an animal and by means of this identification with his prey increased the yield of the hunt, the first stone-age man who marked a tool or a weapon by a special notch or ornament, the first chieftain who stretched an animal's skin over a lump of rock or the stump of a tree in order to attract animals of the same kind – all these were the forefathers of art.

The power of magic

The exciting discovery that natural objects could be turned into tools capable of influencing and altering the outside world was bound to lead to another idea in the mind of early man, always experimenting and slowly awakening to thought: the idea that the impossible, too, could be achieved with magic tools – that nature could be 'bewitched' without the effort of work. Overwhelmed by the immense importance of similarity and imitation, he deduced that, since all similar things were identical, his power over nature – by virtue of 'making alike' – could be limitless. The newly acquired power to grasp and control objects, to prompt social activity and bring about events by means of signs, images, and words, led him to expect the magical power of language to be infinite. Fascinated by the power of the will – which anticipates and brings about things that are not yet there but exist only as an idea in the brain – he was bound to ascribe an immensely far-reaching, boundless power to acts of will. The magic of tool-making led inevitably to the attempt to extend magic to infinity.

In Ruth Benedict's book *Patterns of Culture* (Routledge, 1935) there is a good example of the belief that imitation must bring power. A sorcerer on the island of Dobu wants a fatal illness to strike an enemy.

In communicating the spell the sorcerer imitates in anticipation the agony of the final stages of the disease he is inflicting. He writhes upon the ground, he shrieks in convulsion. Only so, after faithful reproduction of its effects, will the charm do its destined work.

And we read further:

The charms themselves are almost as explicit as the action that accompanies them. . . . The following is the incantation for causing gangosa, the horrible disease which eats away the flesh as the hornbill, its animal patron from which the disease is named, eats the tree trunks with its great rending beak:

> Hornbill dweller of Sigasiga
> in the lowana tree top,
> he cuts, he cuts,
> he rends open,
> from the nose,
> from the temples,
> from the throat,
> from the hip,
> from the root of the tongue,
> from the back of the neck,
> from the navel,
> from the small of the back,
> from the kidneys,
> from the entrails,
> he rends open,

> he rends standing.
> Hornbill dweller of Tokuku,
> in the lowana tree top,
> he* crouches bent up,
> he crouches holding his back,
> he crouches arms twined in front of him,
> he crouches hands over his kidneys,
> he crouches head bent in arms twined about it,
> he crouches double twined.
> Wailing, shrieking,
> it† flies hither,
> quickly it flies hither.

Art was a magic tool, and it served man in mastering nature and developing social relationships. It would be wrong, however, to explain the origins of art by this element alone. Every newly formed quality is the result of a set of new relationships, which may sometimes be highly complex. The attraction of shining, gleaming, glittering things (not only for human beings but also for animals) and the irresistible attraction of light may have played their part in the birth of art. Sexual allurement – bright colours, pungent smells, splendid coats and feathers in the animal world, jewels and fine clothes, seductive words and gestures among humans – may have provided a stimulus. The rhythms of organic and inorganic nature – of heartbeat, breathing, sexual intercourse – the rhythmic recurrence of processes or elements of form and the pleasure derived from these, and, last but not least, working rhythms – may have played an important part. Rhythmical movement assists work, coordinates effort, and connects the individual with a social group. Every disturbance of the rhythm is disagreeable because it interferes with the processes of life and work; and so we find rhythm assimilated in the arts as the repetition of a constant, as proportion and symmetry. And, lastly, an essential element of the arts is the fearsome, the awe-inspiring, and that which is supposed to confer power over an enemy. Clearly the decisive function of art was to exert power – power over nature, an enemy, a sexual partner, power over reality, power to strengthen

* The victim.
† The immaterial power of the charm.

the human collective. Art in the dawn of humanity had little to do with 'beauty' and nothing at all to do with any aesthetic desire: it was a magic tool or weapon of the human collective in its struggle for survival.

It would be very wrong to smile at the superstitions of early man or at his attempts to tame nature by imitation, identification, the power of images and language, witchcraft, collective rhythmic movement, and so on. Of course, because he had only just begun to observe the laws of nature, to discover causality, to construct a conscious world of social signs, words, concepts, and conventions, he arrived at innumerable false conclusions and, led astray by analogy, formed many fundamentally mistaken ideas (most of which are still preserved in one form or another in our language and philosophy). And yet, in creating art, he found for himself a real way of increasing his power and enriching his life. The frenzied tribal dances before a hunt really did increase the tribe's sense of power; war paint and war cries really did make the warrior more resolute and were apt to terrify the enemy. Cave paintings of animals really helped to build up the hunter's sense of security and superiority over his prey. Religious ceremonies with their strict conventions really helped to instil social experience in every member of a tribe and to make every individual part of the collective body. Man, the weak creature confronting dangerous, incomprehensible, terrifying Nature, was greatly helped in his development by magic.

The original magic gradually became differentiated into religion, science, and art. The function of mime altered imperceptibly: from imitation intended to bestow magic power it came to replace blood sacrifice by enacted ceremonies. The song to the hornbill on the island of Dobu, which I have quoted, is still pure magic; but when certain Australian aboriginal tribes appear to prepare for an act of blood vengeance while, in fact, appeasing the dead by means of mime, this is already a transition to drama and to the work of art. Another example: Djagga Negroes felling a tree. They call it the sister of the man on whose plot of land it is growing. They represent the preparation for felling as preparations for the sister's wedding.

On the day before the tree is actually felled they bring it milk, beer, and honey, saying '*mana mfu* [departing child], my sister, I give you a husband, he shall marry you, my daughter'. And when the tree has been felled the owner breaks out in lamentations: 'You have robbed me of my sister.' Here the transition from magic to art is clear. The tree is a living organism. By felling it, the members of the tribe prepare for its rebirth, just as initiation and death are regarded as the individual's rebirth out of the maternal body of the collective. It is a performance delicately balanced between serious ceremonial and artistic play; the owner's simulated distress carries echoes of an ancient dread and magical imprecations. Ceremonial rite has been preserved in drama.

The magic identity of man and earth was also at the root of the widespread custom of sacrificing the king. The status of a king originated, as Frazer proved, first and foremost in fertility magic. In Nigeria, kings were at first only the queens' consorts. The queens had to conceive so that the earth might bear fruit. After the men – who were seen as earthly representatives of the moon god – had done their duty, they were strangled by the women. The Hittites sprinkled the blood of the murdered king over the fields and his flesh was eaten by nymphs – the queen's followers, wearing masks of bitches, mares, and sows. As matriarchy developed into patriarchy, the king took over more and more of the queen's power. Wearing female dress and equipped with artificial breasts, he represented the queen. An *interrex* was killed instead of him and finally this *interrex* was replaced by animals. Reality became myth, the magic ceremony became religious enactment, and finally magic itself became art.

Art was not an individual but a collective production, although the first characteristics of individuality began to declare themselves tentatively in the sorcerer. Primitive society meant a dense, close-knit form of collectivism. Nothing was more terrible than to be cast out of the collective and to remain alone. Separation of the individual from the group or tribe meant death; the collective meant life and the content of life. Art in all its forms – language, dance, rhythmic chants, magic ceremonies – was the social activity *par excellence*, common to all and raising all men above nature and the animal world. Art has never wholly lost this collective character, even long after the primitive collective had broken down and been replaced by a society of classes and individuals.

Art and the class society

Stimulated by the discoveries of Bachofen and Morgan, Marx and Engels described the process of disintegration of collective tribal society, the gradual growth of productive forces, the progressive division of labour, the birth of barter trade, the transition to patriarchal rule, and the beginnings of private property, social classes, and the State. Countless scholars have since analysed every detail of this process on the basis of abundant evidence. George Thomson's *Aeschylus and Athens* and *Studies in Ancient Greek Culture* are of immense importance in this field. In ancient Greece, increased labour productivity led to a situation in which labourers, the *demiurgoi*, 'those working for the community', were accepted as part of the community consisting of the chief, the elders, and the land cultivators. The chief was empowered to dispose of any surplus agricultural products. The chiefs received regular tribute. Barter of goods developed imperceptibly out of friendly relations between tribes. Gifts and counter-gifts assumed the character of barter. Chiefs and labourers were the first to discard the bonds of the clan: the former became landowners, the latter organized themselves in guilds. The tribal village was transformed into a city state ruled by the landowners. That was the beginning of class society.

Just as magic corresponded to man's sense of unity with nature, of the identity of all existing things – an identity implicit in the clan – so art became an expression of the beginnings of alienation. The totemistic clan represented a *totality*. The clan totem was the symbol of the immortal clan itself, the ever-living collective from which the individual emerged and to which he returned. The uniform social structure was a 'model' of the surrounding world. The world order corresponded to the social order. Some races call the lowest social unit the *womb*. The social collective is a union of the living and the dead. Father van Wing writes in *Études Bakongo*:

The land belongs, undivided, to the entire tribe, that is to say not only to the living but also – or rather, primarily – to the dead, i.e. the Bakulu. The tribe and the land on which it lives form an indivisible whole, and this whole is ruled by the Bakulu.

G. Strehlow wrote of the Aranda and Loritja tribes in Central Australia:

As soon as a woman knows that she is pregnant, i.e. that a *ratapa* (totem) has entered her, the grandfather of the expected child … goes to a *mulga* tree and cuts off a small *tjurunga* (the secret, hidden totem body that unites the individual with his ancestors and with the universe), on which he carves, with an opossum tooth, signs connected with the totem ancestor or his totem. … The totem, the totem ancestor and the totem descendant, that is to say the performer (who, in the ceremonies, embodies the totem by his ornaments and his mask) appear in the *tjurunga* songs as a single unit. …

The perfect unity of man, animal, plant, stone, and source, of life and death, collective and individual, is a premise of every magic ceremony.

As human beings separated themselves more and more from nature, as the original tribal unity was gradually destroyed by division of labour and property ownership, so the equilibrium between the individual and the outside world became more and more disturbed. Lack of harmony with the outside world leads to hysteria, trances, fits of insanity. The characteristic posture of the maenad or bacchante – the body arched, the head thrown back – is the classic posture of hysteria. In a letter written from prison on 15 February 1932, the great Italian Marxist Antonio Gramsci spoke of the psycho-analytical method, which, he thought, could only be usefully applied to the social elements described in Romantic literature as

the insulted and the injured … who are much more numerous than is traditionally believed. That is to say, applied to persons caught up in the iron contradictions of modern life (to speak only of the present, but every age has had a present in contrast to a past), who cannot, without help, come to terms with those contradictions, overcome them and find a new moral peace and freedom, i.e. they cannot strike a balance between the impulses of the will and the aims to be attained. ...

There are times of crisis in which the contrast between the present and the past assumes extreme forms. The transition from the primitive social collective to the 'iron age' of class society with its small stratum of rulers and its masses of 'insulted and injured' was such a time.

The condition of being 'beside oneself', i.e. of hysteria, is a forcible re-creation of the collective, of world unity. As social differentiation progressed, so, on the one hand, there occurred periods of collective demoniacal possession and, on the other hand, there were individuals (often actually forming associations or guilds) whose social function it was to be possessed or 'inspired'. It is the task of these possessed individuals, both the blessed and the damned, these prophets, sybils, and singers, to restore a disturbed unity and harmony with the outside world. We read in the *Ion* of Plato:

For the epic poets, all the good ones, have their excellence, not from art, but are inspired, possessed, and thus they utter all these admirable poems. So it is also with the good lyric poets; as the worshipping Corybantes are not in their senses when they dance, so the lyric poets are not in their senses when they make these lovely lyric poems. No, when once they launch into harmony and rhythm, they are seized with the Bacchic transport, and are possessed – as the Bacchantes, when possessed, draw milk and honey from the rivers, but not when in their senses.*

God speaks in the possessed, said Plato. God is a name for the collective. The content of demoniacal possession was the collective reproduced in a violent manner within the individual, a sort of mass essence. Thus, in a differentiated society, art developed out of magic precisely as a result of differentiation and of the increasing alienation to which it led.

In a class society the classes try to recruit art – that powerful voice of the collective – into serving their particular purposes. The verbal eruptions of Pythia in her state of ecstasy were very

* Translated by Lane Cooper, Oxford University Press, 1938.

skilfully, very consciously 'edited' by aristocratic priests. Out of the chorus of the collective developed the chorus leader; the sacred hymn became a hymn in praise of the rulers; the clan totem was sub-divided into the aristocracy's gods. Finally the chorus leader with his gift of improvisation and invention developed into a bard, singing without a chorus at the king's court and, later, in the market place. On the one hand we find the Apollonian glorification of power and the *status quo* – of kings, princes, and aristocratic families and the social order established by them and reflected in their ideology as a supposedly universal order. On the other hand there was the Dionysian revolt from below, the voice of the ancient, broken collective which took refuge in secret associations and secret cults, protesting against the violation and fragmentation of society, against the *hubris* of private property and the wickedness of class rule, prophesying the return of the old order and the old gods, a coming golden age of commonwealth and justice. Contradictory elements were often combined within a single artist, particularly in those periods when the old collectivism was not yet too remote and still continued to exist in the consciousness of the people. Even the Apollonian artist, herald of the young ruling class, was not entirely free from this Dionysian element of protest or nostalgia for the old collective society.

The sorcerer in the primitive tribal society was in the most profound sense a representative, a servant of the collective, and his magic power entailed a risk of being put to death if he repeatedly failed to fulfil the collective's expectations. In the young class society the sorcerer's role was shared between the artist and the priest, later to be joined by the doctor, the scientist, and the philosopher. The intimate bond between art and worship was only very gradually loosened, eventually to be discarded altogether. But even after this had happened, the artist remained a representative or spokesman of society. He was not expected to importune his public with his own private affairs; his personality was irrelevant, and was judged only by his ability to echo and reflect common experience, the great events and ideas of his people, his class and his age. This *social*

function was imperative and unchallengeable, just as the sorcerer's had been earlier. The artist's task was to expound the
profound meaning of events to his fellow-men, to make plain
to them the process, the necessity, and the rules of social and
historical development, to solve for them the riddle of the
essential relationships between man and nature and man and
society. His duty was to enhance the self-awareness and life-
awareness of the people of his city, his class, and his nation; to
liberate men, as they emerged from the security of a primitive
collective into a world of division of labour and class conflict,
from the anxieties of an ambiguous, fragmented individuality
and from the dread of an insecure existence; to guide individual
life back into collective life, the personal into the universal; to
restore the lost unity of man.

For man had indeed paid a colossal price for his rise to more
complex and more productive forms of society. As a result of
the differentiation of skills, the division of labour, and the
separation of classes he was alienated, not only from nature,
but from his own self. The complex pattern of society meant
also the breaking-up of human relationships; increasing social
enrichment meant, in many respects, increasing human
impoverishment. Individualization was secretly felt to be a
tragic guilt, the longing for a lost unity was inextinguishable,
the dream of a 'golden age' and an innocent 'paradise' shone
through a dark and distant past. This is not to say that looking
back to utopia was the only or the essential content of poetry
during the development of class society. The opposite motif –
affirmation of new social conditions, praise of 'new gods' – was
also powerfully present. In the *Oresteia* of Aeschylus, for
example, this is the decisive element. All social problems and
conflicts were reflected in literature, usually in the form of some
mythological 'alienation' and with shifting emphasis. Those
who glorified the past as a 'golden age' were usually the
oppressed or disinherited among the poets. Later, with the
decay of the ancient world, the theme was also taken over by
privileged poets (Virgil, Horace, Ovid) and, as in the *Germania*
of Tacitus, used as an argument against the forces of decay. But
the feeling that was present from the outset and came up again

and again during the process of differentiation and class division was the fear of *hubris*, the belief that man had lost all balance and measure and that the birth of individuality inevitably led to tragic guilt.

The individualization of human beings was bound in the end to spread to the arts. This happened when a new social class, that of seafaring traders, came into being – the class that had so much to do with evolving the human personality. The aristocratic landed gentry, those grave-diggers of the old tribal collective, had also thrown up a few personalities, but their natural element was war, adventure, heroism. An Achilles or an Odysseus could only be conceived of away from their native soil: at home they were not individual heroes but merely representatives of their noble families, merely the mortal frame of the eternal landowner, impersonal links in a long chain of ancestors and heirs. The seafaring trader was something very different: a reckless self-made man used to staking his life again and again, and owing no allegiance to the conservative land with its unalterable pattern of sowing and harvest but only to the inconstant, moody, perpetually moving sea that could bring him as low as it had swung him high on the crests of its waves. Everything depended on individual skill, determination, mobility, cleverness – and luck. But the difference went still deeper than that. The landowner and his land did not confront each other as strangers; they were closely bound together, so that a piece of land was almost the extension of its owner's person. Everything came from the earth and was returned to the earth. The trader's relationship with his property was very different. They were *alienated* from each other. It was the very nature of that property not to remain itself but to be constantly exchanged, and therefore transformed. Never in the history of the ancient world – which had regarded the incursions of money into the natural economy as an evil thing – had exchange value triumphed so completely over utility value as it did in the capitalist world. The concrete qualities of the exchanged object – whether it happened to be metal, linen, or spices – became secondary for the merchant; its abstract quality – value – and the most abstract form of property – money – became the essential things. But just because a product was now a commodity, something detached and alien, the merchant's attitude to it was that of a sovereign individual. The depersonalization of property gave him the freedom required to become a personality. In the trading coastal cities of the ancient world we always come across the great merchant prince, the individual 'tyrant', confronting the aristocratic families, defying the traditional privileges, and claiming his rights as a strong, efficient, and successful personality. Wealth in its monetary form recognized no traditional bonds. It did not care for nobility or loyalty. It fell to the boldest – and the luckiest.

This invasion of money and trade into the conservative feudal world had the effect of dehumanizing relationships between people and loosening the structure of society still further. The self-reliant and self-dependent 'I' came to occupy the foreground of life. In Egypt, a country where work was respected and the worker was not discriminated against as in Greece, profane poetry concerned with individual destinies came into being at an early stage, side by side with sacred poetry and the literature of the collective. Let me quote one of the many love songs of ancient Egypt:

> My heart holds you dear.
> When I lie in your arms
> I do whatever you wish.
> My desire is my mascara:
> When I see you, my eyes shine.
> I cling close to you so as to see your love:
> You, the husband in my heart.
> This hour is beautiful above all others.
> May this hour swell to eternity.
> Since I have slept with you,
> You have raised up my heart.
> Whether my heart be plaintive or jubilant,
> Do not go away from me!

In other countries of antiquity it was trade that brought subjectivism into literature. The individual experience became so important that it could hold its own by the side of the tribal chronicle, the heroic epic, the sacred chant, and the war song.

The Song of Songs, ascribed by legend to King Solomon, was an expression of this new age. In the Greek world – a world of sea traders – Sappho wrote poetry full of individual passion, lamenting her own fate and her own sorrows. Later, Euripides revolutionized the magnificent collective drama created by his predecessors by portraying individual human beings instead of collective masks. The myth, once the mirror of a collective of which the individual had been but an anonymous particle, gradually became a formal disguise for individual experience.

This new individualism, however, was still contained within a larger collective framework. The personality was the product of new social conditions; individualization was not something that happened to one man, or a few, but was a development shared by many and therefore communicable, for all communication presupposes a common factor. If there existed in the whole world only one self-aware 'I' pitted against a collective, it would be senseless to try to communicate this unique plight. Sappho could not have sung of her fate had it been hers alone: intensely subjective though she was, she had something to say which, as yet unsaid, nevertheless applied to others. She expressed an experience common to many – that of the lonely, wounded, rejected personality – in a language common to all Greeks. It was not simply an inarticulate lament: her *subjective* experience was rendered *objective* in the common language, so that it could be accepted as a universally human one. More than that: the famous poem to Aphrodite is, by its nature, a prayer – a magic means of influencing the gods, that is to say, of exercising some power over reality; it is a magic, a sacramental act. The purpose or function of such poems is to affect either gods or men: not merely to describe a condition but effectively to change it. That is why the subjective poet submits to the objective discipline of metre and form, to magic ceremony and religious convention. The fact that a human being does not just cry out in formless protest against the pain and passion of individual fate but deliberately obeys the discipline of language and the rules of custom seems inexplicable – until we realize that art is the individual's way back to the collective.

The new 'I' emerged from the old 'we'. The individual voice

broke away from the chorus. But an echo of that chorus still lingers on in every personality. The social or collective element has become subjectivized in the 'I', but the essential content of personality is and remains social. Love, the most subjective of feelings, is also the most universal instinct of all – that of the propagation of the species. But the specific forms and expressions of love in any particular age reflect the social conditions that allow sexuality to develop into more complex, richer, and more subtle relationships. They reflect either the atmosphere of a society based on slavery, or the atmosphere of a feudal or bourgeois society. They also reflect the degree of feminine equality or inequality, the structure of marriage, the current idea of the family, the contemporary attitude to property, and so on. An artist can only experience something which his time and his social conditions have to offer. Hence an artist's subjectivity does not consist in his experience being fundamentally different from that of others of his time or class, but in its being stronger, more conscious, and more concentrated. It must uncover new social relationships in such a way that others will become conscious of them too. It must say *hic tua res agitur*. Even the most subjective artist works on behalf of society. By the sheer fact of describing feelings, relationships, and conditions that have not been described before, he channels them from his apparently isolated 'I' into a 'we', and this 'we' can be recognized even in the brimming subjectivity of an artist's personality. Yet this process is never a return to the primitive collective of the past. On the contrary, it is a reaching out into a new collective full of differences and tensions, where the individual voice is not lost in a vast unison. In every true work of art, the division of human reality into the individual and the collective, the specific and the universal, is suspended; but it remains as a suspended factor in a re-created unity.

Only art can do all these things. Art can raise man up from a fragmented state into that of a whole, integrated being. Art enables man to comprehend reality, and not only helps him to bear it but increases his determination to make it more human and more worthy of mankind. *Art is itself a social reality*. Society needs the artist, that supreme sorcerer, and it has a right to demand of him that he should be conscious of his social function. This right was never doubted in any rising, as opposed to decaying, society. It was the ambition of the artist full of the ideas and experiences of his time not only to represent reality but also to shape it. The Moses of Michelangelo was not only the artistic image of Renaissance man, the embodiment in stone of a new, self-aware personality. It was also a commandment in stone to Michelangelo's contemporaries and patrons: 'That is what you ought to be like. The age in which we live demands it. The world at whose birth we are all present needs it.'

Usually the artist recognized a twofold social mission: the direct one imposed by a city, a corporation, or a social group; and the indirect one arising from an experience which mattered to him, i.e. from his own social consciousness. The two missions did not necessarily coincide, and when they conflicted with each other too often, it was a sign of increasing antagonisms within that particular society. But, generally, an artist who belonged to a coherent society and to a class that was not yet an impediment to progress did not feel it as any loss of artistic freedom if a certain range of subjects was prescribed to him. Such subjects were very rarely imposed by an individual patron's whim, but usually by tendencies and traditions deeply rooted in the people. By his original handling of a given subject, an artist could express his individuality and at the same time portray the new processes taking place within society. His ability to bring out essential features of his time and to disclose new realities was the measure of his greatness as an artist.

It has nearly always been characteristic of the great periods of art that the ideas of the ruling class or of a rising revolutionary class have coincided with the development of the productive forces and with the general needs of society. At such periods of equilibrium, a new, harmonious unity has seemed to be just round the corner, and the interests of a single class have seemed to be the common interest. The artist, living and working in a state of magic illusion, anticipated the birth of an all-embracing collective. But as the illusory nature of this expectation became clear, as the apparent unity disintegrated, as the class struggle flared up again, and as the contradictions and injustices of this new situation created acute uneasiness, so the situation of the arts and of the artist became more difficult and more problematic.

In a decaying society, art, if it is truthful, must also reflect decay. And unless it wants to break faith with its social function, art must show the world as changeable. And help to change it.

CHAPTER THREE

ART AND CAPITALISM

THE artist in the capitalist age found himself in a highly peculiar situation. King Midas had turned everything he touched into gold: capitalism turned everything into a commodity. With a hitherto unimaginable increase in production and productivity, extending the new order dynamically to all parts of the globe and all areas of human experience, capitalism dissolved the old world into a cloud of whirling molecules, destroyed all direct relationships between producer and consumer, and flung all products on to an anonymous market to be bought or sold. Previously the artisan had worked to order for a particular client. The commodity producer in the capitalist world now worked for an unknown buyer. His products were swallowed up in the competitive flood and carried away into uncertainty. Commodity production extending everywhere, the increasing division of labour, the splitting up of the job itself, the anonymity of the economic forces – all this destroyed the directness of human relationships and led to man's increasing alienation from social reality and from himself. In such a world art, too, became a commodity and the artist a commodity producer. Personal patronage was superseded by a free market whose workings were difficult or impossible to comprehend, a conglomerate of nameless consumers, the so-called 'public'. The work of art was subjected more and more to the laws of competition.

For the first time in the history of mankind the artist became a 'free' artist, a 'free' personality, free to the point of absurdity, of icy loneliness. Art became an occupation that was half-romantic, half-commercial.

For a long time capitalism regarded art as something suspect, frivolous, and shady. Art 'did not pay'. Pre-capitalist society had tended towards extravagance, carefree spending on a vast scale, lavish entertainments and the promotion of the arts. Capitalism meant sober calculation and the puritanical slide-rule. Wealth in its pre-capitalist form had been volatile and expansive; capitalist wealth demanded constant accumulation and concentration, incessant self-increase. Karl Marx gives this description of the capitalist:

Fanatically bent upon the expansion of value, he relentlessly drives human beings to production for production's sake, thus bringing about a development of social productivity and the creation of those material conditions of production which can alone form the real basis of a higher type of society, whose fundamental principle is the full and free development of every individual. Only as the personification of capital is the capitalist respectable. As such, he shares with the miser the passion for wealth as wealth. But that which in the miser assumes the aspect of mania, is in the capitalist the effect of the social mechanism in which he is only a driving-wheel. Furthermore, the development of capitalist production necessitates a continuous increase of the capital invested in an industrial undertaking; and capitalism subjects every individual capitalist to the immanent laws of capitalist production as external coercive laws. Competition forces him continually to extend his capital for the sake of maintaining it, and he can only extend it by means of progressive accumulation.*

And further on:

Accumulate! Accumulate! That is Moses and all the prophets. 'Industry furnishes the material which saving accumulates' (Adam Smith, *Wealth of Nations*). Therefore you must save, you must save, you must reconvert the largest possible proportion of surplus value or surplus product into capital. Accumulation for accumulation's sake, production for production's sake, this was the formula by which the classical political economists gave expression to the historical mission of the bourgeois period.

Of course the capitalist's increasing wealth also brought new luxuries with it, but, as Marx pointed out, '. . . the capitalist's extravagance never has the genuine character of unbridled prodigality which was typical of certain feudal magnates . . . behind it there lurk sordid avarice and anxious calculation'. For the capitalist, luxury may mean the purely private satisfaction of his desires, but it also means the chance of displaying his

* *Capital*, op. cit.

wealth for prestige reasons. Capitalism is not essentially a social force that is well-disposed to art or that promotes art; in so far as the average capitalist needs art at all, he needs it as an embellishment of his private life or else as a good investment. On the other hand, it is true that capitalism released tremendous forces of artistic as well as economic production. It brought into being new feelings and ideas and gave the artist new means with which to express them. It was no longer possible to cling rigidly to any fixed, slowly evolving style; the local limitations within which such styles are formed had been overcome, and art developed in expanded space and accelerated time. And so, while capitalism was basically foreign to the arts, it nevertheless favoured their growth and the production of an enormous range of many-sided, expressive, and original works.

Furthermore, the acutely problematic condition of the arts in the capitalist world did not become fully manifest so long as the bourgeoisie was a rising class and the artist who affirmed bourgeois ideas was still part of an active progressive force.

During the Renaissance, on the first wave of the bourgeois advance, social relationships were still relatively transparent, the division of labour had not yet taken the rigid and narrow forms it was to assume later, and the wealth of new productive forces was still stored up as a potential within the bourgeois personality. The newly successful bourgeois and the princes who collaborated with him were generous patrons. Whole new worlds were then open to a man of creative gifts. Naturalist, discoverer, engineer, architect, sculptor, painter, and writer were often combined in one person, who passionately affirmed the age in which he lived and whose fundamental attitude was summed up in: 'What joy it is to be alive!' The second wave came with the bourgeois–democratic revolt which reached its climax in the French Revolution. Here again, the artist in his proud subjectivity expressed the ideas of the age, for it was precisely this subjectivity of the free man championing the cause of humanity and of the unification of his own country and mankind as a whole in a spirit of liberty, equality, and fraternity that was the banner of the age, the ideological programme of the rising bourgeoisie.

True, the inner contradictions of capitalism were already at work. It proclaimed liberty while practising its own peculiar idea of freedom in the form of wage slavery. It subjected the promised free play of all human capabilities to the jungle law of capitalist competition. It forced the many-sided human personality into narrow specialization. And these contradictions were beginning to pose problems even then. The sincere humanist artist was bound to feel profound disillusionment when faced with the thoroughly prosaic, thoroughly sobering, yet disquieting results of the bourgeois–democratic revolution. And after 1848, the year of that revolution's collapse in Europe, we may speak of something like a disenchantment in the arts. The brilliant artistic period of the bourgeoisie was at an end. The artist and the arts entered the fully developed world of capitalist commodity production with its total alienation of the human being, the externalization and materialization of all human relationships, the division of labour, the fragmentation, the rigid specialization, the obscuring of social connexions, the increasing isolation and denial of the individual.

The sincere humanist artist could no longer affirm such a world. He could no longer believe with a clear conscience that the victory of the bourgeoisie meant the triumph of humanity.

Romanticism

Romanticism was a movement of protest – of passionate and contradictory protest against the bourgeois capitalist world, the world of 'lost illusions', against the harsh prose of business and profit. The harsh criticism by Novalis, the German Romantic, of Goethe's *Wilhelm Meister* was characteristic of this attitude (although Friedrich Schlegel, another Romantic, was full of praise for the great novel). In *Wilhelm Meister*, Goethe presents bourgeois values in a positive spirit and traces the path from aestheticism to an active life within the prosaic bourgeois world. Novalis would have none of this.

Adventurers, comedians, courtesans, shopkeepers and philistines are the ingredients of this novel. Whoever takes it properly to heart will never read another.

From Rousseau's *Discourses* until *The Communist Manifesto* of Marx and Engels, Romanticism was the dominant attitude of European art and literature. Romanticism, in terms of the petty-bourgeois consciousness, is the most complete reflection in philosophy, literature, and art of the contradictions of developing capitalist society. Only with Marx and Engels did it become possible to recognize the nature and origin of those contradictions, to understand the dialectic of social development, and to realize that the working class was the only force which could surmount them. The Romantic attitude could not be other than confused, for the petty bourgeoisie was the very embodiment of social contradiction, hopeful of sharing in the general enrichment yet fearful of being crushed to death in the process, dreaming of new possibilities yet clinging to the old security of rank and order, its eyes turned towards the new times yet often also, nostalgically, towards the 'good old' ones.

To begin with, Romanticism was a petty-bourgeois revolt against the Classicism of the nobility, against rules and standards, against aristocratic form, and against a content from which all 'common' issues were excluded. For these Romantic rebels there were no privileged themes: everything was a fit subject for art.

The extremes and excrescences [Goethe, the admirer of Stendhal and Mérimée, said as an old man on 14 March 1830] will gradually disappear; but at last this great advantage will remain – besides a freer form, richer and more diversified subjects will have been attained, and no object of the broadest world and the most manifold life will be any longer excluded as unpoetical.*

Opposed though he was to everything that Goethe stood for, Novalis, too, saw that Romanticism encouraged the poetic treatment of hitherto forbidden themes. 'Romanticizing,' he wrote, 'means giving a lofty significance to that which is common, a mysterious appearance to the ordinary, and the dignity of the unknown to the familiar.' Shelley wrote in *The Defence of Poetry*: 'Poetry . . . makes familiar objects appear as

* Goethe: *Conversations with Eckermann.* Everyman Edition, J. M. Dent & Sons, London and Toronto, 1930.

if they were not familiar.' Romanticism led out of the well-tended park of Classicism into the wilderness of the wide world.

Yet Romanticism opposed not only Classicism but also the Enlightenment. In many cases it was not a total opposition but one directed only against mechanistic ideas and optimistic simplifications. It is true that Chateaubriand, Burke, Coleridge, Schlegel, and many others – especially among the German Romantic school – solemnly dismissed the Enlightenment; but Shelley, Byron, Stendhal, and Heine, whose insight into the contradictions of social development was more profound, carried on the Enlightenment's work.

One of the basic experiences of Romanticism was that of the individual emerging alone and incomplete from the ever-increasing division of labour and specialization and the consequent fragmentation of life. Under the old order, a man's rank had been a kind of intermediary in his relations with other men and with society at large. In the capitalist world the individual faced society alone, without an intermediary, as a stranger among strangers, as a single 'I' opposed to the immense 'not-I'. This situation stimulated powerful self-awareness and proud subjectivism, but also a sense of bewilderment and abandon. It encouraged the Napoleonic 'I' and at the same time an 'I' whimpering at the feet of holy effigies, an 'I' ready to conquer the world yet overcome by the terror of loneliness. The writer's and artist's 'I', isolated and turned back upon itself, struggling for existence by selling itself in the market-place, yet challenging the bourgeois world as a 'genius', dreamed of a lost unity and yearned for a collective imaginatively projected either into the past or into the future. The dialectic triad – *thesis* (unity of origin), *antithesis* (alienation, isolation, fragmentation), and *synthesis* (removal of contradictions, reconciliation with reality, identity of subject and object, paradise regained) – was the very core of Romanticism.

All the contradictions inherent in Romanticism were carried to their extreme by the revolutionary upheaval of which the American War of Independence was the prologue and Waterloo the final act. The revolution and the attitudes adopted to it as a whole and to its separate phases are a key-subject of the

Romantic movement. Again and again, at each turning-point of events, the movement split up into progressive and reactionary trends. Each time the petty bourgeoisie proved itself to be, as Marx wrote to Schweitzer, 'contradiction incarnate'.

What all the Romantics had in common was an antipathy to capitalism (some viewing it from an aristocratic angle, others from a plebeian), a Faustian or Byronic belief in the insatiability of the individual, and the acceptance of 'passion in its own right' (Stendhal). In proportion as material production was officially regarded more and more as the quintessence of all that was praiseworthy, and as a crust of respectability formed round the dirty core of business, artists and writers attempted more and more intensively to reveal the heart of man and to hurl the dynamite of passion in the face of the apparently well-ordered bourgeois world. And as the relativity of all values was made increasingly clear by capitalist production methods, so passion – intensity of experience – became increasingly an absolute value. Keats said that he believed in nothing so much as in the 'heart's affection'. In the preface to *The Cenci*, Shelley wrote: 'Imagination is as the immortal God made flesh for the redemption of mortal passion.' Géricault, 'extreme in all things' as Delacroix said of him, wrote in an essay of the 'fever of exultation which overthrows and overwhelms everything', and of the 'fire of a volcano which must irrepressibly break through to the light of day'.

Romanticism was indeed a gigantic breakthrough. It led to the wild and the exotic, to limitless horizons: but it also led back to one's own people, one's own past, one's own specific nature. The greatest of the Romantics all admired Napoleon, the 'cosmic self', the unbounded personality; yet at the same time the Romantic revolt merged with the national liberation struggles. Foscolo greeted Napoleon with an ode entitled *A Bonaparte Liberatore*. In 1802 he pleaded with Napoleon to proclaim the independence of the Cisalpine Republic, i.e. of Italy. In the end he turned, full of loathing, against Napoleon the conqueror. Leopardi, similarly embittered and disillusioned by the French liberator's failure to set his country free, exclaimed in the *Canzoni*:

. . . l'armi, qua l'armi! io solo
Combatteró, procomberó sol io.
Dammi, o ciel, che sia foco
Agli italici petti il sangue mio.

Arms, bring arms! I alone shall fight, I alone shall fall. Heaven provide that my blood be an inspiration to Italian hearts.

And in Eastern Europe, where capitalism had not yet triumphed and where the people were still labouring under the yoke of a decaying medievalism, Romanticism meant rebellion pure and simple, a trumpet call to the people to rise against foreign and home-bred oppressors, an appeal to national consciousness, a struggle against feudalism, absolutism, and foreign rule. Byron carried these countries by storm. The Romantic idealization of folk lore and folk art became a weapon for stirring up the people against degrading conditions, Romantic individualism a means of freeing the human personality from medieval bondage. The bourgeois–democratic revolution, as yet unaccomplished in the East, flashed like distant lightning through the works of the Romantic artists of Russia, Hungary, and Poland.

But for all these differences in its manifestation in various countries, Romanticism everywhere had certain features in common: a sense of spiritual discomfort in a world with which the artist could not identify himself, a sense of instability and isolation out of which grew the longing for a new social unity, a preoccupation with the people and their songs and legends ('the people' being endowed with an almost mystical unity in the artists' minds), and the celebration of the individual's absolute uniqueness, the unbounded Byronic subjectivism. The 'free' writer rejecting all ties, setting himself up as an opponent of the bourgeois world, and at the same time, though himself unaware of this, recognizing the bourgeois principle of production for the market, made his first appearance at the time of Romanticism. In their Romantic protest against bourgeois values and in their emancipation which ultimately forced them into the role of Bohemians, such writers made of their works precisely what they wanted to denounce: a market commodity. Despite its invocation of the Middle Ages, Romanticism was an eminently bourgeois movement, and all the problems regarded as modern today were already implicit in it.

Because of Germany's central position between the capitalist world of the West and the feudal world of the East and because of the 'German wretchedness', *die deutsche Misere*, which was the result of disastrous historical developments, German Romanticism was the most contradictory of all the Romantic movements. The capitalist 'disenchantment in the arts' had set in before the bourgeois–democratic revolution had spread to Germany; illusions were lost before they had been properly accepted; and so, in its disgust with the capitalist aftermath of revolutionary upheavals, German Romanticism turned against those upheavals themselves and their postulates and ideas. Heine recognized here the element of anti-capitalist protest.

Perhaps it was distaste with the money cult of today [he wrote] and disgust with the ugly face of egoism which they saw lurking everywhere, that first led some poets of the Romantic school in Germany, whose intentions were honest, to seek refuge from the present in the past and to call for the return to the Middle Ages.

The German Romantics said 'No' to the developing social reality of their day. Bare negation can never be a permanent artistic attitude; to be productive, such an attitude must point to a 'yes' as a shadow points to the object which casts it. But this 'yes' cannot, in the last analysis, be anything other than affirmation of a social class in which the future is embodied. In Western countries, the working class was beginning to rise behind the bourgeoisie. In the East, the entire people – peasants, workers, bourgeois, and intellectuals – opposed the ruling system. But the German Romantics, already seeing the bourgeois businessman as a repellent figure, could not yet detect in the wretched German working class any force capable of building a future, and therefore tried to escape into an idealized feudal past. In doing so they were able to set certain positive features of that past against corresponding negative features of capitalism, e.g. the producer's, artisan's, or artist's close bond with the consumer, the greater directness of social relationships, the stronger collective sense, the greater unity of the human personality due to a more stable and less narrow division of labour. But these elements were taken out of their context, idealized, and turned into a fetish, before they were opposed to the justly criticized horrors of capitalism. The Romantics, yearning for a 'totality' of life, were unable to see through the real totality of social processes. In this respect they were true children of the capitalist bourgeois world. They did not understand that precisely by wiping out all social stability, destroying all fundamental human relationships, and atomizing society, capitalism was in fact preparing the way for the possibility of a fresh unity – whilst itself being utterly incapable of forming a new whole out of the fragments.

Novalis, the most original of the German Romantics and a man who combined great talent with an outstanding intellect, was quite aware of the positive aspects of capitalism and wrote the following astonishing sentences:

The spirit of commerce is the *spirit of the world*. It is the *magnificent* spirit, pure and simple. It sets all things in motion and connects all things. It creates countries and cities, nations and works of art. It is the spirit of culture, of the perfection of mankind.

But the brilliance of such thoughts as this was often overshadowed by his dread of the mechanization of life, of the machine in all its forms. Novalis attacked the new, commercial, bourgeois State emerging in Germany: 'The moderate form of government is half State, half nature; it is an artificial, very fragile machine – and therefore highly repellent to all great minds – but it is the hobbyhorse of our time. If this machine could be transformed into a living, autonomous being, the great problems would be solved.' This is the concept of the 'organic', which all the Romantics opposed to the 'mechanical': 'The beginning of all life must be anti-mechanical – a violent breakthrough – opposition to the mechanism.' In the works of E. T. A. Hoffmann this antithesis was intensified until it became a ghostly duel between man and automaton, and the whole of Hoffmann's output was, as Heine said, 'nothing but a scream of fear in twenty volumes'. The Romantic idealization of everything 'organic', everything that had grown or taken form 'naturally', became a reactionary protest against the outcome of the revolution: the old social classes and relationships were regarded as 'organic', the movements and conditions created by the new classes as wickedly 'mechanical'. The 'world's sleep' must not be disturbed. The ancient night must not be replaced by the new day. In *Hymns to the Night* Novalis asked:

> Must the morning always come again?
> Does the power of earthly things never end?
> Unholy industry consumes
> The heavenly mantle of night.

Friedrich Schlegel argued against the phrase 'the Dark Ages', saying that 'that remarkable period of humanity' might indeed be compared to the night,

but what a starry night it was! Today, it seems, we are living in a confused, clouded interim state of half-light. The stars which illuminated that night have paled and for the most part vanished, but day has not yet dawned. More than once, the imminent appearance of a new sun of universal understanding and bliss has been announced to us. But the reality has in no way confirmed the rash promise, and if cause there be to hope that it will soon be fulfilled, that cause is only the appreciable cold which, in the morning air, usually precedes sunrise.

Side by side with the motif of 'lost illusions' we find that of the 'cold', the sense of a lonely and inhospitable world – and this note, struck for the first time by Romanticism, has never since been stilled; on the contrary, it has become more and more pronounced throughout the development of the capitalist world, in the increasing alienation of life. Hand in hand with this feeling goes the yearning for a return to warmth and security, to a condition which, in the imagination, resembles the mother's womb; and also for the voluptuousness of death, that death-wish peculiar to German Romanticism. Unity, an all-embracing totality, is identified with death:

> One day all will be body,
> *One* body,
> In heavenly blood
> The happy couple swimming.

> O that the ocean
> blushed already
> and the cliff swelled
> to fragrant flesh!

The universal sexuality and death-wish of Romanticism anticipate certain ideas of Siegmund Freud, just as Friedrich Schlegel, with his concept of 'Dionysian' and 'Apollonian', anticipated Friedrich Nietzsche. 'The organs of thought,' wrote Novalis, 'are the sexual organs of nature, the world's genitals.' Or again: 'It is curious that the association of sexual pleasure, religion, and cruelty has not long since drawn attention to their close relationship and their common tendency.'

For the Romantic mind, social reality was, if not 'abolished', then at least extravagantly distorted and dissolved in irony. Friedrich Schlegel wrote:

> German poetry is delving more and more deeply into the past; its roots are in legends, where the stream of fantasy still flows fresh from the source; it can only grasp the present of the real world through humour, if at all.

And Novalis wrote:

> The world must be romanticized. Thus the original meaning is discovered again ... by giving a lofty meaning to the commonplace, a mysterious appearance to the ordinary, the dignity of the unknown to what is known, the semblance of infinity to the finite. ... The fact that we cannot see ourselves in a faery world is due only to the weakness of our physical organs and perceptions.

This 'faery world' behind the real one cannot be approached by realistic means but only when the conscious is switched off and dreams take over. And so Novalis suggests a new theory of art:

> Stories without connexion but with associations, like dreams; poems merely melodious and full of beautiful-sounding words, but also entirely without meaning and connexion, only a few verses comprehensible at most; all these must be fragments of absolutely different things.

This feeling of living in a broken world, a world of fragments, this flight from reality into associations without sense or connexion as a means of apprehending a mystical reality, all these ideas, proclaimed for the first time by the early Romantics, were later to become accepted artistic principles in the bourgeois world.

The Romantic protest against bourgeois–capitalist society, the escape into the past, did also, however, have a positive side. There was a 'day' as well as a 'night'. This was expressed in a profound longing for unity and a noble belief in man's potential ability to become master of his fate.

> Community [wrote Novalis], *pluralism* is our very essence. The tyranny that oppresses us is our spiritual indolence. By widening and cultivating our activities we shall become our own fate. . . . If we establish harmony between our intelligence and our world, we are *equal to God*.

And a vision is glimpsed: 'The world judgement – the beginning of a new, cultivated, poetic era.'

Finally, the negative, backward-looking aspects of German Romanticism turned many Romantic writers into bigoted Catholics and reactionaries. Friedrich Schlegel preached an art of 'purely Christian beauty of feeling' and condemned the 'false glamour of daemonic enthusiasm, an abyss towards which Lord Byron's muse is more and more inclined'. And so it happened that while Byron died of marsh fever fighting for freedom in Greece, while Stendhal supported the national liberation movement in Italy, while Pushkin sympathized with the Decembrists, many a German Romantic became an acolyte of Metternich's and fully deserved Heine's contemptuous verdict: 'Theirs is the party of lies, and they are the henchmen of the Holy Alliance, the restorers of all the wretchedness, the horrors, and the follies of the past.'

When considering German Romanticism and all later, similar movements, we must analyse their internal contradictions and recognize both their negative and positive roles. There is always the same conflict: on the one hand, a deeply-felt protest against bourgeois values and the machinery of capitalism; on the other hand, fear of the consequences of revolution and escape into mystification which inevitably leads to reaction. German Romanticism was the prototype of all the divided movements which later flourished among the intelligentsia of the capitalist world, including, in our own time, Expressionism, Futurism, and Surrealism. The conflict in such movements is also reflected in the fact that by no means all the artists concerned become reactionaries. Of the German Romantics, Heinrich Heine and Nikolaus Lenau became revolutionaries; and others such as Uhland and Eichendorff never associated themselves with the 'party of lies'.

It must also be remembered that part of Romanticism developed into realist criticism of society. Romanticism and realism are closely intertwined in the works of many great writers – Byron and Scott, Kleist and Grillparzer, Hoffmann and Heine, Stendhal and Balzac, Pushkin and Gogol – with sometimes the Romantic element predominant and sometimes the realist. Thomas Mann, the great realist writer of the late bourgeois world, was deeply rooted in the traditions of German Romanticism, and particularly in the glittering variety of meaning contained in irony – irony which Mann himself described as 'refraction of the fundamental instincts'.

Folk art

The concept of 'folk lore' and 'folk art' was developed by Romanticism – not only German Romanticism but Romanticism in general – and constitutes one of its most important elements. In its search for a lost unity, for a synthesis of the personality and the collective, in its protest against capitalist alienation, Romanticism discovered folk songs, folk art, and folk lore, and straightaway proclaimed the gospel of 'the people' as an organically developed, homogeneous entity. This Romantic concept of *the people* seen as a kind of essence outside and beyond class divisions and possessed of a collectively creative 'folk soul' has gone on causing confusion right up to the present day, and many of us frequently use the word 'the people' without a clear idea of what we mean. Folk

art was contrasted to all other kinds of art as a 'natural' phenomenon as opposed to 'manufactured' ones, and its 'anonymity'
was taken to be a proof of its spontaneous creation by a
mysterious 'community' without individuality or consciousness. The Romantics were led astray by verses like this:

> *Wer hat das schöne Liedel erdacht?*
> *Es haben's drei Gäns' übers Wasser gebracht,*
> *Zwei graue und eine weisse.*

Who made up the pretty song? Three geese brought it from across
the water, two grey ones and a white.

This may be poetic but it is not acceptable as either truth or
symbol. Undoubtedly folk art expresses something common to
many and so reflects the ideas of a community; but that is true
not only of folk art but of all art. Art originated in a collective
need. But even in the Stone Age, it was the individual – the
sorcerer or witch-doctor – who transformed what the collective
needed into words or shapes. Not only the cave paintings and
the epics of the distant past but folk songs, too, are the products
of individual authors – helped, certainly, by an abundance of
traditional patterns. The Romantic attitude to folk songs was
highly uncritical. *Des Knaben Wunderhorn*, the collection edited
by Brentano and Arnim, is a ragbag of fine, original poems
side by side with insignificant ones of little value.

Many of these poems might be quoted to support the anti-
Romantic theory that folk art is only a derivative or by-product
of 'high' art (just as many modern scientists do not regard the
virus as transitional from inert to living matter but as the result
of a retrogressive development). I consider this theory to be as
one-sided as the Romantic one. Folk songs may have been, in
many cases, the result of a retrogressive development – fragments of heroic epics, religious poems, or troubadour lyrics
converted into popular form – but to say this is not enough. We
must not forget that the heroic epic itself had its origins in
ancient myths and legends, originating in social conditions
where there was not yet a ruling class and therefore no 'people'
as its antithesis. Art then expressed a relatively homogeneous
collective. Folk songs and folk art must, in many cases, have

the same kind of origin, without having gone through the intermediate stage of 'high' art, expressing the needs of a ruling class. Folk songs and folk art are partly (more in some countries, less in others) produced by the peasantry, among whom ancient traditions tend to persist for a long time; very largely, however, they are a product of the highway with its journeymen, runaway clerics, wandering students, apprentices, showmen, and magicians of all kinds.

Neither folk songs nor folk plays are ever found in a definitive, 'authentic' form. They have always been altered many times in the process of transmission, sometimes enriched by these changes but often cheapened, coarsened or unbearably sweetened by them. Béla Bartók made the attempt of purifying Hungarian folk music, getting rid of additions and deformations, restoring the freshness and strength of the originals. Something of the same kind might well be done for folk art as a whole, bearing in mind, however, that it can very rarely be stated with certainty that this or that form is the 'original' one, since it is the very nature of folk art to occur in different versions. What *is* possible – and that was Bartók's great achievement – is to clear away superimposed elements of *kitsch*, of coarseness and sentimentality, although these elements, one must add, may also well be 'popular'.

In folk songs, the tradition of a far distant collective is often mixed with elements which come from the conflict between the 'people' and the ruling class. A characteristic example of this mixture of the traditional (in this case, traces of witchcraft and blood sacrifice) and the peasants' class struggle against the landowner is quoted by Frazer in *The Golden Bough*:

In some parts of Pomerania (at harvest time) every passer-by is stopped, his way being barred with a corn-rope. The reapers form a circle round him and sharpen their scythes, while their leader says:

> 'The men are ready.
> The scythes are bent,
> The corn is great and small,
> The gentleman must be mowed.'

Then the process of whetting the scythes is repeated. At Ramin, in the district of Stettin, the stranger, standing encircled by the reapers, is thus addressed:

> 'We'll stroke the gentleman
> With our naked sword,
> Wherewith we shear meadows and fields.
> We shear princes and lords.
> Labourers are often athirst;
> If the gentleman will stand beer and brandy
> The joke will soon be over.
>> But if our prayer he does not like,
>> The sword has a right to strike.'

Three elements are clearly recognizable here: prehistoric magic still surviving among a primitive peasantry as yet untouched by capitalism; the peasant's anger with the lords and princes who are to be 'mown down'; and a brokenness of spirit following the failure of several peasant risings, a readiness to be bought by beer and brandy, a coarse, sullenly threatening desire for material benefits. In many folk songs, a prehistoric core has been overlaid with a number of later motifs arising partly from class struggles and revolts and partly from the degradations and corruptions inherent in class society. How much unbroken rebelliousness we find, for instance, in the ballads of Robin Hood, how much defiance in many German folk songs such as the song of poor Schwartenhals:

> I took my sword into my hand
> and strapped it to my side.
> Alas, poor fellow, I had to walk
> because I had no mount.
> Far and wide I walked,
> I took the broad highway.
> A rich man's son then came along
> his purse he had to leave me.

Or the song of the obdurate bride:

> I don't like eating barley
> I don't like rising early.
> I am to be a nun
> and that's not my wish at all.

> Whoever wants the poor girl that I am
> to be locked in a convent
> I wish them as much misfortune
> over again.

Yet other songs, included side by side with these in *Des Knaben Wunderhorn*, are full of tame servility, empty mysticism, crumbs from the lords' table. What, for instance, of the flat doggerel of 'The Mystic Root':

> O miracle! In God's true son
> two natures joined in one person.

Or, in the 'Song of Eternity':

> Hear me, O Man: as long as there is God
> so long will last the pain of hell
> so long will last the joy of heaven.
> O lasting pain, o lasting joy!

Or the mannered song about the 'Dainty Shepherd's Life', so obviously derived from aristocratic pastoral themes:

> Nothing on earth
> can be compared
> with the shepherd's pleasure.
> In green meadows
> and flowery pastures
> there are true joys:
> I know it well.

These profound differences in the fundamental attitude and the quality of folk songs refute the Romantic theory of a single, unified 'folk soul' and prove that these songs are not only expressions of different classes and social conditions but also the work of individuals of different degrees of talent and integrity. The people have absorbed and reproduced all kinds of things over the centuries. All kinds of things – good and bad, original and inferior – have become 'popular'. We cannot share the uncritical Romantic admiration for *all* folk art. We can only judge it by the same standards as any other form of art: by its social content and its quality.

Furthermore, we must realize that increasing industrialization irrevocably destroys folk art. The possibility of folk art now renewing itself by drawing upon the content and means of expression of the peasantry and the wandering artisans has become extremely remote. The working class represents a new content and demands new means of expression. New 'folk songs' – the 'Marseillaise', the 'Internationale', songs of the partisans in their struggle for freedom – have grown out of revolutionary movements. Songs composed with a very high degree of conscious skill, such as those by Bertolt Brecht and Hanns Eisler, have become the new 'folk songs' of the revolutionary working class. A homogeneous 'people' possessed of a mysteriously creative 'folk soul' is a Romantic concept in the capitalist world, for it is a world of opposing classes, and only in class struggle against the ruling class will a 'people' gradually rise again from the Medea's cauldron of our society's fragments. The German Romantic idealization of 'the people' was not merely an illusion: it was reactionary in its consequences. It not only attacked the bourgeoisie but also all manifestations of class struggle, and eventually petered out in a babble of 'social partnership' and the preaching of a false and hypocritical 'brotherhood'.

The Romantic protest against the bourgeois–capitalist world is, as we have already said, a constantly recurring one. But it is only one of the artist's possible reactions to a reality which he can no longer affirm. With astonishing force and perseverance, bourgeois writers and artists have developed the method of Realism, a method whereby a society whose contradictions have been recognized as such is represented critically. England, France, Russia, and America are the countries where the attempt to represent social reality dialectically and without mystification has been most strikingly successful. Just as the Romanticism of Germany and Austria was different in character from that of other countries, so also their development of Realism was more inhibited and its works less rich than in countries where the breakthrough of capitalism had come earlier and taken revolutionary forms, or where extreme economic and social backwardness had united all classes and people at all social levels against the ruling system, so that explosive tensions were created under intolerable pressure and revolutionary energies were irrepressibly built up.

L'art pour l'art

L'art pour l'art was a movement related to Romanticism. It was born in the post-revolutionary bourgeois world, side by side with Realism, whose aim is to explore and criticize society. L'art pour l'art – the attitude adopted by that great and fundamentally realistic poet, Baudelaire – is also a protest against the vulgar utilitarianism, the dreary business preoccupations of the bourgeoisie. It arose from the artist's determination not to produce commodities in a world where everything becomes a saleable commodity. Walter Benjamin, the outstanding German essayist who committed suicide in 1940 as a refugee from Hitler and whose works still await translation, tried to prove the opposite in an original interpretation of Baudelaire. He wrote:

Baudelaire's behaviour on the literary market: Baudelaire's thorough understanding of the nature of commodities enabled or obliged him to recognize the market as an objective test. . . . Baudelaire wanted to find a place for his works and so he had to elbow others out. . . . His poems were full of special devices intended to put all other poets into the shade.

Against this opinion I should like to reaffirm something I myself wrote years ago:

Baudelaire set up the sacred effigy of beauty in opposition to the smug world of the bourgeoisie. For the vulgar hypocrite and the anaemic aesthete, beauty is an escape from reality, a cloying holy picture, a cheap sedative: but the beauty which rises out of Baudelaire's poetry is a stone colossus, a stern and inexorable goddess of destiny. It is like the angel of wrath holding the flaming sword. Its eye strips and condemns a world in which the ugly, the banal, and the inhuman are triumphant. Dressed-up poverty, hidden disease, and secret vice lie revealed before its radiant nakedness. It is as though capitalist civilization had been brought before a kind of revolutionary tribunal:

beauty holds judgement and pronounces its verdict in lines of tempered steel.

Benjamin, however, develops his striking analysis as follows: the decisive element in the picture we have of Baudelaire is that

he was the first to realize – and this realization had immense consequences – that the bourgeoisie was in the process of withdrawing its
commission from the artist. What steady social commission could
take its place? No class was likely to supply it; the likeliest place from
which a living could be earned was the investment market. It was not
the obvious, short-term demand that occupied Baudelaire but the
latent long-term one. . . . But the nature of the market, where this
demand was to be discovered, was such that it imposed a manner of
production, as well as a way of life, very different from those of
earlier poets. Baudelaire was obliged to claim a poet's dignity in a
society which had no more dignity of any kind to give away.

The essential point here is that the bourgeois world was
incapable of 'commissioning' Baudelaire's work even in an
indirect sense, and that he produced for a nonexistent, anonymous market – hence 'art for art's sake' – but that he did so in
the expectation of some eventual, unknown public or consumer. Many remarks of Baudelaire's bear witness to his
ambivalent attitude and so support both Benjamin's interpretation and mine. His art would have nothing to do with the bourgeois world, it arrogantly dismissed and repulsed the bourgeois
reader; yet nevertheless it set out to fascinate him by its startling
shock effects. Baudelaire spoke of his disgust with reality and,
at the same time, of the 'aristocratic pleasure of displeasing'.
His disgust with reality meant a withdrawal into *l'art pour l'art*,
his aristocratic pleasure meant a desire to terrorize the despised
bourgeois mind by a fearful beauty, by glittering instruments of
torture. He refused to produce for the bourgeois buyer and yet
he believed in and produced for a literary market as the final
'test'. We may recall that Marx quoted the principle established
by capitalist economists – production for production's sake –
the counterpart of which is 'science for science's sake' or 'art
for art's sake'. In each case the market is lurking in the background. And so we recognize in *l'art pour l'art* the illusory

attempt to break out single-handed from the capitalist bourgeois world and at the same time a confirmation of its principle of 'production for production's sake'.

The element of Romantic protest, the sharp edge of accusation, is unmistakably present in Baudelaire's work, and ideas which Novalis was the first to formulate recur again and again in his theories of art. Mallarmé, the most consistent spokesman of *l'art pour l'art*, put into practice in his poems what Novalis had outlined as a principle of Romanticism: '. . . only melodious and full of beautiful words . . . a few verses comprehensible, no more . . .'. Hugo Friedrich in *The Structure of Modern Lyric Poetry*, which contains a subtle analysis of Mallarmé's poetry, sums up as follows:

Mallarmé's lyric poetry is the embodiment of total loneliness. It wants none of the Christian, the humanist, or the literary tradition. It denies itself any intervention in the present. It keeps the reader at arm's length and will not allow itself to be human.

Mallarmé tried, as Hugo Friedrich says, to escape from the 'flood of banality':

In the eyes of others my work is what clouds are in the twilight, and the stars: useless. . . . Expunge reality from your song, for it is common. . . . The only thing the poet has to do is to work mysteriously with his eye turned upon Never.

In this *poésie pure*, this poetry stripped of all palpable reality, there is nothing left of Baudelaire's revolt; protest has turned to silent retreat; and where in Baudelaire the call for death, the 'old captain', and the leap into nothingness still carried a sense of plunging into the new and unknown, in Mallarmé's work we breathe pure nothingness thinly disguised in ghostly veils and magic arabesques, no longer even the 'faery world' in which Novalis believed he could see himself, but a world so ice-cold that even faery creatures could not exist in it. Here *l'art pour l'art* leads into a vacuum. The same process is at work as with German Romanticism. The negative element predominates as time goes on. *L'art pour l'art* culminates in Mallarmé's expiring melodies, in the tenuous lyricism of Heredia, and finally in the aristocratic contempt of Stefan George, who retreated into a narrow circle of disciples and glorified the elect personality against the common mass.

Impressionism

Impressionism also was a revolt, an attack by men of genius against the inflated pomposity of official academic art. Under the title of *Twenty Years of Great Art, or the Lessons of Foolishness*, Francis Jourdain has published a collection of the paintings that won official prizes in France in the last quarter of the nineteenth century. Appended to the book is a list of French artists of the same period who won no prizes and enjoyed no official recognition. The list includes the names of Degas, Sisley, Pissarro, Cézanne, Monet, Renoir, Rousseau, Gauguin, Toulouse-Lautrec, Bonnard, Matisse, Rouault, and Dufy. Their art has survived their period. The collection of the academicians' works, on the other hand – works by the approved and acclaimed – is a cosy inferno of smug pretentiousness, pompous insignificance, and well-fed hypocrisy. There are stuffy historical canvasses side by side with jolly *genre* scenes, gallantly saluting soldiers, and naked women whose flesh is as smooth and glutinous as gelatine, polite portraits of statesmen exuding the dignity of their office from every pore, bearded worthies being wooed by muses seconded to Parnassus from the Moulin Rouge, coy nymphs and crucified saints groomed for martyrdom at a *salon de beauté*.

This kind of academic art with its empty classicism, its pilfering of old forms whose content had long been lost, its made-to-order idealism, and its sentimentality which moistens the eye with false emotion while artfully revealing a bosom and a leg, was one of the most repellent products of the bourgeois world in process of disintegration. It was made up of lies, empty phrases, and hypocritical invocations of classical and Renaissance traditions in an age where replete respectability went whoring with naked commerce. It was to be found not only in art but everywhere: the reactionary politician holding forth on 'liberty, equality, and fraternity' of a Sunday afternoon, the tricolour of the Revolution wrapped like a napkin round his stomach, differs only in the degree of the crudity of his impudence from the painter who borrows the forms and intonations of classicism in order to deceive the public about the nature of the world they live in. Those academic heroes who degraded Titian and Racine to the status of cliché-makers, who had 'the beautiful' and 'the sublime' forever on their lips and on their canvasses, who were always bursting with indignation at the 'decadence' of others, were themselves the embodiment of the worst and most shameful form of decadence. For it is utterly decadent, in a world gone out of joint, to behave as though everything were in perfect order, as though all that mattered was to repeat, with every kind of polite flourish, what the classics had once expressed with the full force of their originality as the true experience of their age.

It was against this artistic counterfeit, hung with medals and disguising its private parts with laurel leaves, that Impressionism revolted. When Courbet, who was later to take part in the Paris Commune, wrote his proud letter to the Minister of Fine Arts declining the Cross of the Legion of Honour offered him, it was as though an opening chord were struck.

At no time, in no case should I have accepted it. Still less should I accept it today, when treason multiplies itself on all sides and human conscience cannot but be troubled at so much self-seeking and disloyalty. . . . My conscience as an artist is no less repelled by accepting a reward which the hand of the Government is pressing upon me. The State is not competent in artistic matters.

Further on in the letter Courbet says that it is fatal for art if it is 'forced into official respectability and condemned to sterile mediocrity'. This was a declaration of war on official, academic art. Courbet, who broke out of 'official respectability', who painted peasants and working men, landscapes, fruits, and flowers with a vigorous naturalism, handling his brush like a trowel, was no Impressionist, but his leap over the museum wall into nature, into the people's midst, into the freshness of light and colour gave an example to the Impressionists. Cézanne said of him:

A stonemason. A rough-and-ready plasterer. A colour grinder. . . . There is none other who could eclipse him in this century. He may roll up his sleeves, tilt his hat over one ear, overthrow the Vendôme column, his brushstroke is that of a classic. . . . He is profound, serene, gentle. There are nudes of his, golden as ripe corn: I'm mad about those nudes. His colours have the fragrance of corn. . . . Those girls! An *élan*, a breadth, a happy languor, a repose that Manet in his *Déjeuner* never gave us.

Courbet was a painter of nature and of the people. The Impressionists who followed him were also the discoverers of a new reality and were obsessed by the desire to paint the people and objects of their age. The elegant Manet, friend of Baudelaire and later of Zola, suggested to the Préfet of Paris that the walls of meeting-rooms at the Hôtel de Ville should not be covered with academic historical paintings but with figures and motifs of the new age, with markets, railway stations, Seine bridges, and public parks swarming with people. Like naturalism in literature, its exact contemporary, Impressionism turned its eyes upon the present day, contemplating ordinary things without reticence, even though they might be ugly. Manet formulated this attitude:

The painter today does not say 'look at faultless works'. He says 'look at sincere works'. It is sincerity that bestows on paintings the character of a protest, although the painter may only have been concerned to record his impression.

Manet added that he had not set out with the intention of protesting, but the violent reaction of the academicians, and of the public corrupted by them, had forced him to protest against such intolerance. In 1874, Claude Monet exhibited a painting in the Salon des Refusés, which he entitled *Soleil levant. Impression*. The name 'Impressionism' stems from this picture, which provoked screams of foolish rage. The rebellious character of the new movement was obvious.

Yet Impressionism, too, was a dual phenomenon, and Cézanne, whose intelligence equalled his genius and who carried the new movement to its peak and, at the same time, to its end, was aware of this inner contradiction. He said of the old masters:

They are capable of contemplating detail. All the rest of the picture will always follow you, will always be present. It is as though you could hear the whole melody of it in your head, no matter which detail you happened to be studying. You cannot tear anything out of the whole. . . . They did not paint patchwork as we do. . . .

And, gazing at Delacroix's *Femmes d'Alger*, he exclaimed: 'All of us are there in that man Delacroix! . . . Everything is connected, worked *from the whole*.' Only patchwork, no longer all of a piece: Cézanne recognized that the grand unity had been lost, not only in art but in social reality. Delacroix, in whom the flame of the Revolution had not yet been extinguished, whose Romantic pathos expressed a tremendous feeling for struggling humanity, was the last painter in whom the conception of man as a totality, so typical of the Renaissance, manifested itself in original form and with the vehemence of a fever. Baudelaire said of him:

The achievement of Delacroix sometimes seems to me like a kind of *art of recollecting* the grandeur and natural passion of man. . . . A good picture, true to the vision which has begotten it, should be brought into being like a world. . . . The principal characteristic of Delacroix's genius is precisely the fact that he does not know decadence; he shows only progress. . . . Eugène Delacroix never lost the traces of his revolutionary origin.

Baudelaire goes on to compare Delacroix with Stendhal, in whom enlightenment, revolution, and Romanticism were closely interwoven, and passion and reason, individual arrogance and social consciousness, warmth of feeling and austerity of form combined into a unity that was full of tension. This unity was lost with Delacroix, and the 'patchwork' art of which Cézanne speaks reveals a fragmented world. Cézanne formulated the new Impressionist principle many times:

The artist is merely a recording apparatus for sensory perceptions. . . . No theories! Works . . . Theories corrupt men. . . . We are a shimmering chaos. I come in front of my theme, I lose myself in it. . . . Nature speaks to everyone. Alas! Landscape has never been painted. Man ought not to be present, but completely absorbed into the landscape. The great Buddhist invention, Nirvana, solace without passion, without anecdotes, colours!... Impressionism – what does it mean? It is the optical mixing of colours, do you understand? Disintegrating the colours on the canvas and reuniting them in the eye.... Nothing is more dangerous for a painter, do you know, than to get mixed up with literature. [Yet Delacroix had himself been passionately 'mixed up' with literature!] A painting represents nothing, should not, at first, represent anything but colours. [cf. Mallarmé: 'A poem consists not of thoughts but of words.']

Impressionism, dissolving the world in light, breaking it up into colours, recording it as a sequence of sensory perceptions, became more and more the expression of a very complex, very short-term subject–object relationship. The individual, reduced to loneliness, concentrating upon himself, experiences the world as a set of nerve stimuli, impressions, and moods, as a 'shimmering chaos', as 'my' experience, 'my' sensation. Impressionism in painting corresponds to positivism in philosophy. This, too, allows the world to be no more than 'my' experience, 'my' sensation, not an objective reality existing independently from the individual's senses. The element of revolt in Impressionism is counteracted by another element, that of a sceptical, evasive, non-militant individualism, the attitude of an observer concerned only with his impressions, who does not intend to change the world and to whom a bloodstain means no more than a patch of colour and a red flag no more than a poppy in a wheatfield.

And so Impressionism was, in a sense, a symptom of decline, of the fragmentation and dehumanization of the world. But at the same time it was, in the long 'close season' of bourgeois capitalism between 1871 and 1914, a glorious climax of bourgeois art, a golden autumn, a late harvest, a tremendous enrichment of the means of expression available to the artist. And we must see both sides of the conflict, of the inner contradiction. In order to do justice to Impressionism, we must recognize its socially conditioned character and honour its imperishable achievement.

Naturalism

Literary naturalism was more decisively a movement of protest and revolt than Impressionism, but it was marked by similar inner contradictions. Zola coined the term 'naturalism' to describe a special and radical form of realism, in order to mark off the new movement from all sorts of well-meaning fools who tried to pass off their literary products as 'realistic'. Yet the actual originator of naturalism was Flaubert, whose *Madame Bovary* blazed the trail for the new movement. Zola wrote:

Flaubert has helped the true, the right word in literature, the word that everyone was waiting for, to break through. *Madame Bovary* is of such clarity and perfection that this novel represents a type, a fundamental model for this form of art.

It might seem strange at first glance that Flaubert, who loved beauty as much as Baudelaire and for whom the theme of his novel was a kind of torture, should have presented the dull, torpid reality of provincial petty-bourgeois life with such precision and artistic dedication. But his *impassibilité* was an expression of the same loathing of the banality, stupidity, and meanness of the bourgeois world that moved Baudelaire to summon them to judgement in poems of supreme beauty. Flaubert wrote to George Sand that an artist has no right

to express his opinion on anything, no matter what. Has God ever expressed an opinion? . . . I believe that great art is scientific and impersonal. . . . I want neither love nor hatred nor pity nor anger. . . . Is it not time to introduce justice into art? The impartiality of description would then become equal to the majesty of the law.

In fact, however, this apparent impartiality amounted to a colossal hatred of bourgeois society as a whole, of the right and the left, of shopkeepers and working men. The result was total disillusionment with human beings, with mankind.

The unchangeable barbarity of mankind fills me with black grief. . . . The immense disgust I feel for my contemporaries drives me back into the past. . . .

What remains is this:

> For an artist there is only one thing: to sacrifice everything to art. He must regard life as a means, nothing else, and the first person he dismisses is himself. . . . The earth has limits, but people's stupidity is boundless.

The outcome of this attitude is the hopelessness, the utter despair of Madame Bovary: she tries to escape to a dream world of romantic hysteria, but her environment refuses to set her free and strangles her with cruel thoroughness. This brilliant, inexorable novel is the prototype of naturalism.

Zola, too, subscribed to the doctrine of the 'scientific novel', although he added that 'dispassionate contemplation of the world is not desirable, indeed it is impossible'. 'Our century,' he said, 'is the century of science.' The writer must apply 'the discoveries of Darwin and Claude Bernard': 'the doctrine of the origin of species, the law of the determining influence of environment, the laws of heredity . . .' He did not know Marx and Engels: and so he did not recognize the class struggle or the trends of social development, but only the human person as a passive, animal creature of heredity and environment, incapable of escaping a predetermined fate; man was, for him, not so much the subject as the object of already existing circumstances. It is an interesting point that Mallarmé, the representative of 'pure poetry', admired the novel *The Killer* and its author's 'depersonalization', concluding his comments with the words: 'We are living in an age where truth is becoming the popular expression of beauty.' Despite the extreme contrast between naturalism and *l'art pour l'art*, a secret relationship can be traced between the two.

Zola, who revealed social misery with complete ruthlessness and laid bare the Second Empire down to its very entrails, refused for many years to draw political conclusions.

> We have only got as far as analysis, it is a long way yet to synthesis. . . . It is the legislator's business to intervene; let him think about it and put things right. It hasn't anything to do with me.

Only much later, after the Dreyfus case and his magnificent

J'accuse!, did Zola's attitude change, so that he was able to say, anticipating a fundamental doctrine of socialist realism: 'Detailed investigation of the reality of today must be followed by a glance at the development of tomorrow.' Only now, recognizing at last the need for socialism, did he write in his notebook:

The bourgeoisie is betraying its revolutionary past in order to protect its capitalist privileges and maintain itself as the ruling class. Having captured power it is unwilling to abdicate it to the people. And so the bourgeoisie must gradually become fossilized. It is becoming the ally of reaction, clericalism, and militarism. I must emphasize again and again that the bourgeoisie is played out; it has gone over to the reaction in order to maintain its power and its wealth. All hope lies in the forces of tomorrow, which are with the people.

All these things – the decay of the bourgeoisie, the wretchedness of the common people, the resistance of the working class – Zola depicted in his novels, but without hope of a solution, as a nightmare never to be shaken off. In this 'objective' portrayal of appalling social conditions and in this refusal to describe them as changeable lie both the strength and the weakness of naturalism. Here is to be found its duality. There comes a moment of decision when naturalism must either break through to socialism or founder in fatalism, symbolism, mysticism, religiosity, and reaction. Zola chose the former path; many of his companions took the latter. Taine, horrified out of his wits by the Commune, became a champion of respectable religious art. Huysmans sought an escape, first in the realm of the pathological, and later in the bosom of the Catholic church. Paul Bourget retreated into the twilight of a sentimental Christianity. If we consider also that Ibsen and Gerhard Hauptmann embraced symbolism and mysticism, and that Strindberg plunged into neo-Romanticism and wild superstition, we come to recognize the problematic nature of naturalism and its highly ambiguous position. From this position it is equally possible to go this way or that, forwards or back.

Symbolism and mysticism

When naturalism developed into symbolism and mysticism, this had social causes but was also determined by the method particular to it. In all intellectual and artistic revolts within the bourgeois world there always comes a moment of decision when a revolutionary movement – not merely a movement of protest – stirs the masses, i.e. when the classes take action. The French Revolution, the revolution of 1848, and the Paris Commune were turning-points in literature and art as well as politics. Each time artists were forced to take sides, to align themselves with progressive or reactionary tendencies. The first proletarian revolution, the first transient grasping of power by the working class under the Paris Commune, had a lasting effect. The panic that seized the bourgeoisie affected Hippolyte Taine, an old man, at one end of the scale, and the young Friedrich Nietzsche, to whom the Commune came as an unforgettable shock, at the other. The more decisively the working class emerged into the foreground, the more difficult it became to remain satisfied with revolts *within* the bourgeoisie – always bedevilled as they were by contradictions – and the more sharply did the class struggle force intellectual rebels to make a choice. Either they had to ally themselves with the working class, or else to join the reaction; the third choice was illusory – by opting for the apparent independence of social nihilism they were in fact supporting the *status quo* against the forces of the future.

Naturalism believed that it depicted social conditions with 'scientific objectivity'. But this 'objectivity' was deceptive. Like Impressionism, naturalism failed to see those conditions as a struggle between the past and the future but saw them as an unchangeable present, not in their dialectical context but as a fixed moment in time. When Taine was still a progressive, he wrote to the young Zola:

If you shut yourself up in a vacuum and depict for the reader the hopeless story of a monster, a madman or a diseased wretch, you will only succeed in putting him off. . . . The true artist must possess wide knowledge and a superior attitude, which will help him to see the overall pattern. The writers of today specialize too much, shut themselves off from the world and concern themselves with microscopic examinations of individual parts instead of fixing their eye upon the whole.

The artist had lost 'the whole', as Cézanne, too, pointed out. For naturalism there was no order of priorities in reality; the incidental and the characteristic detail claimed the same amount of attention. A decisive conversation or event, and the buzzing of a bee or the entrance of a woman selling eggs that happened to interrupt it, were considered equally 'real' and therefore equally important. This photographic recording of conditions, thought of statically rather than dialectically, created a feeling of meaninglessness, an oppressive, discouraging atmosphere of passivity. In a certain sense naturalism anticipated the dehumanization, the dull and despairing surrender to *things* made omnipotent by the inhuman laws of capitalist production, which later were to find still more blatant expression in the arts. Naturalism revealed the fragmentation, the ugliness, the surface filth of the capitalist bourgeois world, but it could not go further and deeper to recognize those forces which were preparing to destroy that world and establish socialism.

This is why the naturalistic writer, unable to see beyond the patchwork shoddiness of the bourgeois world, was bound – unless he moved towards socialism – to embrace symbolism and mysticism, to fall victim to his desire to discover the mysterious whole, the meaning of life, behind and beyond social realities.

Alienation

Jean-Jacques Rousseau was the first to use the concept of 'alienation'. His experiences in Calvinist-Republican Geneva led him to recognize that when a people is 'represented' by deputies it becomes alienated from its own collective and so ceases to be a people. The community, he found, could be the instrument of government but never of the common will, for then it was bound to become alienated from itself within the State.

The people ... is not and cannot be represented by deputies. Sovereignty ... cannot be represented; it lies essentially in the general will, and does not admit of representation; it is either the same, or other; there is no intermediate possibility. [*Contrat Social*]

Conditions, however, had become too complex and States too large; division of State power and the fiction of 'popular representation' could not, therefore, be abandoned, but from this followed alienation, concentration of power, and loss of freedom and democracy.

Hegel and the young Marx developed the concept of alienation philosophically. Man's alienation begins when he parts company with nature through work and production. Through his work 'man makes himself twofold, not only intellectually, as in the conscience, but in reality, through his work, and hence contemplates himself within a world made by himself...' (Karl Marx). As man becomes more and more capable of mastering and transforming nature and the entire world around him, so does he confront himself more and more as a stranger in his own work, and find himself surrounded by objects which are the product of his activity yet which have a tendency to grow beyond his control and to become more and more powerful in their own right.

This alienation, necessary for Man's development, needs to be continually overcome, so that men can become conscious of themselves in the process of work, find themselves again in the product of their work, and create new social conditions so as not to be the slaves of their own production but its masters. The artisan, who is creative, can feel at home in his work and can have a personal feeling for his product. But with the division of labour in industrial production this becomes impossible. The wage-earner can have no sense of unity with his work or with himself to set against his 'alienation'. His attitude towards the product of his work is that 'towards an alien object having power over him'. He is alienated from the thing he makes and from his own self, lost in the act of production. Then, as Marx puts it,

activity appears as suffering, strength as powerlessness, production as emasculation, and the worker's *own* physical and spiritual energy, his personal life – for what is life if not activity? – as an activity turned against himself, independent from himself, and not belonging to himself.

In primitive social conditions, e.g. in the natural economy of the early Middle Ages, the social relationships between people (landowner to peasant, customer to artisan, etc.) appear as their own *personal* relationships. In a developed commodity-producing society they are disguised as *social relationships between objects*, i.e. between work products. An artisan produces a particular object for a particular customer. But for the industrialist it is immaterial what his factory produces and for whom; any product is, for him, merely the means of profit. Those engaged in commercial exchange are totally alienated from one another, and the product is likewise totally alienated from the man who puts it on the market. Bertolt Brecht makes this point very strikingly in the 'Trader's Song' from *Die Massnahme*:

> How should I know what rice is?
> How should I know who knows what it is?
> I've no idea what rice is.
> I only know its price.

We speak of price trends, stock-exchange prices, and by so doing we acknowledge the inhuman, autonomous movement of objects, a movement that carries human beings along as a stream carries twigs of wood. In a world governed by commodity production, the product controls the producer, and objects are more powerful than men. Objects become the strange thing that casts long shadows, they become 'destiny' and the *daemon ex machina*.

Industrial society is distinguished not only by this *objectification* of social relationships, but also by an increasing division of labour and specialization. Man as he works becomes fragmented. His connexion with the whole is lost; he becomes a tool, a small accessory to a huge apparatus. And as this division

of labour makes a man's role more partial, so his field of vision
becomes more limited; the more ingenious the work process,
the less intelligent is the work required and the more acute the
individual's alienation from the whole. The tag from Terence –
'*Nihil humanum mihi alienum est*' – is reversed, and the tremendous expansion of production is accompanied by a shrinkage of
the personality.

Franz Kafka, who felt the alienation of human beings more
intensely than any artist before him, said in a conversation with
Janouch about 'Taylorism' (a system which visualized the total
transformation of the worker into a machine part by conveyor-
belt mass production): 'It defiles and degrades not only the
work but, above all, the human being who is a component of it.
This kind of Taylorized life is a terrible curse from which only
hunger and misery can grow, instead of the longed-for wealth
and profit. There's progress for you. ....' 'Progress towards
the end of the world,' suggested Janouch. Kafka shook his
head: 'If that, at least, were certain! It is not certain. ... The
conveyor-belt of life carries you on, no one knows where. One
is more of an object, a thing, than a living creature.'

Not only is the human being more and more obliterated by
his own special knowledge and training – by his existence as a
detail – but also the social relationships and conditions around
him become more and more difficult to comprehend.

Men's living together has become so broad and thick [wrote Robert
Musil in *The Man Without Qualities*] and their relationships are so
endlessly intertwined, that no eye and no will can any longer penetrate
an area of any size, and every man outside the narrowest circle of his
activities must remain dependent on others like a child; never before
was the underling's mind so limited as it is today, when it rules all.

In a note on Rousseau, Musil wrote:

The great undivided life-force must be preserved. .... The culture
of social and psychological division of labour which smashes this
unity into innumerable fragments is the greatest peril for the soul.

Ulrich, the 'man without qualities', remarks that in the past
'one had an easier conscience about being a person than one

has today'. Responsibility today, he finds, 'has its centre of gravity not in the human being but in relationships between objects . . .'. And elsewhere he says: 'The inner drought, the uncanny mixture of keenness about details and indifference to the whole, the human being's immense abandonment in a desert of detail. . . .'

A ghostly anonymity envelops everything. The abbreviated names of large firms and organizations have the effect of hieroglyphics used by some mysterious power. The individual is faced by enormous, incomprehensible, impersonal machines whose strength and size fill him with a sense of his own impotence. Who decides? Who is in charge? To whom can one turn in search of justice and help? These are the questions that recur again and again in Kafka's great works *The Trial* and *The Castle*. Enigmatic, unidentifiable holders of power summon Josef K., try him, sentence and execute him. The bureaucracy of Count West-West, the owner of the inaccessible castle which K. vainly tries to approach, passes all understanding. Bureaucracy is an essential element of man's alienation from society. There are no human relationships for the bureaucrat, only files, i.e. objects. Man himself turns into a file. A dead man is identified by an index number. Even when a man is personally summoned he is not a person but a 'case'.

In *The Trial*,* the Advocate explains to K. that the first plea is not read in court but is simply filed. It is supposed to be examined later,

but unluckily even that was not quite true in most cases, the first plea was often mislaid or lost altogether and, even if it were kept intact until the end, was hardly ever read; that was, the Advocate admitted, merely a rumour. The proceedings were not only kept secret from the public, but from the accused as well. . . .

They were also kept secret from the minor officials, so that these could hardly ever follow the cases they worked on through to the end. 'The most important thing was the Advocate's personal connexions; in them lay the chief value of the Defence.'

* Secker & Warburg, 1945.

A man who has become a 'case' only comes into contact with junior representatives of the system; the senior representatives are remote and wrapped in mystery. A senior official such as Klamm in *The Castle** is virtually invisible. Barnabas, who serves under Klamm, is never sure whether he is really talking to Klamm. 'He speaks to Klamm, but is it Klamm? Isn't it rather someone who is a little like Klamm?' Barnabas does not dare to ask 'for fear of offending in ignorance against some unknown rules and so losing his job'. The junior bureaucrats, such as the two 'assistants' whom the Castle sends to watch the stranger, are present only within the limits of their function; otherwise they are without personality, that is to say without presence. K. compares their faces:

'How am I to know one of you from the other? The only difference between you is your names, otherwise you're as like as ...' He stopped, and then went on involuntarily, 'You're as like as two snakes.'

They are pure function, shadows of a task, servants of a secret power looming in the background. The 'case' is decided upon in impenetrable darkness.

This sense of the powerlessness of the individual who, as he confronts the apparatus of power, is from the start the accused, the culprit, not knowing what is the accusation against him nor what is the nature of his guilt – this feeling, so characteristic of the ordinary man under the Hapsburg monarchy, has since spread over continents. The great decisions are removed from the elected representatives of the people and placed in the hands of a small group of rulers. The State is alienated from the average citizen, who generally thinks of it as 'the powers that be' or 'them up there', never as 'us'. His alienation is reflected in his poor opinion of politics and politicians. He is convinced that the whole business is a pretty dirty one, yet feels that nothing much can be done about it – that he must, in fact, accept it as it is. 'Lie low and keep quiet' is quickly becoming a universal social motto. The *citoyen*, the active citizen, is disappearing fast. Retreat into private life is the order of the day.

* Secker & Warburg, 1953.

The contradiction between the findings of modern science and the backwardness of social understanding also encourages a sense of alienation. Modern knowledge about the structure of the atom, the Quantum and Relativity theories, the new science of cybernetics, have made the world an uneasy place for the man in the street – far uneasier than the discoveries of Galileo, Copernicus, and Kepler made the world for medieval man. The palpable becomes impalpable, the visible becomes invisible, behind the reality perceived by the senses there is a vast reality that escapes the imagination and can only be expressed by mathematical formulae. Vigorous, forceful reality with all its shapes and colours – the 'nature' Goethe saw as a scientist as well as a poet – has become an immense abstraction. Ordinary men no longer feel at home in such a world. The icy breath of the incomprehensible chills them. A world that can only be understood by scientists is a world from which they are alienated.

There are moments when technical achievements – the flight into the cosmos, which is the realization of an ancient, magic dream – can enchant men. But it is precisely this same power over the forces of nature that also intensifies a sense of powerlessness and arouses apocalyptic fears. And indeed the discrepancy between social consciousness and technical achievement is alarming. A single misreading of a radar report, a mistake by a simple technician may mean world disaster. Humanity may be destroyed and no one will have wanted it to happen.

Alienation has had a decisive influence on the arts and literature of the twentieth century. It has influenced the great writings of Kafka, the music of Schoenberg, the Surrealists, many abstract artists, the 'anti-novelists' and 'anti-dramatists', Samuel Beckett's sinister farces; and also the poetry of the American beatniks, one of which reads:

> Now listen to this
>   a do-it-yourself laparectomy set
>   the hydrogen strophe
> the best fallout possible.
>   Think of the funny embryonic mutations
>   generous, genial, genocide.

> It's democratic too
>   it'll take fragmented man
>   everyone will move upward
>   in the free world
>   equally
>   in that final illumination. . . .
>   (Carl Forsberg: *Lines on a Tijuana John*)

The sense of total alienation veers into total despair, veers into nihilism.

Nihilism

Nietzsche, who understood decadence if anyone did, recognized nihilism as one of its essential features. He announced the 'rise of nihilism': 'The whole of our European culture has been moving, for a long time past, with a tortured tension that increases from decade to decade, towards something like a catastrophe: restlessly, violently, precipitously. . . .' And this is how he described the times into which we have been 'thrown' (this idea of being 'thrown' into one's time was to become one of the themes of existentialism):

... a time of great inner decay and disintegration .... Radical Nihilism [he declared] means being convinced that existence is absolutely untenable. . . . Nihilism is an intermediary pathological state (the colossal generalization, the conclusion that there is *no sense at all* is purely pathological): whether it be that the productive forces are not yet strong enough – whether it be that decadence is still hesitating and has not yet found its auxiliary means. . . . Nihilism is not a cause but only the logic of decadence.

Here nihilism is clearly diagnosed as a result, an expression of decadence. But, blind to social dialectics, Nietzsche failed to recognize the connexion with outworn capitalism. Nihilism, already foreshadowed by Flaubert, is a genuine attitude for many artists and writers in the late bourgeois world. But we must not overlook the fact that it helps many uneasy intellectuals to reconcile themselves to iniquitous conditions – that its radical nature is often only a form of dramatized opportunism. The nihilist writer says to us: 'The capitalist bourgeois world is wretched. I say so without mercy and I carry my opinion to its most extreme consequences. There is no limit to this barbarity. And whoever believes that there is something in this world worth living for or worthy of mankind is a fool or a swindler. All human beings are stupid and wicked, the oppressed as much as the oppressors, those who fight for freedom as much as the tyrants. To say this needs courage.' Let me continue now with words actually written by Gottfried Benn:

The thought occurs to me that it is perhaps far more radical, far more revolutionary, far more of a challenge to a man who is strong, hard and fit, to tell mankind: You are like that and you will never be any different; this is how you live, have lived, and always shall live. If you have money, you keep your health; if you have power, you need not perjure yourself; if you are strong, you are doing right. That is history! *Ecce historia!* . . . Whoever cannot bear this thought lies among the worms that nest in the sand and in the dampness which the earth lays upon them. Whoever boasts, as he looks into his children's eyes, that he still has a hope, is covering the lightning with his hand, yet cannot save himself from the night that snatches the nations away from their cities. . . . All these catastrophes born from destiny and freedom: useless blossoms, powerless flames, and behind them the impenetrable with its boundless No.

All this sounds much more radical than any Communist Manifesto – and yet the ruling class only occasionally has any objection to such 'radicalism'. More than that: in times of revolutionary upheaval, nihilism such as this becomes virtually indispensable to the ruling class, more useful, indeed, than direct eulogies of the bourgeois world. Direct eulogies provoke suspicion. But the radical tone of the nihilist's accusation strikes 'revolutionary' echoes and so can channel revolt into purpose-lessness and create a passive despair. Only when the ruling class thinks itself unusually secure, and particularly when it is preparing a war, does its satisfaction with anti-capitalist nihilism evaporate: at such times it requires direct apologetics and references to 'eternal values'. Nihilistic radicalism then runs the risk of being branded as 'degenerate art'.

The nihilist artist is generally not aware that he is, in effect, surrendering into the hands of the capitalist bourgeois world,

that in condemning and denying *everything* he condones that
world as a fit setting for universal wretchedness. For many of
these artists, who are subjectively sincere, it is by no means easy
to grasp things that have not yet come fully into being and to
translate these things into art. There are two good reasons why
it is not easy: first, the working class itself has not remained
entirely uncorrupted by imperialistic influences in the capitalist
world; secondly, the overcoming of capitalism, not only as an
economic and social system but also as a spiritual attitude, is a
long and painful process, and the new world does not come
forth gloriously perfect but scarred and disfigured by the past.
A high degree of social consciousness is needed in order to
distinguish between the death-throes of the old world and the
birth-pangs of the new, between the ruin and the as yet
unfinished edifice. Equally a high degree of social consciousness is needed in order to portray the new in its totality without
ignoring, or worse still idealizing, its ugly features. It is far
easier to notice only the horrible and inhuman, only the ravaged
foreground of the age, and to condemn it, than to penetrate
into the very essence of what is about to be – the more so as
decay is more colourful, more striking, more immediately
fascinating than the laborious construction of a new world.
And one last word: nihilism carries no obligation.

Dehumanization

Dehumanization in all its forms is another element of late
bourgeois art. To describe such art as anti-humanist is by no
means a Marxist prejudice; art theoreticians who are the very
opposite of Marxist point out the same thing, often applauding
this dehumanization as a quality and a sign of progress. André
Malraux writes:

Art must not, if it wants to come to life again, impose any cultural
idea upon us, because everything humanistic must be excluded from
the start. Humanist art was an adornment for the culture which
supported it; with the advent of a non-humanist art . . . artists closed
their ranks more and more tightly as their separation from the culture
and society of their time became more and more pronounced.

Such a statement implies recognition both of the artist's alienation and of his turning away from society and humanism, not, however, with alarm but almost with satisfaction. The ideas of the Renaissance and of the bourgeois-democratic revolution – reason and humanism, man as the 'measure of all things', as the creator of himself and of a developing social reality – are rejected with repugnance. Malraux speaks of a 'return of the demons', adding:

> The demonic realm: that is everything in man that longs for the annihilation of man. The demons of the Church, of Freud, and of Bikini all have the same features. The more new demons appear in Europe, the more European art must recognize its ancestors in those cultures that knew about the ancient demons. ... The prophetic fetishes squat like the Fates in their museums as these go down in flames, gazing at a West that is as close to them as a brother.

In an alienated world in which only *things* have value, man has become an object among objects: indeed he is, apparently, the most impotent, the most contemptible of all objects. Already with Impressionism the human being was dissolved into light and colour and treated as just another natural phenomenon in no way different from any other. 'Man should not be present,' said Cézanne. More and more man dwindles away, becomes a patch of colour among other patches of colour or is no longer present at all in the lonely landscapes and deserted city streets. Or else he is distorted, not ecstatically as in Gothic art (from which Expressionism in part derives), but as a mechanism that can be dismantled, a puppet akin to technical constructions, an absurd and demonic *thing*. Man, having been alienated from himself, becomes conscious of himself as a fetish, a mask, a bogey. The 'fetish-like character of the commodity' of which Marx spoke has transferred itself to man and has completely taken possession of him.

Dehumanization is also recognizable in the depersonalization which many literary critics single out as an essential feature of modern lyric poetry. The subject – the poet's personality – withdraws from the scene (this withdrawal, we recall, was elevated into a principle by Flaubert) and the poem assumes an impersonal, apparently 'objective' character. This objectivity, however, is not that of writing in which a social collective, a group, or a class finds expression, nor does the poet feel himself to be the instrument of a living community; on the contrary, he invents an 'I' removed from the reach of consciousness, an 'id' as Freud called it, and this 'id', rooted in an archaic or mythical past, becomes the agent of what the poem reveals. Rimbaud is reported to have said: 'My superiority is that I have no heart.' And Rimbaud, too, said about the subject of poetry:

'I' is another. If tin wakes up as a trumpet, that is not its merit. I am present at the flowering of my own thought, I watch it, I listen to it. I make a stroke with the bow, and already the symphony stirs in the depths. It is wrong to say *I think*. One ought to say *I am being thought*.

Depersonalization builds on the illusion that, by trusting the 'id', one can make even speechless objects talk – as for example Joyce tried to do in the abstruse *Finnegans Wake*, where he constructed a language meant to be that of wind and water. It is not the objects that speak, however, it is man treating himself as an object, no longer trusting his consciousness but only the associations of the unconscious. Gottfried Benn refers to Levy-Bruhl's theory that logical thought is far inferior to the pre-logical mind because the latter is 'deeper and comes from farther away'. He goes on to speak of an 'archaically extended, hyperaemically discharging I' as the organ of poetry: 'Come down, oh I, to couple with the All; to me, ye hosts of the enchanted: visions, intoxications, denizens of morning.' In the place of the social collective in which he no longer believes, the decadent poet invents a mythical, archaic, cosmic collective supposed to be the true source of all poetry.

The dehumanization of art and literature can manifest itself not only in the disappearance or distortion of man, not only in the debasement of the 'I', but also in an anti-humanist attitude which sometimes assumes the character of brutally harsh social criticism. Let me quote a glaring example, namely the American type of thriller. This is not the place to discuss the function of the thriller, which is largely a substitute for the heroic epic we no longer have, with its successful 'positive' hero emerging triumphant from all manner of exciting ordeals, with its excess of action, and its total absence of psychological analysis of any kind. I mention it only as a typical instance of dehumanization in literature. Leaving aside the appalling Spillane, let me mention Dashiell Hammett, an original writer who invented a new type of thriller. At the end of his *Maltese Falcon*, a by no means idealized private detective turns his mistress over to justice and the electric chair. He explains to her, with icy logic, why he is doing this: because money, success, and his own life are more important than any feeling. When she asks him: 'Don't you love me any more?', he replies: 'I don't know what that amounts to. Does anybody ever? But suppose I do? What of it? Maybe next month I won't. . . . Then what? Then I'll think I played the sap. And if I did it and got sent over then I'd be sure I was the sap. Well, if I send you over I'll be sorry as hell – I'll have some rotten nights – but that'll pass.' In this and other novels, Dashiell Hammett depicts American capitalism with merciless truthfulness, indeed with loathing and disgust. But his attitude – 'that's how things are' – accepts anti-humanism as a starting-point and presents the process of dehumanization nakedly, without any philosophical frills. There are many other examples, not only among thrillers but among other genres of late bourgeois literature. Man is nothing. Success is all.

Fragmentation

The fragmentation of man and his world has found expression again and again in works of our period. There is no unity left, no wholeness. Discussing American drama of the present day, Arthur Miller was reported to say something like this: 'I believe that we in America have arrived at the end of a development because we are repeating ourselves year after year, and nobody seems to notice it.' He spoke of a 'narrowing field of vision', a 'slackening grip', an 'inability to put the whole world on the stage and shake it down to its foundations, which has always been the aim of great drama'. 'Though we are at present incapable of distinguishing between a big subject and a small one, a wide and a narrow view, we remain absolutely at the mercy of the emotions involved.' It is an inability 'to see things in their proper size'. This is an important symptom of decadence. It is the result of an attitude which does not dare to recognize, in the struggle between an old world and a new, in the growth of socialism despite all its setbacks, the one important thing, the thing that will 'shake the world to its foundations'.

But the problem of fragmentation is bigger than this. It is closely bound up with the tremendous mechanization and specialization of the modern world, with the overwhelming power of anonymous machines, and with the fact that most of us are caught up in jobs which are only a tiny part of a much bigger process neither the meaning nor the functioning of which we are in a position to understand. Already the Romantics had become aware of the fragmentariness of life in the bourgeois world; Heine had written, 'Too fragmentary are world and life. . . .' This awareness increased as capitalism and its problems grew, until the whole world seemed to be a chaos of fragments, human and material, levers and hands, wheels and nerves, the humdrum daily round and the fleeting sensation. The imagination, bombarded by a mass of heterogeneous details, was no longer capable of absorbing them as any kind of whole. The first poets of the modern metropolis, Edgar Allan Poe and Baudelaire, adapted their imagination to the fragmented reality surrounding them, smashing the world to pieces in their own minds in order to fit it together again with sovereign wilfulness. Baudelaire wrote: 'The imagination takes the whole of creation apart; according to laws which spring from the very depths of the soul, it gathers and assembles the parts and makes a new world out of them.' Despite this synthetic method, Baudelaire's poetry still retained an apparent classicism. Its structure was firm, its form homogeneous. Rimbaud was the first to shatter the traditional form and structure of poetry. 'A storm,' he wrote, 'strikes breaches into walls, smashes the boundaries of dwellings.' Breaking away from ordinary reality, the new poetry constructed a new world for itself. In *Le Bateau ivre*, cataracts of images pursue one another, a stream

without beginning or end carries everything along, all the
shreds of a destroyed reality, out of sight, out of mind.

> ... *Qui courais, taché de lunules électriques,*
> *Planche folle, escorté des hippocampes noirs,*
> *Quand les juillets faisaient crouler à coups de triques*
> *Les cieux ultramarins aux ardents entonnoirs;*
>
> *Moi qui tremblais, sentant geindre à cinquante lieues*
> *Le rut des Béhémots et les Maelstroms épais,*
> *Fileur éternel des immobilités bleues,*
> *Je regrette l'Europe aux anciens parapets!*
>
> *J'ai vu des archipels sidéraux! et des îles*
> *Dont les cieux délirants sont ouverts au vogueur:*
> *Est-ce — ces nuits sans fonds que tu dors et t'exiles,*
> *Million d'oiseaux d'or, ô future Vigueur?*

... That raced, dotted with small electric moons, mad board with
black sea-horses for escort, when Julys bludgeoned the blazing-
funnelled, ultramarine sky; I, trembling as I sensed, fifty leagues
away, the groans of behemoths in rut and dense maelstroms, eternal
spinner of blue standstills, I long for Europe and her ancient para-
pets! I have seen starry archipelagoes! and islands whose delirious
skies open to the drifter: is it in those bottomless nights that you
sleep, is it there you banish yourself, a million golden birds, O future
strength?

Poetry such as this had never been written before. Even
Baudelaire's tremendous *Le Voyage*, when compared with such
extremism, seems orthodox like a traditional poem in the
tradition of Ronsard or Racine. The method invented by
Rimbaud, whereby the fragments of a dismembered world,
beautiful and ugly, brilliant and vulgar, legendary and real, are
pressed together, in dreamlike sequences and with a scientist's
boldness, to make a new 'substance', revolutionized what had
previously been meant by poetry. Modern poetry, with its
montage of heterogeneous scraps, with its intellectual irrational-
ism which recurs again and again, be it in the late Rilke or in
Gottfried Benn, in Ezra Pound, Eliot, Éluard, Auden, or
Alberti, stems entirely from Rimbaud. It would be academic
pedantry to go on lamenting this shattering of the traditional
poem, this abandonment of form, this unleashing of associative

fantasy. The development was undeniably the result of decadence, but it is equally true to say that it has led to a great wealth of new possibilities and means of expression. Mayakovsky, too, was a destroyer of old forms – and his poetic method proved magnificently suited for expressing the reality of revolution. And Brecht, too, though with greater formal moderation, applied the method of constructive fantasy – except that his poetic intellect served the rational, not the irrational. That, however, is a matter of mental attitude, not of form. Mayakovsky and Brecht linked the new means of expression with the theme of revolution and class struggle, and by so doing went beyond the meaninglessness of fragmentation.

Mystification

The literature and arts of the late bourgeois world tend towards mystification. Mystification means shrouding reality in mystery.

This tendency is above all the result of alienation. The industrialized, *objectified* late bourgeois world has become so alien to its inhabitants, the social reality seems so questionable, its triviality has assumed such gigantic proportions, that writers and artists are forced to grasp at every apparent means of piercing the rigid outward crust of things. Both the desire to simplify this unbearably complex reality, to reduce it to essentials, and the desire to present human beings as linked by elementary human relationships rather than by material ones, leads to the *myth in art*. Classicism's use of ancient myths was purely formal. Romanticism, in its rebellion against 'prosaic' bourgeois society, resorted to myths as a means of depicting 'pure passion' and all that was excessive, original, and exotic. The danger of the method – in itself a legitimate one – was that, from the outset, it opposed an unhistorical 'essential man' to man as he develops within society; it opposed the 'eternal' to the time-conditioned.

Mystification and myth-making in the late bourgeois world offer a way of evading social decisions with a reasonably clear conscience. Social conditions and the actual phenomena and conflicts of our times are transposed into a timeless unreality, into an eternal, mythical, changeless 'original state of being'. The specific nature of a historical moment is falsified into a general idea of 'being'. The socially conditioned world is presented as a cosmically unconditional one. In this way the 'outsider' not only divests himself of the duty to take part in social processes, but also rises above the world of the 'commons' into that of his 'peers', from where he can gaze down with sarcastic superiority upon the clumsy efforts of his 'committed' brethren.

In his absurdly grandiloquent book *The Outsider*, Colin Wilson calls upon his fellow-artist to refuse to commit himself to anything, to free himself from the 'curse' of all social obligations and try to dedicate himself solely to the redemption of his own existential 'I'. A 'new anti-humanist epoch' must be ushered in, for our civilization has already embraced too much of the Marxist attitude. The book ends with a kind of prophecy: 'The individual begins that long effort as an Outsider; he may finish it as a saint.' Günther Blöker, a more intelligent writer than Wilson, would doubtless acclaim such a conclusion as belonging to the 'true mythical conscience'. In Blöker's book *The New Realities* he chides the 'immature' 'committed' artists who want to change social conditions:

As long as a man assumes that the evils of this earth have their cause in the specific failures of individual persons and individual institutions, he still remains in the stage of intellectual childhood. The moment of maturity comes when he becomes conscious of the innate faultiness of the world, a faultiness that may be mitigated but never wholly removed.

Hermann Broch has said that all literature tends towards the myth. But what is myth? Broch never tires of defining it.

Myth is the *naïveté* of the beginning, it is the language of the first words, of original symbols, which each epoch must discover for itself anew, it is the irrational, the direct world view, the original glimpse of the 'first-time-ever', it is the whole world becoming an indivisible image.

Today it has become internationally fashionable to write newspaper features in the 'language of first words' and to pretend that a quick look at Heidegger serves as 'the original glimpse of the first-time-ever'. These elaborately confused pronouncements have an ever-recurring refrain: namely that it is 'being', not 'doing', that matters. 'Events have lost their interest for people,' Gertrude Stein declared in a lecture. 'People are interested in existence.' Doing is dynamic, being is static. Those who opt for 'being' instead of 'doing', for the myth instead of the changeable social reality, do so – often unconsciously – out of a fear of social upheaval. 'Because things are as they are, they will not stay as they are,' said Brecht. 'Mythical being' is evoked precisely in order to deny this truth.

Romanticism made a cult of 'pure passion'. The myth-making neo-Romantics accept only the totally irrational as the 'being' of man – and by so doing they justify, without always being aware of their own purpose, the rule of social unreason. Man's 'being', says Blöker, is like 'a vast reverberation, an ancient moan, an elemental stammering in which the human essence, literally, makes itself heard before it assumes shape'. This moaning and stammering of the modern mystic – has it not all been said before, with admirable simplicity?

A time to be born, and a time to die; a time to plant, and a time to pluck up that which is planted . . . to kill and to heal . . . to break down and to build up . . . to weep and to laugh . . . to mourn and to dance . . . to cast away stones and to gather stones together . . . to embrace and to refrain from embracing . . . to get and to lose . . . to keep and to cast away . . . to rend and to sew . . . to keep silence and to speak . . . to love and to hate . . . war and peace . . . to everything there is a season, and a time to every purpose under the heaven.

Or in the Book of Job:

Man that is born of woman is of few days, and full of trouble. He cometh forth like a flower, and is cut down: he fleeth also as a shadow, and continueth not. . . . For there is hope of a tree, if it be cut down, that it will sprout again, and that the tender branch thereof will not cease. Though the root thereof wax old in the earth, and the stock thereof die in the ground; yet through the scent of water it will bud, and bring forth boughs like a plant. But man dieth, and wasteth away: yea, man giveth up the ghost, and where is he?

This, in articulate language, is the solemn song of birth and death, killing and curing, finding and losing: what is to be said of man's 'being', of the human condition, is said here without pretence.

But there is more than this to say about the fulness of ever-changing reality. Man is more than the eternal cycle of birth and death, of reproductive urge and weary old age: man is a being that is made and is still making himself, imperfect and incomplete, never to be completed, yet constantly moulding himself by moulding the world around him. There exist plenty of novels, plays, and films in which man's social activity is over-simplified so that the characters are mere puppets of social forces, devoid of inner contradictions, empty of personal dreams and personal sorrows. Every objection to this manner of presenting human beings as though they were *only* social beings is fully justified. But most of those who preach a 'return to the myth' are not concerned with the fulness of reality: on the contrary, they would like to empty reality in another way. They want to divorce man from society and reduce him to a lonely, isolated creature helpless in the power of destiny, a being such as has never existed.

The plunge into the 'world's sleep', into the archaic, the inchoate, and the inarticulate, is mostly an escape into irresponsibility. At the same time, however, the reaction against naturalism and the search for new forms of expression gave rise to Kafka's method of *apparently* transforming social reality into myth. The world owes a tremendous debt of gratitude to Max Brod for saving Kafka's manuscripts: but it is a fact, too, that many have been led astray by Brod's misinterpretation of Kafka's works. Kafka did not write of man's anguish in 'the cosmos' or in the 'origin of things', but in a particular social situation. He invented a marvellous form of fantastic satire – dream interwoven with reality – to present the revolt of the lonely individual hopelessly struggling against obscure powers in an alien world, and longing for some form of community, even the ambiguous one of *The Castle*. Brod interpreted these images of social conditions as symbols for supposedly 'eternal' ones. He constructed a mystical whole out of a scattered handful of mystical elements in Kafka's work, and presented the new means which Kafka employed to describe life under the Hapsburg monarchy – a life both real and ghostly – as a kind of cabbala, a mysterious coded record of religious experience and illumination. Kafka, thus misinterpreted, has done a great deal of harm and has encouraged many mystifiers.

Brecht's method of presenting social conflicts in the simplified form of parables has much in common with Kafka's. But they had very different attitudes, these two great writers. Kafka's attitude was one of indecision. He was on the side of the insulted and injured, and against the power-wielders. But he did not believe in the ability of the people he championed to alter the world. At the back of each new hope in his mind there was a new fear, at the back of every answer a new question. Brecht had the courage to answer. His parables were didactic pieces. His conviction that the world could be changed, that it could become better and more rational, was unshakable. Of course he, too, knew that every answer leads to a new question and that nothing on earth is final. But, unlike Kafka, he was not oppressed but encouraged by this knowledge. Kafka, desperately lonely, did not fundamentally believe in progress but only in the same things recurring for ever. Brecht believed that new things must arise against all odds.

Both Kafka and Brecht depicted social reality in their parables. They 'alienated' this reality, and just as ancient myths represented the quintessence of the historical past, so their works were attempts to distil the essence of the historical present. But this is not the case with the works of writers, ranging from Camus to Beckett, who set out to divorce man from society, to dissolve his identity and to wrap him in mystery as the agent of 'eternal being' and 'formless original forces'. Any man is more than the mere mask of a social character. But the tendency to turn him into a hieroglyphic in a play of cosmic mysteries, to blot out his social as well as his individual face in a mystical archaic fog, leads to nothingness. A man who does not belong to any society loses all identity, becomes a reptile crawling between nothing and nothing. Thus, reality is made unreal, and man inhuman.

The flight from society

The de-socialization of art and literature produces the recurring motif of flight: the motif of deserting a society which is felt to be catastrophic in order to attain a supposed state of 'pure' or 'naked' being. When Gertrude Stein repeats 'a rose is a rose is a rose is a rose' like a monotonous magic incantation, the intention is precisely this: to persuade us to stand aside from any form of social reality, to dissolve all connexions, to concentrate upon a single object magically transformed into a 'thing-in-itself'. Ernest Hemingway, Gertrude Stein's successful disciple, discloses the technique of this flight from reality particularly clearly in his fifteen early stories called *In Our Time*. In short paragraphs between the stories, the catastrophic events of our age are hinted at – war, murder, torture, blood, fear, cruelty, all the things that modern obscurantists try to dismiss under the heading of the 'senselessness of history'; the stories themselves consist of apparently uneventful incidents, empty of content, taking place beyond and apart from what moves the world – and this 'beyond' and 'apart' is regarded as the *real* existence. One of the stories, a poetically memorable one, describes Nick putting up his tent, alone at night:

He had made his camp. He was settled. Nothing could touch him. It was a good place to camp. He was there, in the good place. He was in his home where he had made it. . . . It was quite dark outside. It was lighter in the tent.

In a sense this is no different from 'a rose is a rose is a rose'. It also reflects the philosophy of a man fleeing from society. Put up your tent, far from the world. No other way is worth while. The world is dark. Crawl into your tent. It's lighter inside.

Hemingway's attitude is typical of a widespread longing in the late bourgeois world. Millions of people, particularly young people, seek to escape from unsatisfying jobs, from daily lives they feel to be empty, from a boredom prophetically analysed by Baudelaire, from all social obligations and ideologies, away, away on roaring motor-cycles, intoxicated by a speed that consumes every feeling and thought, away from their own selves, into a Sunday or holiday in which the whole meaning of life is somehow concentrated. As though driven by approaching disaster, as though sensing an imminent storm, whole generations in the capitalist world flee from themselves, to put up, somewhere in the midst of the unknown, a flimsy tent where it will be brighter inside than it is in the outer darkness.

What makes the problems of the de-socialization and dehumanization of the arts all the more acute is the fact that the improving techniques of mechanical reproduction, which began with photographs and records, have created a colossal entertainment industry serving vast masses of art consumers. The barbaric character, anti-humanist content, and brutal sensationalism of many artistic items manufactured for mass consumption under capitalism are well known; to analyse such products and their effects would require a book in itself. I should like to make only two points. First, writers and artists of some stature often supply the models that are later imitated, in cruder form and cheaper execution, by the art-manufacturing industries – so that, as it were, the *haute couture* of anti-humanism influences the mass-producing trade. Secondly, an art which arrogantly ignores the needs of the masses and glories in being understood only by a select few opens the floodgates for the rubbish produced by the entertainment industry. In proportion as artists and writers withdraw more and more from society, more and more barbaric trash is unloaded on to the public. The 'new brutalism' extolled as an admirable quality of modern art by certain aesthetes has in fact a free commercial run in the late bourgeois world.

Realism

The feature common to all significant artists and writers in the capitalist world is their inability to come to terms with the social reality that surrounds them. All social systems have had their great apologists in art (side by side with their rebels and accusers): only under capitalism has *all* art above a certain level of mediocrity always been an art of protest, criticism, and revolt. Man's alienation from his environment and from himself has become so overwhelming under capitalism, the human personality released from the bonds of the medieval system of guilds and classes is so violently aware of having been cheated of the freedom and fulness of life it might have enjoyed, the transformation of all earthly goods into market commodities, the all-embracing utilitarianism, the total commercialization of the world, have provoked such intense repugnance in anyone possessed of an imagination that the imaginative have inevitably found themselves emphatically rejecting the victorious capitalist system.

The process began with the Romantic revolt and Jean-Jacques Rousseau's attack on bourgeois civilization. Hegel spoke of the 'increasing power of estrangement' and added: 'When the unifying force disappears from the lives of men and when contradictions lose their context and acquire independence, then the need for philosophy is born.' Shelley, in *The Defence of Poetry*, argued the necessity of poetry from the same premises: 'The cultivation of poetry is never more to be desired than at periods when, from an excess of the selfish and calculating principle, the accumulation of the materials of external life exceeds the quantity of the power of assimilating them to the internal laws of human nature.' The lonely 'I' opposed to the banality of bourgeois life became a central theme. Thus Byron's *Manfred*:

> I said with men, and with the thoughts of men,
> I held but small communion; but instead
> My joy was in the wilderness – to breathe
> The difficult air of the ice mountain tops. . . .
> These were my pastimes, and to be alone . . .
>   I disdain'd to mingle with
> A herd, though to be leader – and of wolves.
> The lion is alone, and so am I. . . .

Or Franz Grillparzer's *Libussa*:

> *Der eigne Nutzen wird dir zum Altar,*
> *Und Eigenliebe deines Wesens Ausdruck. . . .*
> *Durch unbekannte Meere wirst du schiffen,*

Ausbeuten, was die Welt an Nutzen trägt,
Und allverschlingend sein, vom All verschlungen. . . .

Self-interest becomes your altar, self-love the expression of your nature. . . . You will sail unknown seas, exploiting whatever the world has to offer that is useful, and you will be all-consuming and consumed by everything.

Or Stendhal:

Each man for himself in this desert of self-love that is called life. . . . Men of substance and coarse pleasures who have earned a hundred thousand francs in the year that precedes their opening this book [*De l'amour*] should shut it again very quickly, especially if they are bankers, manufacturers, or respectable industrialists, that is to say men with eminently positive ideas. . . .

Or Heine:

> *O lasst uns endlich Taten sehn,*
> *Verbrechen, blutig, kolossal,*
> *Nur diese satte Tugend nicht*
> *Und zahlungsfähige Moral!*

O let us see deeds at last, crimes bloody and colossal, but no more of this well-fed virtue and solvent morality.

Out of the Romantic revolt of the lonely 'I', out of a curious mixture of the aristocratic and plebeian denials of bourgeois values, came *critical realism*. The Romantic protest against bourgeois society turned more and more into criticism of that society – without, however, losing the nature of the protesting 'I'. Romanticism and realism are by no means mutually exclusive opposites; Romanticism is, rather, an early phase of critical realism. The attitude has not fundamentally changed, only the method has become different, colder, more 'objective', more distant.

Byron's most important work, the unfinished *Don Juan*, combines a Romantic protest with realistic social criticism. It is no longer the work of a poet talking to himself: the protagonist has been supplied with an antagonist, and is shown in conflict with social reality. The 'I' is no longer unbounded. Cynicism in the grand manner keeps the Romantic extravagance under control. Don Juan is still the old Romantic hero in his boldness, his thirst for life, and his anti-morality; but he is no longer fighting God and Satan. He is, in all his adventures, a living criticism of the world of cant, hypocrisy, and meanness around him, an embodiment of the longing for sincere, uncontaminated passion.

Balzac and Stendhal were still less prepared than Byron for any form of conciliation, whether with the post-revolutionary bourgeois world or with the State controlled by aristocrats, financiers, and the clergy. In his late novels, Balzac came to accept the victory of bourgeois capitalist society, though his distaste for its typical representatives remained undiminished. Again and again, men who retire in resignation from the 'great' world or artists obsessed by their work – like Wenceslaus in *La Cousine Bette* who, in his visions, 'led, as it were, the life of a courtesan who abandons herself to an extravagant imagination' – are shown as antagonists of the bourgeoisie. Again and again, realist criticism leads to Romantic protest, to the Romantic antithesis of noble resignation and tainted success, the genius and the bourgeois.

The boldest and most consistent of the novels that burst the confines of Romanticism was Stendhal's *Lucien Leuwen*. In its social insight and in the ruthlessness of its criticism, this unfinished novel surpasses all Balzac's works. The bourgeois revolution has been accomplished. There is no going back to the Jacobins or to the young Napoleon. And forward? Lucien sympathizes with the republicans and the Saint-Simonists but their cause seems hopeless to him; and the bourgeois-democratic republic as the superstructure of capitalism repels him much in the same way as it did that witty conservative, Alexis de Tocqueville. 'In New York, the cart of State has merely fallen in the gutter on the opposite side of the street, not ours. Universal franchise rules like a tyrant, and a tyrant with dirty hands.' In *Lucien Leuwen* one finds a merciless maturity bereft of illusion, a contradictory criticism that is not only moral but also aesthetic. The novel breaks off with Lucien's flight from the 'coldness of heart' of Paris, first to Lake Geneva, where he visits 'the spots made famous by *La Nouvelle Heloïse*', then to Italy, where a 'gentle melancholy' opens his soul to art. The final sentences are very curious:

> Bologna and Florence threw him into a state of tenderness and sensibility to the slightest detail which would have caused him the keenest remorse three years earlier.
>
> In fact, on reaching his post at Capel, he had to lecture himself in order to adopt, towards the people he was about to see, a proper degree of frigidity.*

An anti-Romantic novel – and such a reversion to Romantic sensibility? We do not know where Stendhal eventually intended to take his Lucien. But the fragment suggests that (to use Marx's words) the Romantic view would always exist side by side with the bourgeois view as a 'justifiable contrast'.

The concept of realism in art is, unfortunately, elastic and vague. Sometimes realism is defined as an attitude, as the recognition of an objective reality, sometimes as a style or a method. Often the dividing line between the two becomes blurred. Sometimes the term 'realist' is applied to Homer, Phidias, Sophocles, Polycletus, Shakespeare, Michelangelo, Milton, and El Greco; then again, it is reserved for the method practised by a specific kind of writer or painter, from Fielding and Smollet down to Tolstoy and Gorky and from Géricault and Courbet down to Manet and Cézanne. If we are to regard the recognition of an objectively given reality as the nature of realism in art, we must not reduce that reality to a purely exterior world existing independently from our consciousness. What exists independently from our consciousness is *matter*. But reality includes all the immense variety of interactions in which man, with his capacity for experience and comprehension, can be involved. An artist painting a landscape obeys the laws of nature discovered by physicists, chemists, and biologists. But what he portrays in art is not nature independent from himself. It is a landscape seen through his own sensations, his own experience. He is not merely the accessory of a sensory organ apprehending the outside world, he is also a man who belongs to a particular age, class, and nation, he possesses a

* John Lehmann, 1951.

particular temperament and character, and all these things play a part in determining the manner in which he sees, experiences, and depicts the landscape. They all combine to create a reality far larger than the given assembly of trees, rocks, and clouds, of things that can be measured and weighed. This reality is determined, in part, by the artist's individual and social point of view. The whole of reality is the sum of all relationships between subject and object, not only past but also future, not only events but also subjective experiences, dreams, forebodings, emotions, fantasies. A work of art unites reality with the imagination. The witches in Shakespeare and Goya are more real than the idealized peasants and artisans in many a genre painting. The humdrum round of daily life heightened to fantastic pitch in Gogol or Kafka reveals more about reality than many a naturalistic description. Don Quixote and Sancho Panza are more real, to this day, than hundreds of neat, prosaic characters in novels 'drawn from life'. If we choose to define realism not as a method but as an attitude – as the depiction of reality in art – we shall find that almost all art (with the exception of abstract art, tachism, etc.) is realist art.

It seems more practically useful, therefore, to confine the concept of realism in art to a particular *method*, taking good care – and we should never forget this – not to convert the definition into a qualitative judgement. The realist novel and the realist play correspond to a specific social development – to a no longer 'closed', hierarchically ordered society, but to an 'open', bourgeois one. As science develops, it attains an ever greater degree of perfection. Not so the arts. The contents multiply and the horizons broaden out, but Stendhal and Tolstoy are no more perfect than Homer, Géricault and Constable no more perfect than Giotto and El Greco. Even within the work of a single artist – such as Ibsen – the consistently realistic *Doll's House* is no more perfect than the fanciful *Peer Gynt*. Likewise, within a single historical period, the strictly realistic plays of our age are by no means more perfect than Brecht's dramatic parables. Realism (in the narrower sense) is simply a possible form of expression, not the one and only.

There are many different points of view within the scope of critical realism itself ('critical' as an attitude, 'realism' as a method): from the aristocratic contempt with which Fielding viewed the rising bourgeoisie (an element not lacking, either, in Byron, Stendhal, or Balzac) to a total condemnation of post-revolutionary society (Stendhal, Flaubert) and the reformist hopes and schemes of Dickens, Ibsen, and Tolstoy. In all these there is a critical attitude to society as it is, but the approach may be contemptuous, satirical, reformist, or nihilist. Nor is each personal approach necessarily tied to a particular form of expression. For example, the early novels of Thomas Mann (who at that time was an arch-conservative), especially *Buddenbrooks*, were written in a realistic style modelled on Tolstoy and Fontane, whereas the late novels, written when Mann was beginning to be interested in new social ideas and to overcome the heritage of Schopenhauer and Nietzsche (the magnificent *Doctor Faustus* and *The Holy Sinner*) go far beyond the limits normally ascribed to realism. Thomas Mann himself, in his account of how *Doctor Faustus* was written, points out its kinship with the novels of James Joyce. The characteristic attitude of most 'critical realists' is that of an individual, Romantic protest against bourgeois society, and this element of Romanticism is unmistakable not only in Stendhal and Balzac but also in Dickens, Flaubert, Tolstoy, Dostoyevsky, Ibsen, Strindberg, and Gerhard Hauptmann.

Socialist realism

It was Gorky who coined the term 'socialist realism' as opposed to 'critical realism', and the antithesis is now accepted by Marxist scholars and critics.

The concept of 'socialist realism', perfectly valid in itself, has frequently been abused and misapplied to academic historical and genre paintings and to novels and plays in fact based on propagandist idealizations. For this reason, as well as for certain others, the term 'socialist art' seems to me to be better. It clearly refers to an attitude – not a style – and emphasizes the socialist outlook, not the realist method. 'Critical realism' and, even more widely, bourgeois literature and art as a whole (that is to say, all great bourgeois literature and art) imply criticism of the surrounding social reality. 'Socialist realism' and, even more widely, socialist art and literature as a whole imply the artist's or writer's fundamental agreement with the aims of the working class and the emerging socialist world. The fact that the distinction is the result of a new attitude, not simply of new stylistic standards, was often obscured by the methods of administrative interference in the arts practised during Stalin's lifetime. After the Twentieth Congress, rigid adherence to a 'monolithic' Marxist theory of the arts was no longer obligatory, and although the conservative tendencies are still strong, a variety of different artistic concepts now confront each other within the fundamental framework of Marxism.

Here is an example. Ilya Fradkin, a young Soviet theoretician, wrote in the journal *Art and Literature* (No. 1, Moscow, 1962) that it would be wrong to believe that

any dogmatic formula has attained the status of an unchallengeable truth just because it was often repeated during the years of the personality cult. . . . How unselectively, with how little justification, was the merciless verdict of 'decadence' pronounced on the most widely different phenomena of Western art in those years! The art and literature of the period after 1848, and particularly of the twentieth century, were regarded as decadent through and through, and all the 'isms' were summarily dismissed. . . . The question of the artistic movements of the twentieth century is bound up with the wider question of the mutual relationship between realism and other artistic movements and methods. In this field, too, everything was often reduced, in the years of the personality cult, to the temptingly simple but basically dogmatic and, in a scientific sense, vulgar formula: progressive realist art on the one side, various anti-realistic, essentially reactionary trends on the other. But in that case, what of artists of undeniable greatness such as the Classical playwrights Molière and Racine, the Romantics Hölderlin and Walter Scott, or the Post-Impressionists van Gogh and Gauguin? A simple way out of the difficulty was usually found: the greatness of such artists was recognized, but only despite their association with the above-mentioned movements, only in so far as and to the extent that elements of realism could be detected in their work. But can such an approach do full justice to the problem? Did not Classicism, Romanticism, and Impressionism contain their own, their specific artistic truths side by side with their specific historic and aesthetic limitations? Was not Racine's greatness at the same time the greatness of the classical ideals of morality and humanism embodied in his tragedies? Was not Hölderlin's greatness connected with the magic of the poetic dreams of revolutionary Romanticism?

In the next issue of the journal there was a reply by one of the leading cultural policy-makers of the German Democratic Republic, saying that Fradkin's article made 'a big circle' round the subject without touching the heart of the matter.

It sets forth a few, to put it mildly, highly subjective ideas of the author's. . . . He looks backwards in search of an allegedly necessary *post facto* revision of previous judgements. There is, for example, that poor innocent little flower, decadence . . . unless we are mistaken, important Russian artists and thinkers such as Saltykov-Shchedrin, Stassov, Plekhanov, and, not least, Maxim Gorky worked to expose and condemn the phenomenon of decadence, partly in their own time, partly in the years that followed. . . . For various reasons, the decadence of bourgeois art which began in France towards the end of the last century was able to exercise a terrible and destructive effect on the development of the arts in Germany. . . . We should be grateful if Soviet art historians helped us to arrive at a genuinely scientific analysis of that decadence. . . . Artistic scholarship should not abdicate its right to judge works of art in the light of their ideological and political content and their aesthetic quality. Neither should official cultural policy cease to have a direct influence, based on such considerations and judgements, upon artistic production, making individual artists conscious of errors and shortcomings in their work and, in special cases, intervening administratively, as happened in the Soviet Union with Boris Pasternak's novel. . . .

I have chosen this example because it shows very clearly the contrast between the two main schools of thought within the Marxist world today. Ehrenburg judges differently from Gerassimov. Art journals edited by Italian, French, and Polish Communists differ considerably from those published in the German Democratic Republic. In the Soviet Union, a modern sculptor like Neizvestny opposes the old academic painters. The tendency is becoming more and more pronounced not to lay down artistic ideas by decree but to form them and let them develop in the process of work, in the free play of movements and methods, in a diversity of argument and discussion. A new art does not come out of doctrines but out of works. Aristotle did not precede the works of Homer, Hesiod, Aeschylus, and Sophocles: he derived his aesthetic theories from them.

As a greater wealth of means of expression becomes available to us, a common element will emerge more clearly. The antithesis 'critical realism – socialist realism' is an over-simplification, but it implies an essential truth. Against the definition of socialist realism as a method or style, the question immediately comes to mind: whose style, whose method? Gorky's or Brecht's? Mayakovsky's or Éluard's? Makarenko's or Aragon's? Sholokhov's or O'Casey's? The methods of these writers are as different as they can be; but a fundamental attitude is common to them all. This new Socialist attitude is the result of the writer's or artist's adopting the historical viewpoint of the working class, and accepting socialist society, with all its contradictory developments, as a matter of principle.

Even the most uncompromising desire to be objective, to show society in all its intricacy and reality 'as it really is', can be only approximately fulfilled, and even then only in a way that escapes proof. Franz Kafka was aware of this when he wrote: 'Only a party to a case can really judge, but, being a party, it cannot judge. Hence there is no possibility of judgement in the world but only the glimmer of a possibility.' Kafka was right to see that no one can perceive or judge except from a specific standpoint, and that adopting a standpoint, whether deliberate or unintentional, means taking sides. Therefore only one of the parties to a dispute can really judge. But when Kafka adds that, being a party, it cannot judge, he overlooks the possibility of a committed view which nevertheless, in broad outline, coincides with social reality. You can choose a viewpoint from which you will see nothing but fragments slipping into oblivion, or one from which you can survey a wide range of reality in the process of creating new realities. The 'glimmer of a possibility' of judgement that Kafka speaks of can be the glimmer of a dying nightlight – or the first light of dawn. And so the source of light will determine the value of the judgement, its degree of approximation to the truth.

For example, the judgement of Stendhal, the Jacobin, upon the post-revolutionary social reality of his time was incomparably truer than that of the backward-glancing Romantics, not only because he had more talent than they, but also because his chosen viewpoint enabled him to see further and more clearly. Certainly it is true that even Stendhal, the major progressive writer of his time, was incapable of objectively presenting the total process of reality, and retreated again and again, quite consciously, into subjectivism. The most that can be hoped for is that the viewpoint chosen by the artist will *partly* coincide with the development of social reality.

In our age a possibility of far-reaching objectivity is offered by taking sides with the working class and with the national struggles for independence – by adopting the viewpoint of an undogmatic Marxist. Certainly, it is only a possibility: in order to present reality in the process of developing, it is not enough to be convinced of the victory of socialism or to have a knowledge of general social principles. It is necessary to present the forms of transition – of change – in all their contradictory concreteness. Much as a grand vision is needed to cast the 'glimmer' of a light required for true judgement, all objectivity is jeopardized if the writer's desire that tomorrow and the day after tomorrow should fit exactly into a preconceived pattern obscures his view of today; if a wall of dogma, supposed to make his viewpoint 'unassailable', in fact blinds him.

Socialist realism – or rather, socialist art – anticipates the future. Not only what has preceded a particular historical moment, but also what will succeed it, is woven into its fabric. Facts do not alter, but the reality of a moment does alter depending on one's viewpoint. What was once the future merges in the mind with a past event and, by so doing, not only influences the memory but also reveals and, as it were, completes the reality which was partially concealed at the time. The prophetic component, often condemned in the name of realism, has gained new force and dignity in socialist art. Johannes R. Becher was right when he wrote:

When we speak of socialist realism and when we struggle to arrive at a definition, we should not over-complicate and so confuse the issue. The concept of socialist realism is contained in very many statements made before its actual theoretical birth. Thus we find a socialist–realist perspective in Schiller's lines:

> On wings rise bravely
> High above your time
> And faintly in your mirror
> May the future dawn.

And Brecht wrote:

> Dreams and the golden 'if'
> Conjure the promised sea
> Of ripe corn growing.
> Sower, say of the harvest
> You will reap tomorrow
> That it is your own today.

These two statements alone might suffice to define the nature of socialist realism.

Becher over-simplifies the problem somewhat, because, while Brecht's concrete manner reveals a realistic vision of socialist art, that is not true of Schiller's universally utopian view. The age of Romanticism was rich in social utopias and prophetic anticipation, but everything that lay between 'today' and 'the day after tomorrow' was vague. Socialist art cannot content itself with blurred visions. Its task is, rather, to depict the birth of 'tomorrow' out of today, with all the attendant problems. The transition to socialism in all its complexity of interactions and its great variety of unexpected situations is by no means as straightforward as certain simplifiers would have us think.

The socialist artist and writer adopts the historical viewpoint of the working class. But this does not mean that he is in duty bound to approve every decision or action taken by whatever party or character represents the working class in his work. He sees in the working class the determining, but not the only, force necessary for the defeat of capitalism, for the growth of a classless society and the unlimited development of material and spiritual forces of production to liberate the human personality. In other words, he identifies himself fundamentally with socialist society in its process of growth; whereas bourgeois artists and writers, if they are of any importance, inevitably dissociate themselves from the world of the triumphant bourgeoisie. The socialist artist believes man's potential for development to be unlimited, without, however, believing in an ultimate 'paradise state' – without, indeed, even wanting the fruitful dialectic of contradiction ever to come to an end:

Golden age! You will never be. Yet across the earth
fly ahead of us! And may the sea return to the spring that was its
    source.
Deep in the dreams of the world's morning may the future's face be
    mirrored
and may legend become the goal of a mature race.
                    (E. Fischer: *Elegien aus dem Nachlass des Ovid*)

This fundamental acceptance of the new society cannot lack a critical component. What Marx said of proletarian revolutions is also true of periods when socialist societies are being constructed: 'they are . . . ever self-critical; they again and again stop short in their progress; retrace their steps in order to make a fresh start . . .'. True socialist realism is therefore also a critical realism, enriched by the artist's fundamental acceptance of society and a positive social perspective. The artist's personality is no longer engaged in a romantic protest against the world that surrounds him, but the equilibrium between the 'I' and the community is never static; it must be established again and again through contradiction and conflict.

Socialist art, different in its attitude from the art of the capitalist world, requires always new means of expression. In his comments on formalism, Bertolt Brecht wrote:

It would be sheer nonsense to say that no weight should be attached to form and to the development of form in art. Without introducing innovations of a formal kind, literature cannot bring new subjects or new points of view before the new strata of the public. We build our houses differently from the Elizabethans, and we build our plays differently. If we wanted to persist in Shakespeare's method of building, we should, for instance, have to ascribe the causes of the First World War to the desire of an individual (Kaiser Wilhelm) to assert himself, and that desire itself to one of his arms being shorter than the other. Yet that would be absurd. In fact that would be formalism: we should be refusing to adopt a new point of view in a changed world merely in order to maintain a particular manner of building. That being so, it is as formalistic to force old forms on a new subject as new ones.... It is clear that spurious innovations must be resisted at a time when the most important thing is that humanity should rub out of its eyes the dust that is being thrown into them. It is equally clear that we cannot return to things of the past but must advance towards true innovations. What immense innovations are being wrought all around us now . . . how can artists portray it all with the old means of art?

New means of expression are needed in order to depict new realities. It is doctrinaire to prescribe that socialist art must carry on all forms of bourgeois art, and particularly those of the Renaissance and of nineteenth-century Russian realism. The Renaissance produced magnificent artists; but why should socialist art not also learn from Egyptian or Aztec sculpture, from East Asian drawings and paintings, from Gothic art, from the icons, from Manet, Cézanne, Moore, Picasso? The realism of Tolstoy and Dostoyevsky is superb: but why should not the socialist writer also learn from Homer and the Bible, from Shakespeare and Strindberg, Stendhal and Proust, Brecht and O'Casey, Rimbaud and Yeats? It is not a question of imitating any style but of welding the most diverse elements of form and expression into the body of art, so that it may become one with an infinitely differentiated reality. All doctrinaire clinging to particular artistic methods, whatever they may be, is at variance with the task of making a synthesis of the result of many thousands of years of human development, and depicting new content in new forms.

In the socialist world, a discussion of these matters has begun which can no longer be halted. Freed by the clash of opinion, art that is socialist in its content will – of this I am sure – become richer, bolder, more all-embracing in its themes and forms, its endeavours, and the variety of its movements, than any art of the past. Do not be discouraged by obstinacy and mistakes, checks and reverses. Bertolt Brecht's 'In Praise of Dialectics' applies in this as in every other situation.

> If you're still living, never say never.
> What is certain isn't certain.
> Things will not stay as they are . . .
>   and
> Never becomes Before The Day Is Out.

CHAPTER FOUR

CONTENT AND FORM

THE interaction of content and form is a vital problem in the arts, and not in the arts only. Since Aristotle, who first posed the question, and whose answer to it was as mistaken as it was brilliant, many philosophers and philosopher–artists have regarded form as the essential, the higher, the spiritual component of art, and content as the secondary, imperfect component insufficiently purified to attain full reality. Pure form, such thinkers hold, is the quintessence of reality; all matter is driven by an urge to dissolve itself in form to the maximum possible extent, to *become* form, to achieve perfection of form and therefore perfection as such. Everything in this world is a compound of form and matter, and the more form predominates – the less it is encumbered by matter – the greater is the perfection achieved. Thus mathematics is the most perfect of the sciences, and music, they claim, the most perfect of the arts, for in both of them form has become its own content. Form is seen, rather like Plato's 'idea', as something primary in which matter strives to become absorbed – a spiritual principle of order that legislates over matter. This view reflects the experience of the primitive potter: 'First I made a form, and then I poured the amorphous mass into the prepared form.'

This view was developed in scholasticism and the philosophy of Thomas Aquinas, which puts forward the idea of a metaphysical world order. Every being, Aquinas taught, acts for the sake of a metaphysical ultimate purpose. Order – diversity ordered in a unified way – presupposes finality; the idea of order is a final principle. All beings strive towards their final goal; all creatures are ordered among themselves because God has created them. All beings except God are imperfect, and within all beings there is a desire for perfection. This perfection is given to the things of this world as an intrinsic potentiality, and it is the nature of a potentiality to strive to become action or fact. Hence the imperfect must be active in order to attain perfection. The action of each material whole is form: it is the action principle. Every activity is accomplished through form, and every activity aims at perfecting the doer's nature. Every creature attains, within the order of things, its own maximum perfection by action suitable to its nature, i.e. by activity corresponding to its natural form. The formal cause is identical with the final cause; form is striving towards a goal, is *finality*, is the original source of perfection. Thus form is made identical with the essence of things and matter reduced to a secondary, inessential place.

Many art theoreticians of the late bourgeois world derive their confidence and their justification from such doctrines, which continue to influence the arts, the sciences, and the philosophy of our day in a variety of ways. If form is the law-giver for the whole of nature, then it must surely be the decisive element in art, and content an inessential and inferior one. And so, before we examine the problem of form and content in the arts, we are bound to consider nature itself and to ask ourselves what it means precisely to speak of the 'form' of natural organisms and whether it is true that all matter strives towards its final form.

Crystals

Crystals are thought to possess the most perfect form in all inorganic nature. Looking at those marvellously ordered, transparently radiant formations, contemplating their fascinating regularity, admiring their austere beauty, one might indeed come to think that in them inorganic matter has, as it were, become spiritual by attaining a flawless perfection. A naïve, unscientific observer might be tempted to regard them as the works of art of a creative Nature or of a divine Creative Force. That is to say, he might well read something intentional or deliberate into them. This temptation is all the greater as the beauty-lover's attention is not centred upon the crystalline structure of all solids, which is often quite undistinguished, but only upon a small élite of particularly 'noble' crystals. And so we are told by some modern disciples of scholasticism that crystals are 'the embodiment of mathematics', that the structure of the atom is 'immaterial' to the crystal, that symmetry is not due to the properties of the atoms of which a crystal is formed but to a non-material, metaphysical crystalline lattice, that the crystalline lattice is 'beyond substance', that it represents the 'formative order principle', and that form is present as an 'idea', a 'wish for perfection' in every crystal. The substance is, they tell us, 'consumed' by the crystal; the perfect crystal represents the 'ideal' crystal as purely as this is possible in reality; it is really completely homogeneous, 'outwardly a clear form, inwardly a differentiated unity', in which atoms are contained only as a 'potentiality' but not as a reality. Does this metaphysical view correspond to the truth? Is inorganic nature really subject to an autocratic 'formal principle'? Does form really make the crystal? Or is the crystalline form determined by atoms of matter having their own specific properties?

It would go far beyond the scope of this book to re-state the findings of modern crystallography with any degree of completeness. We must confine ourselves to a few characteristic examples. First: the structure of the atoms of which a crystal is composed, far from being immaterial to the structure of the crystal, actually determines it. Crystallographers today are often able to predict the crystalline structure of a given chemical compound on the basis of the properties of its atoms. Let us take the diamond, that radiant apotheosis of carbon which is the strangest and most versatile of all the elements. The structure of the diamond, in which each carbon atom is tetrahedrally surrounded by four adjoining atoms, corresponds exactly to the structure of carbon with its four valency electrons. In other cases, too, the molecular grouping of atoms has been experimentally proved to apply to crystals. The crystal may be regarded as a molecule which is, in principle, infinite, or conversely the molecule may be regarded as a crystal. Further: it is by no means a metaphysically predetermined space lattice that assigns to each atom its place in the crystal in order then to transform it into pure 'potentiality', or unreality. On the contrary, the regular arrangement of the atoms is entirely determined by their properties; what is known as the 'space lattice' is merely the term for a specific relationship in space between specific atoms. Any change in substance is immediately reflected in a change in the space lattice.

The space lattice, or more precisely the ordered complex of associated atoms, is certainly not static. It does not represent a rigid metaphysical 'order principle'. The atoms in a crystal are by no means at rest but are in a state of oscillating movement. Each state of movement has a corresponding temperature. The higher the temperature, the greater the movement and the greater the average spacing of atoms in the crystal lattice. The expansion of the crystal lattice means an expansion of the whole crystalline system. This takes place in different directions to a different extent, depending on the structure of the crystal. As a result, the crystal changes form. At a particular moment, at melting-point or at the point of metamorphosis, quantity is transformed into quality, and the crystalline structure changes or collapses altogether.

What sort of a metaphysically predetermined order principle is it, then, that changes with the properties of matter, with temperature, etc., that cannot impose conditions but is itself governed by material conditions?

Under certain circumstances, matter goes from a disordered into an ordered state and vice versa. Moreover, under certain conditions that are by no means spiritual but, on the contrary, highly material, atoms change their state of order. These changes, prepared by a gradual process, occur instantaneously: particles of matter go suddenly from a chaotic state into an ordered one. Let us, for example, observe the crystallization of liquids. An indeterminate state between liquid and crystal is peculiar to all liquids, provided that the smallest particles of matter are not electrically neutralized. In methyl alcohol and some other benzene derivatives, ordered groups form incessantly and are as incessantly broken up: this is a process of crystallization which produces no permanent crystals. Similarly, in the case of water, the low density of water suggests that there are certain energies opposing the maximum density of molecular compression (which is the characteristic feature of liquids). X-ray observations have shown that in water there is a tendency for a tetrahedral arrangement of molecules similar to that of silica atoms in quartz. But when water changes into ice, i.e. into a permanent crystal, its atoms are arranged according to a quite different structural principle.

Hence a crystal is not a 'finished' or 'final' thing, not the embodiment of a rigid 'idea' of form, but the transient result of continuous changes in material conditions. The processes of transition from non-crystalline to crystalline matter and vice versa can be observed very clearly in carbon dioxide. Carbon dioxide crystallizes at low temperature. But the molecules forming the crystal lattice remain in a state of rotary movement even at low temperature, that is to say they are, as it were, at the ready to abandon their ordered state. In a compound of carbon and four hydrogen atoms, the hydrogen atoms adopt certain positions at temperatures below 18° centigrade (64.4° Fahrenheit), but continue to oscillate incessantly. At temperatures over 22.8° centigrade (73° Fahrenheit) these hydrogen atoms perform rotary movements which, as they increase, increasingly disturb the order of the crystalline lattice and finally cause it to collapse.

What then is the property of atoms that enables them to take up ordered positions under certain circumstances? Each atom in a crystal has its radius of action, its *space requirement*. This is not constant under all circumstances, which is to say it is not a metaphysical 'order principle'; it changes when conditions change, and obeys the dialectic law of interaction. The electric charge of the atom plays an important part. Furthermore, the radius of action increases in proportion with the so-called coordination coefficient. The coordination coefficient expresses the number of adjacent atoms or ions equidistant from an atom. This number may vary from 1 to 12. No case of an atom being surrounded by more than twelve adjacent atoms is known; hence the coordination coefficient of 12 expresses the highest 'atom density', which is characteristic of the metallic elements. The higher the coordination coefficient, the greater is the radius of action of an atom; in other words, the larger the number of adjacent atoms, the more energy is required to keep them off. The coordination coefficient has a decisive effect on the crystalline structure. And so we find that the crystal is formed, not by a disembodied, form-creating crystal lattice, but by the properties and interactions of its atoms. The atoms and ions with their space requirements make the crystal lattice; matter constructs the lattice, and therefore also the crystal itself.

But what of the symmetry of crystals? Is there any explanation for this other than the mysterious 'will for form', the metaphysical order principle? Unfortunately for the metaphysicians, symmetry, too, is not a 'creation of the crystal lattice' but depends on the properties of the particular substance concerned. Without discussing all the symmetries possible in the world of crystals, it should be pointed out that every substance crystallizes in a particular symmetry class, of which there are thirty-two in all. This suggests that the particular symmetry of a crystal is very closely connected with its atomic structure. It could be argued that even if such a connexion exists, the very fact of the existence of strict symmetries in the crystal world justifies the view that we are dealing here with the 'embodiment of mathematics', with a non-material law of form. It is true that regular numerical ratios govern the world of crystals, that atoms of the same kind are always found at the same intervals, that only certain symmetries are possible, and that all symmetries can be expressed by simple numerical formulas. Anyone who finds this mysterious or takes it as an excuse for believing in 'finality', purposive causes, or artistic intentions on the part of nature or super-nature, should try to imagine a world without regular laws or without a definite system of interactions. He would find that such a world cannot exist except perhaps in his imagination. All existence is *eo ipso* a specific existence, i.e. a system of specific interactions. A specific arrangement of atoms can only exist because each atom requires a certain amount of space or has a certain radius of action, which is dependent on its energy potential.

The existence of a specific arrangement of atoms implies that atoms form groups at specific intervals within a specific equilibrium of attraction and repulsion, and that these intervals have the mathematical nature of vectors and can therefore be expressed in natural numbers. Nature does not subordinate itself to the laws of mathematical vectors, but vice versa: vectors are an expression of natural relationships. What we call symmetries are precisely this: series of regular intervals, i.e. specific relationships between specific atoms. These symmetries apply to the world of crystals, not because mathematics would have it so, but because it is the natural property of atoms to form groups at certain intervals under certain conditions. Long before mathematics calculated all possible symmetries, there was nature which produced those symmetries out of the properties of atoms. It is not mathematics but nature which is primary.

Ornaments

Ornaments are in art what crystals are in nature. They are a form of art in which only vectors – intervals of the same kind – are used. Ornamental art was first developed by the Egyptians, who were also highly creative and original in the field of mathematics; and this early ornamental art was so perfect that all later types of ornamentation can be traced back to ancient Egypt. The British Egyptologist Sir Flinders Petrie points out that it is extremely difficult, if not impossible, to find any ornamental pattern that has arisen independently and could not ultimately be traced back to basic Egyptian forms. Such ornamental art is clearly a kind of graphic mathematics. It preceded numbers just as mathematics preceded letters. One might say it was the embodiment of mathematics in art. Group mathematics has concerned itself with ornamental art as well as with crystals, and has calculated the same possible symmetries for both. This, however, is not surprising. Surprising is only the fact that man, without knowledge of the laws of the world of crystals, discovered the sum total of nature's symmetries and put them into ornamental art. If we photograph crystalline structures and superimpose the pictures on each other by projecting them on a flat surface, we obtain extremely beautiful ornamental patterns such as we know from Egyptian art. In both cases the regularity is produced by vectors. In nature, vectors are the expression of natural relationships between atoms. But what gave human beings the impulse to introduce vectors into ornamental art? Undoubtedly this impulse came from land surveying, the mother of geometry; and the pleasure that order gives to human beings must also have had something to do with it. Yet this pleasure, this tendency to find ordered things 'beautiful', has deeper causes. I have already pointed out how rhythm, the repetition of the same sound-pattern, was helpful to life and to work early in the history of man, and I have tried to explain why this was so. Now I should like to raise the question whether the human mind, which reflects the 'order' of human society, does not also reflect the 'order' of nature. Crystals, like ornaments, appear 'beautiful' to us – and the more symmetry they possess, the more beauty we see in them. This increase in beauty, proportional to the increase in symmetry, corresponds to the natural tendency of crystals to realize the highest degree of symmetry.

Such a tendency has been interpreted by metaphysicians as 'upward striving' and a 'will towards form'. However, what we find in crystals (and not only in crystals but also in atoms and molecules and in matter of every kind) is not an ideal 'striving' or mysterious 'will', but a tendency towards maximum equilibrium and conservation of energy. The greater the symmetry of a crystal, the more its energy is confined and the firmer is its equilibrium, i.e. its structure. And so what we call symmetry is nothing other than the expression of a more or less stable energy condition. The most stable atoms are those of the noble gases (such as helium or argon). It is precisely these atoms which have the highest degree of symmetry in their electron-shell structure. Similarly, in the world of crystals, the most stable structures are those of the highest symmetry, namely cubic and hexagonal.

There is no such thing as a 'will towards form'. It could be claimed with equal justification that there is a 'will towards formlessness' or a 'will towards chaos'. Both claims are deceptive. Words should not be misused.

Goethe once said:

The idea of metamorphosis is a most respectworthy, but also a most dangerous gift from on high. It leads to formlessness, destroys knowledge, dissolves it. It is like the *vis centrifuga* and would become lost in the infinite were we not provided with its counterweight: I mean the urge towards specification, the tough persistence of what has once become reality, a *vis centripeta* which cannot, in its deepest essence, be affected by anything external.

This expresses, in both poetic and philosophical form, the two mutually contradictory, fundamental tendencies of nature and reality. What Goethe calls the *vis centrifuga* and Hegel calls 'repulsion' is the tendency of particles of matter to fly out into the infinite at constant velocity – the tendency towards evaporation and dissolution. This tendency is counteracted by the *vis centripeta*, the Hegelian 'attraction', the tendency towards association, unification, the forming of groups, the agglomeration of energy. Both tendencies operate in all organized, ordered matter: the conservative tendency, the 'tough persistence', the clinging to a form of organization once it has been achieved, inertia: and the revolutionary tendency, perpetual movement, the inability to remain at rest, the continuous change of state. Without the infinite contradictions of these two tendencies and without the constant removal of contradiction by the states of relative equilibrium attained by matter and energy there would be no reality, since reality is just that: *a state of suspended tension between being and non-being, in which both being and non-being are unreal and only their incessant interaction, their becoming, is real*.

The dialectic relationship between form and content can be observed very precisely in crystals, i.e. in the structure of solid, ordered matter. What we call form is only a specific grouping, a specific arrangement, a relative state of equilibrium of matter; it is the expression of the fundamental conserving and conservative tendency, the temporary stabilization of material conditions. But content changes incessantly, at times imperceptibly, at other times in violent action; it enters into conflict with the form, explodes the form, and creates new forms in which the changed content becomes, for a while, stabilized once more.

Form is the manifestation of the state of equilibrium attained at a given time. The inherent characteristics of content are movement and change. We might, therefore, though it is certainly a simplification, define form as conservative and content as revolutionary.

Living organisms

The fundamental tendencies of nature are most readily detectable in the relatively simple relationships of inorganic matter; they become more complex as the substances become more complex. In the organic world, heredity is the conservative tendency, and variation the revolutionary one. In human society, which has risen above nature and evolved its own laws, we may generally recognize the conservative tendency in the relations of production, that is to say in the forms taken by production, and the revolutionary tendency in the productive forces, i.e. in the developing, forward-thrusting economic content of all social formations. Always and everywhere, the form, structure, or organization that has already been attained offers resistance to the new – and everywhere the new content bursts the confines of old forms and creates new ones.

Living organisms assimilate the conditions of the outside world in a variety of ways. This assimilation of external conditions and their transformation into internal ones, this absorption and digestion of the outside world (not only of nourishment but also of an entire system of relationships) is one of the essential characteristics of living matter. For example, in the roots of plants the force of gravity has been transformed from an external into an internal condition. Like all mass, the root obeys the law of gravity – it 'falls' towards the centre of the earth – but it does not simply 'fall', it grows towards the centre of the earth with a force several times greater than gravity. Gravity has here become a 'stimulus' producing a chain of inner processes and reactions. The direct effect of gravity becomes an indirect one.

The formation of a plant is the sum of a series of form changes. Each of these changes comes about through a process of irregular growth which may often be extremely inconspicuous and slight. It may, for instance, consist in the local growth of a cell wall or in one side of an organ developing more strongly than the other, etc. These processes can be promoted or inhibited at will by altering the conditions, e.g. by irradiation or by special nourishment, and this will substantially affect the form of the plant. To consider just one example of the extent to which conditions of metabolism can affect the formation not only of plants but of animals, Hartmann has experimentally proved that all the young of the marine worm *Ophryotrocha puerilis* are males. If their body grows to more than fifteen or twenty segments they become females, their form changing considerably. If these animals are starved, not only do all the males remain males but those which were already females shrink back into males. The same result is achieved by increasing the proportion of potassium ions in the nutritive liquor. Thus in this particular case the metabolism conditions determine not only the form but actually the sex of a biological organism.

This extraordinary adaptability and changeability of biological matter is counteracted by a conservative, form-retaining tendency. If a biological organism has adapted itself to relatively stable conditions and has found a form of relative equilibrium with the outside world, that form is then preserved in each cell nucleus and transmitted by heredity. Without such relative stability of form no biological organism could exist. This has nothing to do with striving towards an end. It merely means that any living organism unable to offer resistance to the surrounding world must disappear after a very brief period of existence, in the same way as many chemical compounds disintegrate almost as soon as they are formed. Only those organisms that are capable of existence – i.e. those that are adaptable and resistant at the same time – survive. The cell nuclei, in which the structure of an organism, the entire system of its interactions, and its 'form', are preserved, show a considerable capacity for resistance, and maintain a 'stubborn conservatism' against the outside world. And yet this 'hereditary mass' is not unchangeable and exempt from all interaction with the outside world – any more than the crystal lattice is 'beyond substance' or represents an 'extra-spatial order principle'.

The 'form' of living organisms is not immutable. If we give a plant a new 'content' (by changing its nourishment in the broadest sense, by cross-breeding, or by grafting, all of which amounts to no more than establishing a special new kind of metabolism by imposing new external conditions in a concentrated manner), its form will change too. And though the tendency to revert to the old form is very strong, new forms nevertheless become firmly established in their turn and acquired characteristics can under certain conditions be inherited. Goethe's words in praise of nature still apply: 'It is forever changing and not for an instant is there any standing still in it. It has no notion of remaining, and it has put its curse on everything static. . . .' Form, 'standing still' in a relatively stable state of equilibrium, is always liable to be destroyed by the movement and change of new content.

Society

The problem of form and content in social reality, though it occurs on a different level and under much more complex conditions than in organic or inorganic nature, is fundamentally the same. The content of society is the production and reproduction of life, ranging from the simple fact that human beings must eat, drink, and be housed and clothed, to the vast array of modern tools, machines, and productive forces: it is the deliberate adaptation of the outside world to the growing material and spiritual needs of *Homo sapiens*. The forms in which this process takes place – social organization, institutions, laws, ideas, prejudices – are highly varied. For a certain time they correspond to the state of the forces of production, then they come into conflict with those forces, become rigid and out of date, and must be renewed again and again.

Karl Marx pointed out in the preface to *The Critique of Political Economy*:

> At a certain stage of their development, the material forces of production in society come into conflict with the existing relations of production, or – what is but a legal expression for the same thing – with the property relations within which they had been at work before. From forms of development of the forces of production these relations turn into their fetters. Then comes the period of social revolution.

Marx and Engels both warned against dogmatic and mechanistic over-simplifications of their fundamental thesis. In a letter to Joseph Bloch, Engels wrote:

> According to the materialist view of history, production and reproduction of real life are, *in the last instance*, the determining factor in history. Neither Marx nor I have asserted more than that. If anybody twists this into a claim that the economic factor is the *only* determining one, he transforms our statement into a meaningless, abstract, absurd phrase. The economic situation is the basis, but all the factors of the superstructure – political forms of the class struggle and its results, constitutions adopted by the victorious class after winning a battle, forms of law, and, more than that, the reflections of all these real struggles in the minds of the people involved, political, legal, and philosophical theories, religious views both in their early and their more developed, dogmatic form – all these factors also influence the course of historical struggles and in many cases play the dominant role in determining their *form*.

And again, in a letter to Starkenburg:

> Political, juridical, philosophical, religious, literary, and artistic developments, etc., are based on economic development. But, in addition, they all react upon one another and also on the economic basis. The economic situation is not an *original cause* which alone is active while all else is merely passive effect. There is, rather, mutual action on the basis of economic necessity, which always proves the determining factor *in the last instance*.

The interactions within society are infinitely more complex than those in organic or inorganic nature, and it would be foolish to try to find the conditions governing the world of crystals repeated in the human world. In principle, however, the laws of dialectical contradiction between the conservative tendencies of form and the revolutionary tendencies of content apply to human society as well, and new, relatively stable states of equilibrium occur again and again when the relations of production coincide with the forces of production.

The basic content of society (i.e. the forces of production – human beings with their tools and their ever-increasing knowledge of production, but also with their material and spiritual needs) is constantly changing and developing. The forms of society show a tendency to remain stable, to be passed down as an inheritance from generation to generation. Always it is the ruling classes with their political and ideological machinery that cling to the traditional forms and make enormous efforts to invest them with the character of something eternal, immutable, and final. And it is always in the oppressed classes that new forces of production rise in revolt against antiquated production relations. The oppressed classes see nothing sacred or morally superior in the traditional forms but only a handicap to human progress. Of course it is not easy even for the oppressed classes to escape the influence and authority of traditional forms, which affect the consciousness of all members of society alike. To develop a political and economic class consciousness that runs contrary to predominant views and conventions is extremely difficult.

Any ruling class which feels threatened tries to hide the *content* of its class domination and to present its struggle to save an outdated *form* of society as a struggle for something 'eternal', unassailable, and common to all human values. Hence the defenders of the bourgeois world do not speak today of its capitalist content but of its democratic form, though this form is cracking at every joint. They try to divert attention from the historic struggle between capitalism and socialism by transforming it, in people's minds, into a struggle between 'democracy' and 'dictatorship'. The fact that social forms do influence the content of a society and of the lives of its members helps them in this. The merely formal character of bourgeois democracy is obvious; yet people who suffered under Fascist rule found that even formal democracy, even the façade of a

legal and political system, was important, so that its loss meant
a loss of true content. Further, the difficulty of evolving new
forms commensurate with the new social content achieved
through the victory of the working class – of evolving, that is
to say, a new democracy that is not formal but actual and socialist – makes it easier for the defenders of capitalism to present
their clinging to an old social content as a struggle to preserve
hallowed forms of existence, forms glorified as though they
were the only content of life worthy of humanity. I point this
out to emphasize how complex is the interaction between basis
and superstructure – between social content and social forms –
and also to remind the reader of the temporary preponderance
which traditional forms can gain in the minds of innumerable
human beings.

In order to save an outdated social content, the ruling class
adopts protective postures towards old forms – although it is
always prepared, at a critical moment, to abandon these in
exchange for undisguised dictatorship. At the same time it
tries to cast suspicion on new forms – which may not yet have
attained full maturity – and so to damn the new social content.
It is becoming more and more embarrassing to glorify or
justify the old social content of capitalism with all its attendant
disasters. And so the champions of capitalism now defend
'only' its social and political forms of expression. This tendency
to overlook the content, this emphasis laid on form as though
it were the essential thing, indeed the only thing worthy of
attention, has also affected a large section of the uneasy
intelligentsia in the capitalist world and has brought into being
the phenomenon of 'formalism' in the sphere of the arts. This
is not really a question of the means of artistic expression (for
there can be objection to experimenting with new means); it is
a question of the deeper, more general problem of 'formalism'
as a phenomenon typical of a social form no longer in keeping
with the times, typical of the fact that a ruling class has outlived
itself.

Subject, content, meaning

I have tried to show how the problem of content and form is not merely confined to the arts, and how the idea that form is primary and content secondary is a typical reaction of every ruling class when its position is threatened. Let us now, within this general framework, go on to examine the question of content and form as it occurs specifically in the arts, bearing in mind that the arts have their own socially conditioned laws and problems.

First we must consider the concept of content in literature and art. Is the term too vague? Does it refer to the theme or subject of a work of art, or to its meaning or message? (But perhaps the term 'message' smacks too much of propaganda, and we should speak only of the *meaning* of a work of art, the meaning which is not revealed in the work's details but in it as a whole.) Although subject and meaning are often mutually connected, they are nevertheless not the same thing. Two artists or writers may interpret and treat a subject so differently that their works will have hardly anything in common. The choice of subject is, of course, very important, and through it, among other things, we may often recognize the artist's or writer's attitude. Goethe knew exactly what he was doing when he chose the subjects of *Faust* and *Götz*. They were subjects directly related to a decisive period in German history, to Germany breaking away from the Middle Ages. But the same subjects can be given a totally different content. (We need only recall the treatment of the Faustus theme in Marlowe, Lessing, Lenau, Grabbe, Thomas Mann, and Hanns Eisler.) The subject alone does not determine a particular form; but content and form, or meaning and form, are closely bound together in dialectical interaction.

Subject is raised to the status of content only by the artist's attitude, for content is not only *what* is presented but also *how* it is presented, in what context, with what degree of social and individual consciousness. A subject like 'harvest' can be treated as a charming idyll, as a conventional genre picture, as an inhuman ordeal or as the victory of man over nature:

everything depends on the artist's view, on whether he speaks as an apologist of the ruling class, a sentimental Sunday tripper, a disgruntled peasant, or a revolutionary socialist.

How the meaning of a subject changes

In the arts of ancient Egypt, men at work were a constantly recurring subject. Mural paintings represented peasants ploughing and sowing. The labouring peasant was generally presented from the master's point of view. The master's eye rested with satisfaction on the swarms of men working on his behalf; the peasant was not the subject of his own activity but an object for the observer, who knew that the harvest was destined for his own granaries; and this manner of seeing created the apparent 'objectivity' of Egyptian art. The ruling class always thinks that its way of seeing is 'objective', that is to say, that it corresponds to the world order. For the ruler there is no such thing as an individual peasant with individual needs; there are only peasants as social units having no right to self-expression but only a function, like a beast of burden or a plough. These Egyptian paintings implied no contempt for work (as Greek works did later), only the unshakable conviction that everyone has his predetermined place and function in life, and a profound belief in the 'pre-established harmony' of a society organized according to ranks and castes. The world is made like that, and behold, it is well made. As the style developed, a new element (or a very old one temporarily suppressed by the ruling class) began to appear: a kind of 'naturalism' that disturbed the expressionless, 'objective' representation of the work being done. In paintings and friezes labourers began to acquire features of individual suffering and exhaustion. Social doubts began to spring up, and the stylized manner began to give way to a critical one. We read in a papyrus:

Shall I tell you of the mason, how he suffers his wretchedness? He is exposed to all weathers when he builds, his body bared to the waist. His arms are weary from the work; his food lies between his excreta; he devours himself, for he has no other bread than his fingers. He is dreadfully tired, for there is always a block of stone that must be dragged to this building or that, a block of six or ten ells; always there is a block that must be dragged, this month or next, all the way to the top of the scaffolding where the bunch of lotus flowers is attached when the house is finished. When the work is quite done, he goes home if he has bread, and his children have been mercilessly beaten during his absence.

Some of this spirit of social criticism and discontent spread to the visual arts of Egypt and found expression in a striking form of realism. It is to the eternal glory of Egyptian art that it did not only create monuments to the ruling class but also included among its subjects those who worked, the downtrodden and the humiliated; that it answered Bertolt Brecht's 'Questions of a Reading Worker' thousands of years before Brecht wrote them:

> Who built Thebes of the seven gates?
> The history books give the names of kings.
> Did kings carry the lumps of rock?

The subject of work is a recurrent one in Egyptian art, but the content, the meaning of the recurrent theme, changed from stylized 'objectivity' to subjective expression (and the style, or manner, changed too from a measured solemnity to a plebeian realism).

In the arts of classical antiquity, work was not regarded as a worthwhile subject. In medieval miniatures (the *Breviarium Grimani*, the work of the Master of Nuremberg) and in Renaissance art (Dürer, Grünewald, Riemenschneider, and others) the theme of work, and particularly the many aspects of agricultural work, began to creep back into art. In a society no longer based on serfdom, the working classes began to make themselves felt in the arts. The peasant's and artisan's working processes began to demand artistic representation. Side by side with this there was a tendency to idealize country life, to make it appear idyllic in contrast to the sophistications and vices of the great world. This tendency, which was predominant in Baroque art, can be traced from Giorgione's sleeping shepherdess to the elegant wine harvest of Goya, otherwise so harshly plebeian in his attitude. The shepherd became a favourite subject because he could be presented as gracefully idle, watching his flock with noble languor – not wretched, devoured by lice, and choked by filth as he in fact was. The same 'return to nature' was cultivated in pastoral plays enacted by bored duchesses with a condescendingly sophisticated 'simplicity'. The nature to which the nobility returned was a nicely mannered, carefully pruned, delicately scented nature; the woods were not real woods; the world was not a real world. The shepherd's function was to play the flute, dance country dances, and serve fruit and wine daintily to his rulers, to act, in other words, as a reassuring member of a virtuous and morally irreproachable 'people'. Peasant risings had given the land-owners a glimpse of the 'wicked' countryman; the good countryman of the pastoral scenes was meant to calm the nerves of an uneasy society. Art became a magic means of deceiving the ruling class about the social dangers which surrounded it.

By no means a central theme in Italian Renaissance art, men at work became so in the art of the Netherlands. Here, a self-aware bourgeoisie drew upon rich artistic means to represent the active plebeian – no longer the poor Lazarus, the passive beggar, the sufferer of Gothic art, no longer the fictitious shepherd of operatic Baroque, but the peasant and artisan in his function as producer, in his social activity. In Brueghel, the working people are always there. The inner relationship between Brueghel and Rabelais, Cervantes, and, above all, Shakespeare, has often and rightly been pointed out. But Shakespeare's attitude was still in part an aristocratic one, especially in many of his comic rustic scenes. There is no trace of such an attitude to be found anywhere in Brueghel's work. The Austrian art historian Max Dvorak was perfectly right when he wrote:

Brueghel was the first artist for whom realistic popular scenes were not merely an external stage setting. Life itself was for him the measure of all human things and his source for the study and dis-covery of the urges, weaknesses, passions, morals, habits, thoughts, and feelings that rule mankind.

The representation of agricultural work and of working people in general in Brueghel's paintings is an unbroken affirmation, without idealization, but also without social protest or approval. The peasant women with their forceful tread, the peasants mowing a dense mass of corn that is like a solidly built red-gold wall, the heat of the harvest day, and the busy matter-of-factness of the harvesters – all this has the effect of a statement: 'That is how it is, and may it stay so!' Brueghel's art finds its own meaning and confirmation within itself, without sentimentality or embellishment of any kind. The working people are not given a glow of false beauty, no invisible halo hovers over their heads, their strong, coarse, characteristic features are drawn with a sure hand, often almost to the point of caricature. But these caricatures are not – as sometimes in Shakespeare – an expression of contempt for the plebeian, but the true realist's determination to represent the people as they are, with their achievements and their vices, their strength and their shortcomings – certainly not as virtuous shepherds or 'nature's gentlemen'. Brueghel, painting like this, was the great spokesman of the rising, self-assured bourgeoisie.

Let us now consider the radical change which the subject of agricultural work undergoes in the paintings of Millet. Millet, an artist of peasant origin who supported the revolution of 1848, presents the work of the peasant in the capitalist world as a modern form of slavery and hideous dehumanization. Lamennais wrote at the same time in his *De l'esclavage moderne*:

> The peasant bears the brunt of the day, exposing himself to rain, wind, and sun in order to prepare the harvest that fills our barns in late autumn. If there is a nation whose esteem for him is lessened because of that, a nation that refuses him justice and freedom, then let a high wall be built round that nation so that its stinking breath may not poison the air of Europe.

The class struggle of the proletariat was beginning – and what Brueghel had seen through the eyes of the rising bourgeoisie, Millet saw through the eyes of a proletarian peasant. He painted the dreariness, the misery, the hopelessness of a peasant's work and life, not from the outside, but as a peasant among

peasants. His shepherd-woman bears no resemblance whatso-
ever to the coy shepherdesses of Rococo and Baroque. She
stands there, dressed in a coarse, shapeless garment, leaning
exhausted on her staff, brooding dully, the wretched ghost of a
human creature. Or take the corn gleaners: no faces are to be
seen, only bowed backs, heads almost touching the ground,
hands grubbing in the dust, degraded figures emptied of all
humanity.

The same bowed backs, the same heads, but still more dreadfully, more hopelessly bent earthwards, recur in the paintings
of van Gogh, who began by copying Millet and who in the
loneliness of his genius went far beyond him. 'I can tell you
that I sketched the ten pages *Travaux des champs* by Millet, and
that I have quite finished one. . . . Besides I have made a drawing of the *Angelus*, after the etching which you sent me,' he
wrote to his brother in 1880. Later, in a letter which describes
his purpose in his own painting:

When you come again to the studio, I think you will see pretty soon
that, though I do not speak so much any longer about that plan of
making workmen's types for lithography, I still keep it in mind. . . .
I have a sower – a mower – a woman at the washtub – a seamstress – a
digger – a woman with a spade – the almshouse men – a benedicite
– a fellow with a wheelbarrow full of manure. There are still more, if
necessary. . . . The secret of Lhermitte must be no other, I think, than
that he thoroughly knows the figure in general, that is, the sturdy,
serious workman's figure, and that he takes his subjects from the
very heart of the people. To attain his height – one must not speak
about that – one must *work*, and try to come as far as possible.

And finally:

This one thing is still there – this faith – you feel instinctively that an
enormous amount is changing and everything is going to change –
we are living in the last quarter of a century that will again end with a
tremendous revolution. But even supposing that at the end of our
lives we may see the beginning of it – we certainly shall not see those
better times of clear air, the whole of society refreshed, *after* that
great storm.

This then is how van Gogh worked. He took his motifs

from the 'heart of the people', sensing enormous social changes ahead; he lived before the great storm, filled with the bitter knowledge that he would not live to see 'those better times of clear air ... after the great storm'. In those days before the great storm, working people were oppressed and ill-treated (van Gogh was immensely moved by Zola's *Germinal* and *Earth*), and only the little time they could spend away from their work allowed them to be human beings at all. Van Gogh's *Reaper* is even further removed from Brueghel's than Millet's is. The young peasant, his body wrenched and twisted by his work, is completely alone: the motif of loneliness declares itself, the abandonment of the lonely individual struggling to scrape a living, always threatened, never assured. His face beneath the coarse mop of hair that is as yellow as the corn itself expresses both effort and exhaustion; another moment, and this reaper may become too heavy for his own strength – and then the earth will drag him down, a thing among inanimate things. These *things* are more powerful than man; it is as though they had awakened to a demonic life of their own. This is no longer the static mass of corn that Brueghel had painted; it is a field gripped by a fever, a field aroused and shaken by a strange tremor. Van Gogh was to discover this 'life' of inanimate objects with ever-increasing intensity, to catch them red-handed as it were – the chair that no one is sitting in now (once Gauguin had sat in it), the landscape without any people in it, a world deserted and charged with dynamite – and behind it the immense sun that may, one day, shine upon men as well as things. A great revolution would come, but the painter of this volcanic age would not – of this van Gogh was sure – live to see those 'better times'.

Bowed backs, bent heads, humiliation and degradation of workers and peasants – these, too, were the subjects of the great Mexican painter Diego Rivera. But he also painted those who humiliated and degraded them, with a punishing hatred like that which had inspired Daumier's merciless drawings; he painted the Spanish oppressors and the 'rich man's meal', the American oil bandits and dollar kings, the bankers parading their Bibles and the high-class whores flaunting their bosoms.

In his works it is no longer an invisible power that bows the backs and bends the heads, but a real and tangible enemy, an enemy that can be faced and beaten. Rivera also went further. He painted the liberated earth, peasants sharing out the land among them, tilling the soil for their own benefit, reaping the maize and the sugar-cane, discussing rational methods of farming with agronomists, bringing the first tractor to the village, enjoying holidays. The working human being, of whom until now we had seen only the bowed back and the straining muscles, suddenly acquired a human face, capable of expressing grim determination or gay confidence. Diego Rivera's bold, grand manner of depicting the struggles, the victories, the meaningful work of the common people has nothing of the style of the old genre painters, no superfluous detail, no trace of narrow naturalism or romantic posturing. This is true socialist realism. Rivera's profound artistic experience allowed him to learn from Giotto, Michelangelo, Daumier, and the modern French masters without falling into imitation. Here the subject of work on the land, and of human work in general, received a totally new content. An old subject received a new meaning and with it a new style.

Interpretation of a picture

We have taken a few examples to illustrate that content is incomparably more than subject or theme, that, important as the choice of subject is, the content of a work of art is determined not so much by what it depicts as by how it does so: how the artist, consciously or unconsciously, expresses the social tendencies of his time. To interpret the content of a painting is sometimes a difficult undertaking, and contradictory conclusions can often be drawn. This, too, I should like to illustrate by an example. Here is how Johannes R. Becher defined the 'content' of El Greco's *Storm Over Toledo*:

An apocalyptic storm is gathering, piling up tremendous banks of cloud on the horizon. Already it casts its shadows over the edge of the city, and the city grows pale and trembles before the end of the world that seems to threaten it. The green hills, too, on which Toledo is built, are changing colour, fading to a ghostly green. In their midst they grip the river that is standing still as though paralysed by the approaching horror, forming an inert, waiting mass round a small island lying naked and bare in the reflection of the terrifying sky. The grass and the trees have been roused by fear, yet they are rigid, motionless: it is the moment of silence before the storm. The clouds on the horizon become darker and darker, the artist makes us hear the rolls of thunder drawing near, makes us sense the flashes of lightning. It is a cosmic storm that approaches – we feel that it is so. And Toledo itself, with its towers and palaces, its bridges and arches, is shaken to its foundations even before the storm has broken with full force, and this trembling has at the same time the effect of a triumph: Toledo will stand fast!

This is a beautiful and optimistic interpretation, but another interpreter could turn the statement 'Toledo will stand fast!' into a question 'Will Toledo stand fast?' (We are not concerned here with the 'real' Toledo but with the work of an artist whose paintings, far from suggesting an optimistic view of the world, bear witness to an apocalyptic dread.) The stones and rocks and green hills that have to face the storm do not seem at all firm and unshakable. The elemental force threatening the city from above is also a concealed, subterranean one. It is not only the reflection of the clouds that gives the stone walls and the whole landscape their ghostly pallor – there is something ghostly in the objects themselves. Looking at the painting one remembers Brecht's lines:

> Of these cities will remain
> Only the wind that swept through them.

A gigantic drama is about to be enacted. Not only the explosive core of nature but the solid, well-built city of man is here shown as infinitely vulnerable, holding its breath in a world of appalling dangers. The stately edifice of today is no more than tomorrow's heap of debris. Terrible things will happen. The day will come when Toledo, too, will fall to the ground. This, perhaps, is what El Greco wanted to say with all the expressive power at his command.

The problematic element in both interpretations is their

subjectivity. The world in which El Greco lived and what we know of his own attitude tend to support the second view. I have omitted argument and proof so as not to overload the example. But it seems appropriate at this point to mention the difficulty of arriving at accurate interpretations at any time. One must always ask what the artist himself wanted to say. But even if the answer can be supplied (which is seldom the case), the second question must inevitably be: 'Why did he want to say this?' What external forces, what influences peculiar to his time was he obeying, consciously or unconsciously? Was he not overpowered by his own unconscious? Does not the meaning he wanted to put into the work conceal a deeper one, a meaning that is, in the last analysis, social – and that may contradict the artist's intention? What objective criteria can the observer refer to? A work of art is steeped in the atmosphere of a period and a personality. But does that atmosphere remain unchanged after centuries? Does not the work itself become different in a different world? Is not the judgement of posterity often truer than that of contemporaries? Cannot something that was no more, at the time, than a faint presentiment of the future, have suddenly and startlingly become today's present? The artistic quality of a painting can be discussed objectively, but its meaning allows of many different readings. There was an 'El Greco' of the sixteenth century; then, for a long time, there was none; today there is an 'El Greco' of the twentieth. Always we reach out for what we need, and a work of art is never a thing in itself. It always requires an interaction with a spectator. We discover the meaning of a work: but we also invest it with one.

But whatever the meaning of the picture (and many works of art allow of different interpretations as times change), it is always more than the mere subject matter (e.g. 'storm clouds gathering over a city'). A naturalistic painter might treat the same subject in such a way that his painting would mean nothing more than a real, 'natural' storm over a real, 'natural' city. The observer would then have no more to do than to acknowledge the accuracy with which the artist had recorded a storm. This reduces the content or meaning of the picture to a minimum, namely the degree of likeness achieved. The work of art becomes a mere copy of reality, seen from the outside, devoid of content or ideas, without itself amounting to a new and important reality. It can still be a well-painted picture, and therein may lie its *raison d'être* – but what is the deeper meaning of a work of art if it does nothing more than copy or record the phenomena of nature, if it does not discover, reveal, 'catch objects red-handed'? In his study on *Truth and Verisimilitude of Works of Art* Goethe wrote, using as his point of departure the classical anecdote told about a painting by Zeuxis:

You surely remember the birds that flew down to pick the great master's cherries. – Well, does that not prove that the cherries were excellently painted? – Not in the least; it proves to me, rather, that those amateurs of cherries were real sparrows. – But need that prevent me from considering the painting excellent? – Shall I tell you a newer story? – I would generally rather hear a story than a piece of reasoning. – A great scholar of nature possessed among his domestic animals a monkey, which he once missed and later found again, after a long search, in his library. The brute was sitting on the floor and had scattered around itself the copper-plate prints of an unbound work on natural science. Astonished at such zealous scholarship on the part of his pet, the master approached and found to his surprise and annoyance that the greedy monkey had eaten all the beetles it had seen depicted here and there. . . .

The greedy monkey will doubtless have discovered to his own 'surprise and annoyance' that real beetles surpass painted ones in taste and nutritive value – in other words, that nature is always more 'natural' than art, and that art cannot hope to achieve, in this respect, what nature so stalwartly performs. And so it clearly cannot be the goal and purpose of art to reproduce nature, and its meaning and content cannot merely be a matter of likeness.

But important as it is to recognize that the meaning and content of a work of art go beyond its subject matter, it is no less essential to grant the subject its due share of importance. The evolution of subjects in literature and the arts is well worth considering, for the choice of subject reflects prevailing social conditions and social consciousness. The change from

mythical to 'profane' subjects, the penetration of the world of
kings and noblemen by the common people, the secularization
of sacred subjects by the depiction of daily life in town and
country, the discovery of human beings at work as a fit theme
for the arts, the replacement of 'noble drama' by 'bourgeois
tragedy' – all these new social subjects indicate a new content
and demand new forms, such as that of the novel. This kind of
development is not governed by any rigid formula and does not
follow a regular sequence of events: first a new subject, then a
new content, finally a new form. Rather it is a matter of complex and multiple mutual influences, and artists of genius such
as Giotto or Cervantes may advance the process suddenly,
leaving out several stages. The staying power of traditional
subjects (especially religious ones), the continuing influence of
an old style, a variety of social, technical, and ideological conditions which may assist each other or temporarily cancel each
other out, the lucky accident of a great artistic personality, all
are factors that may retard or accelerate development, so that
new meanings and new forms may emerge either gradually,
painfully, and with many contradictions, or easily and all at
once. When we analyse any specific work of art, any artistic
movement or period in the arts, we must beware of preconceived opinions. But when we survey the general features
of the history of art as a whole, we cannot fail to observe that
changes in the content and form of the arts are, in the last
instance, the outcome of social and economic changes.
Ultimately it is the new content that determines new forms.

Not infrequently a new content may find expression in old
forms; but it may also destroy the old forms with an almost
explosive violence and bring new ones into existence. The
Swiss critic Konrad Farner quotes Christian art during the
period of late antiquity as an example of a new content
temporarily borrowing old forms. This art, he writes,

made use of old pagan forms to express a new, no longer pagan
content. Christian artists had to use old forms in order to present the
new content in the most direct way possible, since these forms corresponded to familiar ways of seeing – and the prime concern of the
early Christians was to make the Christian message widely known,

in order to create a new world. Generations of artists had to come and go before a new form corresponding to the new content was found, for new forms are not suddenly created, nor are they introduced by decree – which, incidentally, is also true of new contents. But let us be clear about it: the content, not the form, is always the first to be renewed; it is content that generates form, not vice versa; content comes first, not only in order of importance but also in time, and this applies to nature, to society, and therefore also to the arts. Wherever form is more important than content, it will be found that the content is out of date. At the end of the Middle Ages it was scurrilous Gothic, at the time of dying absolutism it was mannered Rococo, and at the time of the decaying bourgeoisie it is empty abstraction.

No one can deny that Christianity brought new ideas into the world. But we should not overlook the fact that, in the early centuries of our era, it belonged to antiquity even so far as its content was concerned. It competed with similar religions, such as the cults of Mithras, Isis, and Serapis – religions which also went far outside local boundaries and attempted to satisfy the Roman Empire's thirst for religious unity. And Christianity, especially in its Alexandrian version, was extremely anxious to establish itself as a movement *within* antiquity and to associate itself both with the arts and the philosophy of antiquity. But none of this is directly relevant to our argument. Farner's main point, with which we must agree, is that new ideas may use old forms in order to express themselves in works of art.

Early Gothic saw a tremendous wealth of new forms and means of expression resulting from a new social content and the rise of new social classes. The process had begun even earlier, in the late Romanesque period. The formal Romanesque world of feudal order was revolutionized. The rigid hierarchy in which there were no human beings but only ranks and castes collapsed. The unapproachable solemnity of feudal lords upon their thrones with vassals at their feet, the gold, red, and blue, the cold brilliance, the measured gestures of aristocratic supermen, all this gave way to the ecstatic realism of early Gothic and late Romanesque art. Christ suffering and tormented, Christ akin to the common people in his poverty and ugliness, displaced the feudal ruler of the heavenly hosts. Mary the Maid, defender of the insulted and the injured, took the place of the Queen of Heaven seated in splendour. And in late Romanesque sculpture, Lazarus was already a central figure, an indictment of the arrogance of the rich and powerful, of the gluttons and the voluptuaries, of the flesh with its pride and its vices. Dogs lick the festering wounds of Lazarus, but the angel is approaching who will lead him into paradise, and death and the devil are preparing a grisly end for Dives, the rich man. The death of Dives is depicted with a fury of avenging fantasy: a demon snatches his soul out of his mouth, another taunts him with his moneybag, an infernal swarm of monsters, birds, dragons, serpents falls upon him to carry his lacerated body down to hell. Friedrich Heer wrote in *The Rise of Europe*:

> Other carvings close by [on the portal of Moissac] depict the punishment of rich men and other sinners in hell. There is the miser writhing on the ground and crouching on his hands and feet like a quadruped; his back is twisted towards the ground, his moneybag is at his side, whilst a satan made up of both human and animal limbs and attended by two devils sinks a claw deep into his body. . . . The *femme aux serpents*, naked, with snakes and toads sucking at her breasts, is a frequent motif in the propaganda of this popular art as the embodiment of the vice of lechery. . . .

Friedrich Heer, a Catholic writer, fully understood how the new art that swept away both the content and the form of feudal Romanesque traditions was conditioned by the social changes and upheavals of the age. Many thousands of landless peasants were on the move, and with them all kinds of other 'wandering folk', runaway monks, pilgrims, students, and vagabonds. The growing power of money was undermining the very structure of feudal society. A new, self-confident class of townspeople, forerunners of the bourgeoisie, was growing up; a new stratum of society, that of the minor gentry, was beginning to develop; large numbers of working men were concentrated for the first time in the workshops of the early medieval textile industry; the social movement of townspeople and minor gentry, peasants and proletarians turned the Bible into a weapon against the rulers of the world and created a militant heretical body; Abelard and others invoked the Holy

Ghost in their struggle against feudal conformism and appealed to the traditions of antiquity against dogmatism and the power of the hierarchy; the influence of Arabic culture further added to the ferment of minds; the embryo of the bourgeois revolution began to stir in the womb of Christian Europe.

The creation of urban building fraternities was one of the symptoms of the new age, and the fraternities themselves became the transmitters of a new style. Heer may be exaggerating when he claims that 'in the crusading enthusiasm of the building movement, the old world of the feudal Middle Ages was melted down and recast'. But the significance of this movement as an element in a broader social trend is self-evident. Heer points out that 'the great turning-point can be seen in individual works and also in the range of subjects'.

At St Julien-en-Brioude, two stone-masons confront us: sturdily realistic faces with rough-hewn features. . . . For the first time in the history of Europe, new strata of society demand to be heard, or rather, at first, to be seen. . . . The dynamism of a new 'people', of new masses, struggles for expression. And now we begin to find representations of real crowd scenes – as for instance in the crypt of the cathedral at Clermont-Ferrand. Common people of all kinds, big and small, crowd round Christ who is performing the miracle of the loaves and fishes. Their hands are outstretched for the bread he is giving them. These figures are drawn with a drastic realism, their gestures and faces outlined with large, firm strokes. Here the mild, sturdy, kindly Christ is already a true 'people's Christ'. . . .

And so, as Romanesque changes to Gothic, as pure feudalism gives way to a social situation in which the bourgeoisie can make advance after advance, a new social content fills the arts and produces new forms and means of expression, the new art being partly realistic and partly ecstatic. The long process of the secularization of the arts has begun – with the songs of the troubadours, with the introduction of popular realism into the visual arts, with the humanization of the Christ figure, with the dawn of reason and of individual protest within the framework of Christian philosophy. The style which had idealized and glorified the feudal world, recognizing only rank and order but not human relationships, became incompatible with the new social movements and upheavals. The new classes' need for expression demanded new means. If we observe the spread of Gothic we see that realistic or even naturalistic methods were used wherever the common people began to play a part in the visual arts. The findings of modern research seem to indicate that the art of primitive classless society started with a primitive naturalism; 'stylization' and abstraction gained the upper hand only in the later Stone Age and were prominent thereafter in all aristocratic systems of government, while contrary movements always originated among the plebeian strata. In Gothic – the first 'bourgeois' movement in art within the still-existing feudal system – the result was highly contradictory: on the one hand a violent, extremely daring realism, on the other a fervent longing for a spiritual, non-material life, for escape from the 'valley of tears' into the beyond. The towers of the Gothic cathedral pointing towards infinity are in themselves ambivalent – an expression of heaven-storming defiance and, at the same time, of an ecstatic yearning for redemption. The social strata dreaming of deliverance were still bound to the feudal system and its traditions. This is what gave rise to the profoundly contradictory nature of Gothic art, so much admired for its boldness, so much abused for its 'barbarian' absurdities. But above all Gothic meant the humanization of sacred themes, although this essential element is partly obscured by grim devilish monsters and a passionate transcendentalism.

Giotto

Giotto was the first master of the new humanism. In Giotto, Christ is truly the son of man. Sacred events have become earthly, the beyond has become a human world. Even the soft gold of the saints' haloes is no longer an echo of the emblazoned supernatural backgrounds of older paintings, but has been transformed into an aura of pure humanity. These frescoes do not proclaim a rigid, immutable world. Everything is shown in movement, as encounter of men with other men. No longer does a revelation beyond and outside history demand unconditional obedience. The story of Christ is told as something so tangible and near that the spectator seems invited to take part in it. Dramatic situations, not changeless images, are depicted; the figures, related to one another, are no longer confined within the two-dimensional plane of the painting but stand out from it, reach forward into space as though they wanted to cast off every bond and to unite themselves with everyone living here and now. A new social reality, a new, undogmatic consciousness makes itself felt in these secularized and humanized images.

Yet when we admire the impressive 'realism' of Giotto's works we should not fall into the error of thinking that Byzantine and early Romanesque art was 'unreal' or that it arbitrarily distorted reality. The arrogant loneliness of the Byzantine emperors and empresses, of the angels and saints in their rigid gold settings, the enormous, majestic Heavenly King surrounded by dwarf-sized vassals, all these were true representations of social reality in Romanesque art. The stiff, inhuman immobility of the figures, the 'unnaturalness' of the proportions were by no means the result of the artists' inability to draw. These artists, servants of the ruling class, intended to represent an 'eternal' world order, to portray masks of a lofty social character, not people engaged in changeable relationships. The attributes of power were more important than the men in whom they were vested. The artist's function was not to praise nature but to praise the 'super-nature' of the social order. What mattered was not natural proportion but the rigid social scale of ranks and classes.

Society and style

I have tried, very briefly, to illustrate by means of an example how a new set of subjects, new forms of expression, a new style, are evolved as a result of changes in social content. But I am fully aware that I have had to over-simplify. A new social content never expresses itself directly but only obliquely, and any attempt at a sociology of art must, unless it is trivial and frivolous, take this obliqueness into account. Here I can only hint at an analysis, and many questions have to remain unanswered: why did Gothic take the particular forms it did – the pointed arch, the flying buttress, cross-vaulting? Why did the two-dimensional image begin to become three-dimensional? How did social, technical, and ideological elements combine to create a new style?

Arnold Hauser, in his stimulating book *The Philosophy of Art History*,* puts a number of such questions:

What was it that first set in motion the change to the Gothic ...? Which came first, cross-vaulting or the idea of vertical composition? Did the builders of the Gothic cathedrals get their 'vertical' conception from the means that had become available for its realization, or did a new vision of height, the Gothic sense of exaltation, wring from the craftsmen the means needed for the translation of this vision into stone and glass?

We must look to specialist studies such as Hauser's for the answers – and even the finest scholars will sometimes be hard put to it to supply absolutely precise answers, for the causes are many and closely interwoven, and it is difficult to judge at what point quantitative changes developed into qualitative ones. We may therefore agree with Hauser when he writes:

Objections to social history of art as a method of interpretation result mostly from attributing to it aims that it neither can nor will carry out. Only the very crudest type of social history would seek to represent a particular type of art as the homogeneous, conclusive, and direct expression of a particular form of society. The art of a historically complex age can never be homogeneous, if only because the society of such an epoch is not homogeneous; it can never be more than the expression of a social stratum, of a group of persons with some common interests; it will exhibit simultaneously just as many different stylistic tendencies as there are different cultural levels within the relevant society.

But since social classes are the most enduring and most effective 'groups of persons with some common interests', the needs and means of expression in art are class conditioned (though we must allow for the fact that a social class is not a windowless fortress, that even antagonistic classes influence

* Routledge & Kegan Paul, 1958.

each other, that the forms and conventions developed by an old ruling class can influence the rising new classes, and that changes and developments take place even within a single class). Hauser is therefore right when he says:

Social history of art merely asserts – and this is the only sort of assertion which it can seek to substantiate – that art-forms are not only forms of individual consciousness, optically or orally conditioned, but also expressions of a socially conditioned world-view.

We should add that even 'optically or orally conditioned' forms of individual experience are not evolved independently from social development. New ways of seeing or hearing are not simply the result of improved or refined sensory perceptions, but also of new social realities. For example, the rhythm, noise, and tempo of great cities stimulate new kinds of seeing and hearing, a peasant sees a landscape differently from a city dweller, and so forth. The point is, however, that social conditions rarely find direct reflection in the arts, and new artistic forms and ideas do not completely coincide with a new social content.

Yet is not what we call 'style' the uniform expression of an age, a social era, in art? Is not the same 'style' recognizable in a general attitude extending to clothes and politics, morals and manners, music and poetry? Is not 'style' the most unequivocal expression of a society? First of all, if we examine the phenomenon of style, we find that a system of forms, conventions, and tendencies has been accepted by artists of different kinds and different temperaments as a law by which they freely choose to be governed. Thus a collective element enters the output of an individual, and though individual works may differ greatly depending on the talent or originality of the artist, the common factor (often difficult to define) is unmistakable. Theorists with a liking for the metaphysical conclude from this that art is a mysterious 'organism', a 'living body' independent from social conditions and developing according to its own laws, either progressing from simple to increasingly complex forms (regardless of whether this contradicts the social developments), or else that art has a life that is subject to a constant cycle of youth and old age, birth and death, so that each 'cultural cycle' produces an entirely new art peculiar to itself, but which nevertheless goes through all the same stages as the art of past 'cultural cycles'. According to such hypotheses, development in art is solely a question of form and of the internal problems of art itself, and style is not the result of social changes and individual achievements but an autonomous power which governs all. Hence the artist, his patron, and the public which is the consumer of his products are, as it were, the executive organs of art; art is created with their help but it also imposes its own laws upon them. If this view were right, every historical age would have had a completely uniform style, style being a divine substance of which individual works of art are the attributes. But if we survey the separate periods of art history, we find that although the development of the arts in any given period tended towards a uniform style, this tendency was invariably opposed by counter-trends. Some branches of the arts developed while others were left behind; there were artists of extreme individuality who opposed the prevailing general style; different movements clashed and intermingled, heterogeneous elements fought or interpenetrated one another (e.g. realism and transcendentalism in Gothic). The picture in fact is much more complex and contradictory than the principle of absolute unity of style can allow.

No one can deny the staying power of old forms and conventions. Artists have a legitimate wish not always to have to start at the beginning but to carry on from a point already attained, to transform an existing style into something new. If we want to understand the style of a period, we must not consider it in isolation but in the context of the history of art as a whole, as a moment in historical development – but this is true not only of the arts but of all social phenomena. The sudden appearance of a new range of subjects and of new artistic methods resulting from it (e.g. the appearance of the working man in art), or the original achievements of artists such as Giotto, El Greco, Brueghel, Goya, or Daumier, cannot be explained by an 'organic' or autonomous development of art. And furthermore the theory collapses when it tries to explain the temporary appearances and eclipses of realism in art – because it persistently ignores the fact that stylized art is bound up with aristocratic systems and realist art with plebeian movements, that the epic declined with the age of chivalry and the novel grew up with the bourgeoisie, that polyphonic music died together with the feudal system and homophonic music developed together with the bourgeois age, and so forth. It would be a complete misunderstanding of the nature of art to assert that formal problems do not exist in art, that all problems are directly connected with social situations. But Hauser is right when he writes:

The greatest danger for art history, and one to which it has been constantly exposed ever since Riegl's historicism laid the foundation of its modern methodology, is that it should become a mere history of forms and problems. . . .

These problems and tasks are real enough; they are neither inventions nor methodological fictions, and any scientific art history must trace them and work them out. . . . The works of art, however, are not brought into being in order to solve these problems; the problems turn up in the course of creating works to answer questions having little connexion with formal and technical problems – questions of world-outlook, of the conduct of life, of faith and knowledge.

And so, if we analyse the artistic achievements of a particular age, we must take account of stylistic and formal problems and of the dominant style, but we must also consider the deviations from that style; in surveying the history of art, we must not regard art as an anonymous whole but as the work of individual artists with their own specific gifts and aspirations. Above all, we must study the social conditions, movements, and conflicts of the period, the class relationships and struggles and the resulting ideas – religious, philosophical, and political – in order to see the art of that period in a real, not an imaginary, context. We must beware of reading into every work of art, or element of style, a direct and unambiguous expression of a class or a social situation. We must take care not to judge a writer's, artist's, or musician's work solely according to whether it is 'progressive' or 'reactionary' (for the two may intermingle, as Lenin pointed out in his analysis of Tolstoy – and besides, the question of quality must enter into *every* judgement). But unless we apply sociology to the arts – unless we examine the social causes for its changing subjects, forms, and content – we are bound to end up in a cloud-cuckoo-land of abstract speculation and aestheticism, miles from reality. An analysis of style, however intelligent it may be and however brilliant its insight into specific problems and details, is bound to fail unless it recognizes that content – that is to say, in the last instance, the social element – is the decisive style-forming factor in art.

Form and social experience

Nevertheless it would be foolish to concentrate all our attention on content and relegate form to the status of a secondary issue. Art is the giving of form, and form alone makes a product into a work of art. Form is not something accidental, arbitrary, or inessential (no more than the form of a crystal is any of those things). The laws and conventions of form are the embodiment of man's mastery over matter; in them, transmitted experience is preserved and all achievement is kept safe; they are the order necessary to art and life.

To understand natural or social phenomena we must find out how they came into being. The form of a social object – a product of work – is directly connected with its function. Primitive man formed a stone, a piece of wood or a bone to make it serve his ends: in other words, form is the expression of social purpose. Countless experiments and attempts at imitation eventually produced certain permanent forms embodying the sum total of past experience in a particular field. Thousands of years before a standard shape for a pot was evolved, pots were made for an *ad hoc* purpose, for the sake of function, not form. Ultimately a particularly useful and practical form was retained, both as a model and as a pattern for more rational production. *Form is social experience solidified.*

Form is also, to some extent, conditioned by materials. This does not mean, as some mystics would have us believe, that a certain form is 'latent' in a particular material, nor that all materials strive towards their own perfection or 'de-materialization', nor that man's desire to form materials is a metaphysical 'will towards form'. But every material has its specific properties which allow it to be formed in specific though possibly varied ways. Thus the forms of human dwellings are largely affected by the material used – by whether the dwelling is made out of plaited grass or rushes or built out of wood, stone, or clay; i.e. the material most readily available partly determines the form of the dwelling. Likewise the proportions and symmetry of a house (or any other product of work) are not the result of an aesthetic 'will towards form' but are determined by the structure of the material and by the past experience of the maker. A jerry-built, lop-sided house will last less well than one that follows certain laws of symmetry. Just as symmetry in crystals is the expression of an equilibrium of energy and hence of a saving of energy, so the symmetry of a house or other man-made object is also an expression of equilibrium. Primitive man did not, it is true, know the theoretical laws that govern matter, but he learned them in practice and came to know the value of measure and order from direct experience. If we bear in mind that his experience in other fields of collective activity also confirmed the value of rhythm and rhythmic repetition, we shall find that the mystical element often read into primitive man's respect for order disappears altogether.

Forms which evolve from collective work processes – forms which are social experience solidified – tend to be extremely conservative. If we study the development of production, building, etc., we find that there is a tendency to preserve old forms even when a new material has been adopted. Sometimes indeed the new material is, as it were, violated by the old form. Elements of the primitive 'style' of grass, mud, or wooden huts are recognizable in the stone buildings of a later age. The forms of stone tools still persist in the tools of the Bronze and Iron Ages, although the new materials lend themselves to more practical shapes. There is nothing surprising about this conservative tendency of form: it is an extension of the tendency of all collectives to hold on to their hard-won social experience, to pass it down from generation to generation as a treasured inheritance. A form evolved by the collective was considered a sacred thing and carried an obligation: *it shall be thus and not otherwise*. To make any change in such forms was sinful and could have dangerous consequences. This conservatism of form was opposed by material production with its constant enrichment of experience, the tendency to make work easier and more efficient by the use of more appropriate tools and materials based on closer observation of nature and increased working skills.

When we speak of efficiency, of which form is the expression, we do not mean only those material structures which we recognize today as efficient, but also the whole enormous range of magic things which, for primitive man, represented the highest form of efficiency. We have already pointed out that man, the productive, nature-changing being, was a magician; that, as he discovered the vast importance of similarity, of 'making alike', of mastering nature through work, through tools and the human will, he tended to overestimate the immediate possibilities of his conquest of nature and so was led to make a bold attempt at influencing reality by magical means. George Thomson remarks in *Aeschylus and Athens* that primitive magic is based on the idea that reality can be controlled by creating an illusion of controlling it. But at the same time, because magic leads to action, it embodies the valuable realization that the outside world can actually be changed by men's subjective attitude towards it. Hunters whose strength has been revived and organized by ritual mime are *in fact* better hunters than they were before.

Discussing the origins and development of totemism, Thomson points out that the totem animal was originally the animal on which the tribe fed. This is made obvious by such facts as that the chief of the Wallaby clan in Australia has to eat some of the totem animal's flesh at his initiation ceremony, i.e. he must 'absorb' the animal. When primitive man fed on a plant or on the flesh of an animal, he felt a regeneration, a surge of vitality. Since the processes of metabolism were unknown to him, he naturally supposed that the 'life force' of the plant or animal was transmitted to him, that his life merged with that of his prey, that a union of their two lives came about. He 'identified' himself through physical metabolism, which he could explain only magically, with the living organisms he ate. But when, as a result of improved hunting techniques, the animal which was the tribe's preferred food became too rare or almost extinct, it was protected by a taboo, a set of strict prohibitive rules. The horde divided itself up into tribes, each with its own hunting ground; the foodstuffs, hunted animals, etc., were in a sense shared out; each tribe was no longer allowed to eat one of the animals or plants that had hitherto been part of its diet, and the nourishment of all the tribes was thereby reasonably assured. Thus a certain animal or plant was 'taboo' for each tribe, and if the tribe violated the taboo it imperilled the very life of the collective, for the existence of human beings was identified with that of their food. As productive forces developed and new sources of nourishment were discovered, the totem and the taboo lost their original economic meaning, but the forms were by then so deeply rooted that they were retained and, in part, invested with a new content. They now became magic rules for safeguarding the traditional structure of society, protecting the tribes and their social property and therefore also regulating sexual relationships.

This hypothesis is attractive, although I am inclined to believe that totem and taboo had a sexual as well as an economic significance from the start. It seems to me characteristic of the primitive collective to regard sexuality, food, and work as an indivisible whole identical with life itself, a life not yet differentiated by the division of labour. Countless rites suggest that in the mind of primitive man, 'metabolism' with the outside world, 'metabolism' between the sexes, and physical metabolism assured by work merged into a single vital process. In almost all initiation rites by which youths are assimilated into the collective – the great collective 'body' – sexual experience is transmitted to the youths together with the principal experiences of work.

We have been speaking of the development of the totem and taboo because a great number of forms evolved from these magic beliefs and because we see them as one of the prime sources of art. Only by realizing that primitive man largely identified himself with the animals and plants he fed on, that is to say with nature itself, and only by becoming aware of the importance that form and similarity of form had for primitive man, can we hope to understand much that would otherwise be incomprehensible. Scholars have pointed this out again and again. I should like to quote a passage from Father Winthuis, although I am by no means in agreement with this anthropologist's conclusions:

Because of his manner of thinking – a concrete manner addressing itself to the whole, never abstract nor abstracting, never analysing the detail nor giving it its due – the decisive element for primitive man is not the inner nature of things but their exterior, their form, what the eye sees. Everything that has the same form has also, to him, the same significance.

Winthuis obviously underestimates the power of abstraction in working human beings whose work irresistibly leads them towards abstraction. But he is right in saying that form was of decisive importance for primitive man.

The magic cave

At this point let us consider a question that is often asked, namely: if the form of human products represents concentrated social experience, how can we explain the magnificent cave paintings of the Middle Stone Age, admirable works of art produced by an extremely undeveloped society? We may regard usefulness as the essence of the form of tools or pots or dwellings, but when faced with the Stone Age rock paintings of Africa, Scandinavia, and Southern Europe are we not bound to think that a mysterious, metaphysical, creative power, a divine inspiration, intuition, or idea, compelled and enabled the primitive men of that time to produce such works of art?

I should like to take as my example the Trois Frères cave discovered by Count Bégouen, with its famous animal paintings and the famous figure of the 'sorcerer' with the animal mask, on which there exists an extensive literature. No one can deny that the buffaloes in this dark cave in the rock are superbly drawn, nor that the sorcerer enthroned over them, disguised as an elk, is extremely impressive. But side by side with these works based on a precise and profound observation of animals, there exist much weaker, inferior rock paintings, and neither their venerable age nor any desire we may have to admire all that is primitive can wholly disguise their feeble execution. This point must be made because some scholars tend to see a demonic quality of 'genius' in all primitive races: a 'genius' which, they claim, civilized man has lost. In reality, however, Middle Stone Age man produced some very mediocre works as well as some outstandingly fine ones.

A comparison with children's drawings may be helpful. Here, too, side by side with clumsy scrawls and glaring inadequacies we sometimes come across instances of astonishing insight into the forms and shapes of the outside world, a marvellous assurance in depicting animals and objects, reminiscent of pre-historic art. This may have something to do with the freshness of a child's brain and with the fact that each individual impression is as yet undisturbed by any awareness of social complexities and conventions. A child sees only a small section of the world, but it sees it with great intensity. But such comparisons should be made with care, for prehistoric man lived in a world very different from that of a civilized child. Even at its most direct and naïve, a twentieth-century child is greatly influenced by the structure of a complex society. An animal, say, means something quite different to a child today from what it meant to a Middle Stone Age hunter.

Before we consider the range of experience reflected in cave paintings we must realize that these works were already the culmination, the result of a long process of artistic development. They were preceded by works of art of a much more primitive kind, clumsy blocks of clay over which the hide of an animal was stretched to counterfeit a living animal and so to avert the vengeance of other creatures of that species. Leo Frobenius, an excellent observer although a theoretician of questionable merit, wrote:

Count Bégouen together with N. Casteret discovered a cave near Montespan in the Haute-Garonne. At the end of a passage he found himself inside a hall in the middle of which there was a figure of an animal made of clay. This was crudely executed, no attention being paid to detail, but showed the animal in a crouching position with the front legs outstretched, and was particularly distinguished by the fact that the head was missing. The whole work was clumsily fashioned rather like the snowmen that children make in winter. Nevertheless, the crudeness of the work could not explain the missing head. . . . The whole figure in its general contours, with the special formation of the legs and the strong, high, rounded rump suggests a bear; and, indeed, a bear's skull was found between the front feet.

Frobenius also writes, this time of the African Kuluballi tribe:

Whenever a lion or leopard devours a man, a bush sacrifice is held and the beast is killed. A special place, called 'Mulikorre Nyama', is then set aside in the bush. This consists of a circular thorn hedge, in the centre of which is placed a headless clay figure representing a beast of prey. The killed lion or leopard is then stripped of its hide but the head, with skull intact, is left on. The hide, with the head, is pulled over the clay figure. Then all the warriors surround the thorn hedge, the animal image being inside but the hunters, dancing, outside. In the meantime the animal's body is buried.

These lumps of clay over which an animal's hide was stretched were evidently the first plastic works in human history. They had little in common with what we call art today; their sole purpose was to propitiate the animal world – i.e. to acquire mastery over reality by means of an image. But once men had begun to reproduce animals for such a purpose, this kind of production like any other was bound to develop and undergo a process of refinement. For magic reasons it was important to achieve the greatest possible likeness, indeed a degree of identification between the image and the model. This identification was first brought about by the hide of the killed animal, but when images began to be made without the hide and head of the real animal (perhaps in the interests of mass production), maximum resemblance became a magic requirement. We may assume that the hide and the head were replaced by the animal's blood. In his conception of magic, primitive man not only accepted the law of *pars pro toto* (a part for the whole), i.e. that you gain mastery of a creature by seizing some part of it, but also regarded blood as the true substance of life. This assumption is supported by many facts, of which we need only quote two. The African hunting tribe of the Kordofans believes that it has gained complete mastery over its prey if the hunter pours the blood of the killed animals into a magic horn. Frobenius reports of the initiation ceremonies of such tribes:

Either at the beginning of the ceremony or during or after it, an antelope or gazelle is killed and one of its horns broken off; this will in future be filled with the blood of the killed game. A buffalo horn may serve as well as an antelope horn. Cave pictures are painted with the blood of the killed antelope.

Through the blood and through their resemblance to the original, the pictures become 'identical' with their models; and if, in addition, a spearhead is painted at the point where one wishes to strike the animal, then the animal is thought to be virtually doomed to death and the success of the hunt to be assured. And indeed, such spearheads can be seen in the buffalo paintings in the Trois Frères cave. Yet how to explain the astonishing resemblance of the image to the animal itself?

This resemblance was a magical obligation. The Stone Age hunter, observing his prey with close attention, was perfectly capable of judging a greater or lesser degree of similarity – and the greater the similarity the more effective he believed the image would be. We are therefore justified in assuming that, just as in the production of tools, patterns gradually came to be made; that the artist working in the cave did not work in complete freedom but was expected to use the most effective available forms, i.e. those having the greatest resemblance to the original. What we call style is, after all, nothing other than the use of accepted, conventional forms. Furthermore, Stone Age man was not only a good observer of his prey; if his hunting was to be successful, he also had to go a long way towards identifying himself with it. And what we call artistic insight is only a by-product of this highly practical 'self-identification'. The hunter imitated the animal; in his hunting dances, he wrapped himself in the animal's hide and reproduced its every step and every movement, identifying himself with it to an extent we can scarcely imagine today. And lastly: the dividing-line between the human and the animal world was not at all sharply defined in the mind of prehistoric man; in many ways he still formed part of the animal world and was but slowly detaching himself from it. The anthropologists Klaatsch and Heilborn write:

The suckling of young animals by women is a widespread custom among primitive peoples. It is as though these savages had not yet acquired a sense of human dignity but felt themselves to be animals among animals. . . . Just as an Australian aboriginal woman gives her breast to the dingo – and Jung points out in this connexion that cases have been recorded where a father has murdered his new-born child in order to give the mother a couple of young dogs to suckle – Polynesian women frequently suckle dogs. The same was reported by Theodat of the Indian women of Canada. In Hawaii, according to Remy, the mothers used to give the breast not only to their children but also to young dogs and pigs. Pigs also feed from the women of the Papuans of New Mecklenburgh and of the Maoris of New Zealand. Moreover, the women of several South American Indian tribes also suckle monkeys, opossums, deer, etc.

When man became a hunter, an abyss filled with blood suddenly opened between the human and animal worlds: man was now the murderer of animals, although he still saw them as being his ancestors or his kin. He had destroyed the unity of life, and though he tried again and again to deceive himself about the nature of his crime by pretending that to eat the killed animal was merely to 'assimilate' it, and that the animal therefore went on living within the human organism, he evidently still feared the vengeance of the animals who were his ancestors and brothers. The woman suckles the animal, the man kills it; thus many hunting tribes came to believe in a mysterious bond between their woman and their prey, with all the contradictions and fears that this implied.

We must take all this into account if we want to understand

the immense significance of animal images for Stone Age man and the powerful compulsion under which the sorcerers strove to gain power over nature by making their images resemble the originals as much as possible. There was no question here of aesthetic creative pleasure – the thing was deeper, more serious, altogether more terrifying than that, a matter of life and death or of the existence or non-existence of the collective. The sorcerer, as we have already said, is enthroned above the buffalo images; he wears an animal mask and stares at all who enter with a huge and frightening eye. Unless all indications are deceptive, the Trois Frères cave was a place where initiation ceremonies were held, where the young members of the tribe were assimilated into the collective. In these ceremonies, the experiences of production (i.e. of the hunt) and of sexuality, and all the rules and obligations evolved by the collective, were passed on to the youths with cruel thoroughness, accompanied by tortures meant to be remembered for life. Thus the young members of the tribe were united with the immortal collective, with the First Ancestor that lived on from generation to generation and was in many cases believed to be bisexual. Frobenius reports of such ceremonies among the Mahalbi of Africa:

The youths may neither enjoy sexual pleasures nor hunt large game before their consecration. For the purpose of the ceremonies of maturity they are brought into the bush. There, dances are organized and confusing noises are made until the boys get into a state of exaltation. At the climax of their ecstasy, a leopard (or a leopard-like creature) appears. Its appearance is terrifying. The boys are frightened almost to death. This creature throws itself upon the boys and wounds them, sometimes in the genitals, so that they bear the traces for the rest of their lives. . . . Days of an orgiastic nature follow. This is the time when certain buffalo horns are prepared that will henceforth have significance for the hunters as magic implements of the utmost importance, until the day of their death. Into these horns they pour the blood of the animals they kill. Women are never allowed to touch these horns: otherwise the killed beasts will turn into very beautiful women to whom the hunter will unknowingly abandon himself, wherepon they will take blood vengeance upon him.

In other tribes, the youths are shut in a cave in the mountains where they must paint pictures on the walls. These pictures are smeared with the blood of a killed antelope. Apparently each youth then has one of his testicles crushed.

The close link between hunting magic and sexual magic is seen again and again in hundreds of similar examples. The prey and the woman merge into one another. The first taboo seems to have been the ban on sexual intercourse during menstruation and pregnancy. A woman in either of these conditions is regarded as both unclean and sacred, a creature from which one retreats in revulsion although she is also considered 'blessed'. George Thomson points out that menstruating or pregnant women in all parts of the world used to smear their bodies with red ochre in order to warn men off and to increase their fertility. In many marriage ceremonies the woman's forehead is marked with red. In Ancient Greece, women who had just given birth were thought to be as unclean as someone who has shed another's blood or touched a corpse. Birth and death became intertwined, a bleeding woman meant death, a pregnant one regeneration.

Among hunting tribes there exists a custom according to which, before the men set out for the hunt, the women must dance and create an atmosphere of sexual excitement; the hunters, however, may not have intercourse with the women at this time but must satisfy their sexual excitement by killing animals. Frazer reports that the Nutka Sound Indians were compelled to refrain from all sexual intercourse during the week of the great whale hunt. A chief who failed to catch a whale was called to account by his tribesmen for having broken the chastity rule. The identification of women with the prey is partly connected with the beginnings of the sex struggle, which may be described as the first class struggle of history; partly, however, its cause goes back to the ancient way of seeing all similar things as identical. Bachofen points out that when prehistoric hunters had sexual intercourse with their women, they would stick a spear into the ground outside their hut or cave, this spear being the symbol of the phallus. Winthuis writes of the dances of Negro tribes:

In each man's system of thinking, by which he identifies himself with the collective, the spear he holds in his hand is no ordinary spear but the living *membrum virile* itself, and the pit before him no ordinary pit but the living personification of the *membrum muliebre*. Each man confirms the other in this conviction by exhibiting his sexual excitement.

The sexual act and the piercing of the prey, the bleeding woman and the bleeding animal, merged in the imagination of primitive man into similar or identical elements of the vital process, and this climate of sexuality no doubt affected also the sorcerer who painted animal pictures on the walls of the cave of initiations.

All this leads up to the belief, encountered again and again among primitive hunting tribes, that a dying animal's glance is something to guard against, and that this glance particularly affects the genitals and destroys virility. Frobenius writes:

Taking possession of a part gives mastery over the whole. It need not take the form of actual grasping with the hands – it may also be performed by a call or cry, and especially by a look. The look is the most sinister. The eye breaking in death is greatly feared.

The eye of a living creature, organ of light and mirror of reality, is where life manifests itself with the greatest intensity. The far-seeing eye of man radiates will-power, and a man pits his will against another's by trying to outstare him. In the eye of a dying animal the hunter senses nature's reproach to the murderer, the destroyer of unity. And this unity of nature lingers on in woman the birth-giver, the source of nourishment: the dying animal and the woman merge into one and the departing life takes vengeance on the sexual organs, which are the organs of life itself. We must bear in mind these interlinking ideas in their entirety in order to understand the image of the sorcerer in the cave and the significant and terrifying look he directs upon those who enter.

To sum up: the Trois Frères cave was, unless all appearances deceive us, a magic place where initiation rites were performed. We may assume that it was the duty of the tribe's sorcerer and his assistants to look after this cave: they were the 'artists' who produced the magic images. It was their duty to make the images resemble reality: the greater the likeness, the greater the efficacy of the image was believed to be. These artists had already inherited a series of traditional forms, 'patterns' retained because of their likeness, i.e. a traditional 'style', and were therefore not forced to depend on any mysterious 'intuition'.

A passage from Herbert Kühn's *The Rise of Humanity* supports this conclusion.

There can be no doubt that the Scandinavian paintings too were made for magic purposes. The sorcerers produced them. To this day, Lapp sorcerers still make quite similar pictures in the same style. In the south-west of Alaska, in an area known as Coop Inlet, and also in the islands of the Kodiak Group, Frederika de Laguna found Eskimo pictures which greatly resemble the engravings of the later stage of the Scandinavian group. They show stylized men, seals, fish, and elks. Eskimos were still living near by, and they were able to tell the explorer who it was that had painted the pictures – adding that the painter was the tribe's sorcerer. She went on to ask why the sorcerers painted such pictures, and was told that these formed part of secret hunting rites and served to put a spell on the animals. Through the pictures, the sorcerer and the hunters acquired power over the prey. . . . It is evident that the sorcerers formed 'schools', just as in the Ice Age. Sometimes one recognizes the same hand at work in different places.

The sorcerers were also considerably helped by the fact that their 'identification' with the original – the collective merging of subject and object – was extremely intense. An atmosphere of collective sexual excitement increased this 'identification' still further, and a state of collective sexual ecstasy may have preceded the actual work. Finally, if we bear in mind that the primitive hunter's attention was totally concentrated upon the prey – not upon the specific or individual features of any particular animal but upon the essential features of the species he set out to hunt; that, in other words, what mattered to him were the contours of the animal and not the manifold details of its appearance – we shall, I believe, have found an adequate explanation for the works of art of the Stone Age. I am fully aware that I am trying to reconstruct conditions and processes concerning which little material is available. It is perfectly possible that I may be overlooking important factors or interpreting facts wrongly. But the point I wanted to make is that no mystical or metaphysical suppositions are needed for an understanding of the origins of early (and consequently also of later) art forms. That is why I have devoted a relatively large amount of space to examining a single example.

Nostalgia for the 'source'

Art forms, once they have been established, put to the test, transmitted, and 'sanctioned' in the full sense of the word, have an extraordinarily conservative character. Even when the original magic meaning has been largely forgotten, people still cling to the old forms with awe-struck reverence: all the word forms, dance forms, pictorial forms, etc., which once had a specific magic and social significance, are preserved in the art of advanced, highly developed societies, and the magic-social law is only very gradually diluted to make an aesthetic one. A new social content has always been needed in order partly to destroy, partly to modify old forms and bring new ones into being. Only in a relatively developed class society, such as Athenian society at the time of the Persian wars, did it become possible for the individual to emerge more powerfully from the chorus of the ancient collective with its strictly prescribed dance movements and magically ordered forms of speech and song; the sacrificial rite was then transformed into the representation of new social events, until finally the religious and collective element was completely dissolved in the freer, more human, and individual one. Without the conflict between the personality (developing out of commodity production and trade) and the privileged land-owning class (whether secular or ecclesiastic), the visual arts would never have been emboldened to loosen the archaic forms originally designed to serve a magic purpose, or to shift their attention upon man as an individual. And the same conflict gave rise to the new lyric poetry which introduced human and subjective elements into the magic chant, the collective prayer, the incantation to the gods or to the dead. New wine was poured into old skins, and it took a long time for the new content to find new forms of expression.

The forms of art, then, are generally found to be conservative, offering resistance to all change. Certain forms in existence today still show traces of the old collective ties and obligations. This is not true of the 'open' form of the novel, and scarcely of modern drama, but to some extent of the visual arts and most certainly of music and lyric poetry. The magic function of art vanished long ago, and its forms, after many struggles, have adapted themselves to new social situations and demands. Yet a ghost of the ancient magic of prehistoric times still haunts modern poetry and music.

The deliberate return to the archaic, the mythical, the 'primitive' in many works and movements of modern art has also something to do with this. The fetish-like character, not only of the commodity but also of a whole world of technical, economic, and social machinery from which the artist is totally alienated, the infinite specialization and differentiation of the late-bourgeois world, all this creates a nostalgia for the 'source', for a unity complete unto itself. The artist's distrust of everything that is easy, slick, and self-complacent leads him into austerity and harshness, into an archaicism that refuses to flatter the senses. The sensuous art of the Impressionists who dissolved the world in light, colour, and atmosphere was followed by a counter-movement, the denial of the shimmering surface, the desire to get at the structure of things, to capture their permanence, not the passing moment. Formal concentration became the aim; the artist's or novelist's work set out to move people 'directly', like music or poetry, not so much through its subject as through its form.

Many factors in this way combined to give a fresh impulse to the romantic longing for the 'source'. In modern lyric poetry there are two opposing tendencies. One sets out to construct the poem in a fully conscious way, free from any 'magic'. The other represents the desire to return to the 'source', to throw off the conventional meanings of words and combinations of words, to restore to them the freshness of youth and a long-forgotten magic meaning. Aragon expresses this in one of his finest poems:

> Je dis avec les mots des choses machinales
> Plus machinalement que la neige neigeant
> Mots démonétisés qu'on lit dans le journal
> Et je parle avec eux le langage des gens
>
> Soudain c'est comme un sou tombant sur le bitume
> Qui fait nous retourner au milieu de nos pas
> Inconscient écho d'un malheur que nous tûmes
> Un mot chu par hasard, un mot qui ne va pas. . . .
>
> Que je dise d'oiseaux et de métamorphoses
> Du mois d'août qui se fane au fond des mélilots
> Que je dise du vent, que je dise des roses
> Ma musique se brise et se mue en sanglots

I use words to say mechanical things, more mechanically than snow as it falls; words uncoined that you read in the paper, and with them I talk as people talk. Suddenly it's like a penny falling on the asphalt, that makes us turn back and retrace our steps – unconscious echo of a disaster we've hushed up, a word that falls by chance, a word that will not do. . . . And if I speak of birds, of slow changes, of August fading amidst the hollyhocks, and if I speak of wind, of roses, my music breaks and changes into sobs.

The poet abhors the word that passes from hand to hand like a copper coin – yet suddenly it falls ringing on the ground, no longer a coin but pure metal, and its resonance rouses associations long buried under the dross of everyday language. A word in a poem has not only objective meaning but also a deeper, in a sense a magic one. The emotion of primitive man who re-created an object by naming it and so made it his own is still implicit in poetry. Many words in a poem spring as it were directly from the 'source' – and their effect is that of having been spoken for the first time here and now, in this particular context, with this particular meaning. A word in a poem is young, clean, untouched, as though a piece of hidden reality has only just crystallized in it. There are earnest people occupied with useful things who regard lyric poetry as childish and useless for this very reason: because it does not confine itself to plain statements but deals in magic, because it traffics with words, because it speaks a language remote from the matter-of-fact idiom of our times. Indeed the suspicion persists that the poet's language is not a 'normal' language at all, as used for ordinary communication between people: and the suspicion is entirely justified. Every poet has felt the desire either to create a completely new language capable of direct expression, or to return to the 'source', to the depths of a language that is ancient, unworn, magically powerful. Most great lyric poets have added new, hitherto unheard-of words to language, discovered forgotten ones, or restored an original, fresh meaning to words in common use. The attempts of many modern poets to absorb slang terms and technical jargon into their poems is closely connected with this desire. This is true of Brecht, who distilled his language from his native Augsburg dialect, from the German of Luther's Bible, from the language of fairground ballads, and other sources.

To express subjective experience in language so subjective that all conventions are destroyed and all communication with others is rendered impossible runs counter to the function of poetry. Even the virtually inexpressible experience of one man is still a human experience and therefore, even at the highest degree of subjectivity, a social one. (Indeed even the extreme isolation typical of artists today is a social experience common to many.) The poet is the discoverer of experience, and through him others are given the power to recognize it – discovered and expressed at last – as their own and so to assimilate it. The discovery of the loneliness of modern cities in Baudelaire's poetry not merely 'brought a new tremor into the world' but also struck a note that reverberated in millions of minds already unconsciously attuned to it. In order to produce this resonance the poet makes use of the existing means of language, but in such a way that every word gains new meaning. The novelty consists in the dialectic, the interaction of the words within the poem and in the fact that each word not only communicates a content but also, as it were, is a content in itself, an autonomous reality. Each word in a poem, like an atom in a crystal, has its place: this makes the poem's form and structure. By seemingly small, unimportant changes of the position of some words, a poem may be rendered ineffective, its structure and form may be destroyed, and the crystallized body may dissolve into an amorphous mass.

The world and language of poetry

In the age of classicism a poem was a vehicle for expressing a thought or an emotion in the most elegant and attractive way. Poetry was a kind of warehouse, a tailor's shop of language, supplying garments made to measure for any given feeling or idea. Consider the confident grace of Alexander Pope:

> But where's the man, who counsel can bestow,
> Still pleas'd to teach, and yet not proud to know? . . .
> Blest with a taste exact, yet unconfin'd;
> A knowledge both of books and human kind;
> Gen'rous converse, a soul exempt from pride;
> And love to praise, with reason on his side?

Or the succinct rhetoric of Racine's morning hymn:

> *Chantons l' Auteur de la lumière,*
> *Jusqu' au jour où son ordre a marqué nostre fin:*
> *Et qu'en le bénissant nostre aurore dernière*
> *Se perde en un midy sans soir et sans matin. . . .*

Let us praise the Author of light, until the day when his command marks our end; and may our last dawn, blessing him, lose itself in a noon without evening or morn.

Then, suddenly, in the midst of this classical scene there appeared the dark and wayward popular ballad. It was a kind of latter-day peasants' rising in a lyrical form, originating from those dispossessed by the early accumulation of capital. In 1765 Bishop Percy compiled the first collection of such ballads. Even earlier, Gray and Macpherson had evoked the old songs of the bards and skalds. Gray admired the precision and clarity of that rhetoric of which Pope was the master; yet at the same time he believed that the one-sided development of the intelligence and the critical faculty, the 'vivacity and spoilt impatience' of his over-refined age were the first signs of decay of the 'glorious arts that rise from the imagination'. He spoke of a 'Gothic Elysium', of a 'magic, wild enthusiasm', of a 'barbaric fancy', of a 'striking and profound harmony of words and rhythms', all arising from imaginations that were 'at home in the cold bleak hills of Scotland some hundreds of years ago' and waiting to be brought back to life.

The village invaded the cities, not only in the shape of wretched and de-classed peasants who had degenerated into a 'mob', but also as fantastic songs and ballads filled with black superstition and ignorance. When Rétif de la Bretonne, the son of a peasant about whose novel *Monsieur Nicolas* Wilhelm von Humboldt said that it was 'the truest book that ever existed', came to Paris, he brought with him not only a plebeian's defiance of the ruling classes but also the robust sensuality, the superstition, the mysticism, and the dark anger of his native countryside. Goya, another peasant's son, carried as his baggage a sack full of witches and demons which he suddenly emptied, with a fury of hatred, over the heads of the duchesses and grandees who were his flatterers.

The Romantic revolt against the rule of the aristocracy and the Church spread to language itself. The rhythm of rebellion thudded beneath the evocations of witches' rides, devils' weddings, and church bells ringing at midnight. The defence of superstition against enlightenment masked a defiance of the cultivated nobility. Old graves were torn open at this beginning of a new age. Gottfried August Bürger's ballad *Lenore* combines all the elements of blood, moonlight, and the eerie breath of the churchyard:

> *Die Flügel flogen klirrend auf*
> *Und uber Gräber ging der Lauf,*
> *Es bleichten Leichensteine*
> *Rund um im Mondenscheine. . . .*

The wings opened with a clash, over the graves they raced; tombstones gleamed pale in the moonlight. . . .

In a 'heart's effusion' on popular poetry, Bürger demanded

that the 'imagination and sensibility' of the people should be explored so that 'the magic wand of the natural epos' might put everything into 'tumult and confusion'. Nature, he said, 'allots the sphere of fantasy and sensibility to poetry, that of wit and reason to a very different lady: the art of verse-making'. Language destroyed the laws of classicism and turned to the unconscious and barbaric to satisfy a new, uneasy awareness. No longer were thoughts clothed in verse; no longer were elegance and wit the admired qualities of poetry; image now followed image in dreamlike, irrational, frightening sequence. The 'tumult and confusion' of the imagination wrought havoc with the rules of classicism. Lyrical poetry was never again to lose the 'magic wand' of romanticism.

No contemporary responded more fully to this new birth of poetry than the young Goethe encountering Gothic art and folk song for the first time as a student in Strasburg. In this early poem the images flash exuberantly by, punctuated by the rhythm of riding:

> *Es schlug mein Herz; geschwind zu Pferde!*
> *Es war getan fast eh' gedacht;*
> *Der Abend wiegte schon die Erde*
> *Und an den Bergen hing die Nacht.*
> *Schon stand im Nebelkleid die Eiche*
> *Ein aufgetürmter Riese da,*
> *Wo Finsternis aus dem Gesträuche*
> *Mit hundert schwarzen Augen sah. . . .*

My heart was beating; quickly to horse! It was done almost before it was thought; evening was already cradling the earth, and night hung on the mountains. Already the oak, a towering giant, stood clad in mist where darkness, with a hundred eyes, was peering out of the scrub.

The poet's 'I' is merged with nature in dream-like associations, in a poetic pantheism; and nature is felt to be instinct with a demonic life whose voice reverberates in poetic language. The same new unity of man and nature expressed itself in a new unity of feeling and language, magically captured by Wordsworth:

As a huge stone is sometimes seen to lie
Couched on the bald top of an eminence,
Wonder to all who do the same espy,
By what means it could thither come, and whence,
So that it seems a thing endued with sense:
Like a sea-beast crawled forth, that on a shelf
Of rock and sand reposes, there to sun itself;
Such seemed this man, not all alive or dead,
Nor all asleep – in his extreme old age. . . .

Unity with nature was frequently identified with erotic union, *union mystica*: that is to say, a union of urban man, no longer capable of naïve religious feeling, with an enchanting but at the same time terrifying being. The abandonment to 'pure passion' – which Stendhal considered to be the essential feature of the Romantic age – thus found expression in a feeling of unity with nature, in sexuality, and in the poet's lonely 'I'. The language of passion, not of serene contemplation – a restless, nervous, often violent, always individual language – fitted the new, individualistic bourgeois age.

Nature seen as a vampire, dangerous yet seductive, as in Goethe's ballads 'The Elm King' and 'The Fisherman'; the voluptuous death dreams of German Romantics such as Novalis and Kleist; the startling images and associations of Blake's poetry – all these elements of Romanticism are combined in Keats's magical 'La Belle Dame Sans Merci'. After the fall of classicism, lyric poetry became a synthesis of nostalgia for the 'source', a longing for the 'pure' intuition of the bards and skalds, extreme subjectivism, egotism, and a refinement of language that aimed at achieving perfect harmony between the theme and the technique of a poem. Keats's poem is a perfect example of this synthesis. In the popular ballad it was the theme that mattered; here the theme is only a symbol for subjective experience, the motivation for the Romantic poet's sense of being consumed, devoured by his destiny.

'O what can ail thee, knight-at-arms,
    Alone and palely loitering;
The sedge is wither'd from the lake,
    And no birds sing.

> 'O what can ail thee, knight-at-arms,
>   So haggard and so woe-begone?
> The squirrel's granary is full
>   And the harvest's done. . . . '

These two verses, both beginning with a cry of anguish and then freezing into stillness as though the poet had no breath left for lamentation, anticipate the ending of the ballad. The lines, passionate at first, the last desperate efforts of a doomed man, begin to stumble, falter, lose themselves in 'loitering' and the withered sedge, lead finally to the grim breathlessness, the hopeless finality of the three short words, their broken rhythm like three blocks of ice piled on one another: '. . . no birds sing.' Then again the vehement cry of the second verse, strangled once more by the past, by cold and bleakness, by an inescapable doom and the dry melancholy of '. . . the harvest's done'.

Now the magic evocation begins. At first there are only vague recollections of fragments, eerily disconnected details: a lily on thy brow, the fading rose of the cheek, dreamy confused associations with the withered sedge. Then suddenly a new key is struck; tortured subjectivity staring at nothingness yields to the apparently objective narrative of an epic popular ballad. But melodious, flowing lines such as 'Her hair was long, her foot was light' are interrupted by the harsh, threatening 'And her eyes were wild', a line that thrusts the whole poem back to the beginning, breaks the flow, and anticipates disaster. The wild sad eyes of La belle Dame sans Merci stare out of the apparent gentleness of brook and meadow, honey wild and manna dew.

The Romantic attitude to nature was contradictory. After the disappointments of the political and industrial revolutions, the destructive, devouring, vampire-like quality of nature – Venus as a she-devil, Diana the huntress seeking blood – became predominant as a reflection of the Romantics' disenchantment with society. La belle Dame sans Merci stares at the poet with a Medusa's eyes; her mouth, which sucks out his life's blood, is the mouth of death. At the same time Shelley wrote of the head of the Medusa:

Its horror and its beauty are divine.
Upon its lips and eyelids seems to lie
Loveliness like a shadow, from which shine,
Fiery and lurid, struggling underneath,
The agonies of anguish and of death. . . .

There is a similar feeling in *Epipsychidion*, that quintessential song of romantic love:

Thou Moon beyond the clouds! Thou living Form
Among the Dead! Thou Star above the Storm!
Thou Wonder, and thou Beauty, and thou Terror!

Nature itself merges into the dream mistress, the Helen conjured up by black magic. Rousseau put such images in the midst of nature. Goethe's Faust called up the phantom of Helen from the underworld. Heine heard the ghostly answer:

Du hast mich beschworen aus dem Grab
Durch deinen Zauberwillen,
Belebtest mich mit Wollustglut –
Jetzt kannst du die Glut nicht stillen.

Press deinen Mund auf meinen Mund,
Der Menschen Odem ist göttlich!
Ich trinke deine Seele aus,
Die Toten sind unersättlich.

You conjured me up from the grave by your magic will, you reanimated me with the glow of your desire, now you cannot quench the glow. Press your mouth upon my mouth, the breath of human beings is divine. I will drain your soul, for the dead are insatiable.

A dream within a dream precedes the fatal awakening in Keats's ballad:

'And there she lulled me asleep,
    And there I dream'd – Ah! woe betide,
The latest dream I ever dream'd
    On the cold hill's side. . . .'

The pain-stricken cry 'Ah! woe betide' shatters the mirror from which the dream woman had stepped, and ghosts that hitherto had remained hidden come rushing out of the darkness. The dreamer learns from them that he is one of many, one of a host of sensual yet eternal lovers, one of the illustrious, obsessed line that includes Geoffroy Rudel, Tannhäuser, Tristan, Lancelot, and Henry II:

> 'I saw pale kings and princes too,
>   Pale warriors, death-pale were they all:
> They cried – "La belle Dame sans Merci
>   Thee hath in thrall!" . . .'

Only in a language so fundamentally suited to poetry as English can you find a verse so charged with poetic meaning. The first two lines of soundless imagery are followed by a mysterious cry out of the darkness. Then again two lines of silent, dreamlike vision:

> 'I saw their starved lips in the gloam
>   With horrid warning gapèd wide. . . .'

The lyrical terror, the sheer intensity of 'La belle Dame sans Merci hath thee in thrall!' cannot be surpassed. Then comes the awakening. The end of the poem reverts to the beginning. We are left with the subjective reality to which the narrated, objective events were no more than the pages of a picture book, turned in a dream. In *The Life of Henri Brulard* Stendhal repeats half a dozen times that memory is like a crumbling fresco – an arm here, a head there, another fragment somewhere else – so that he does not describe *things* but only their effect upon him in a sequence of shining images the connexion between which is lost in darkness. This association of images and sounds, this absorption of the objective by the subjective, is the method of Romantic poetry. Not until the twentieth century was a new lyrical method developed as a conscious antithesis to Romanticism.

Baudelaire's great poem *Le Voyage* obeys the same Romantic principle of associated images. In Keats's ballad, La belle Dame takes shape out of a 'lily . . . with anguish moist and fever dew' and a 'fading rose'. In Baudelaire, the whole world is evoked through a patchwork of maps and stamps. But what a difference between the folksong lilt of Keats and the antithetical rhetoric of Baudelaire, the Englishman's spontaneity and the Frenchman's logic! Classicism in France had been far more powerful than in England; there had been no country squires or stubborn nonconformists to set a limit on the absolutism of the court and the Academy, no glimpse of nature, no wayward English park, to loosen the geometry of the formal yew hedges. Compared with English or German, French was almost a dead language, incapable of change or fancy; and Romanticism in France was introduced, not by the freshness of a Wordsworth, but by the grandiloquence of a Chateaubriand. Recoiling from this pomposity, Stendhal steeped himself in the language of the Civil Code; and Baudelaire, Victor Hugo's disciple, had to fight hard to rid himself of his master's high-flown style.

More than that: Keats's poem is rooted in the ballads of bards and skalds, in the magic refrains of old chants and ballads, whereas Baudelaire's is like a speech delivered in a forum before an invisible audience. The correspondence of Keats's first and last verse is that of a refrain in a folk song; that of the first and last two verses in Baudelaire suggests the preamble and peroration of a speech. The 'Ah!' at the beginning of Keats's first and last verse is a cry from the heart: the 'Ah!' in Baudelaire's third verse is a rhetorical transition from concrete description to antithetic generalization:

> *Ah! que le monde est grand à la clarté des lampes!*
> *Aux yeux du souvenir que le monde est petit!*

Ah! how large the world is by lamplight! in the eyes of memory, how small the world!

Baudelaire's poem does not break with the tradition of Ronsard or Hugo: but the classical pathos is made to break down upon itself, as the new theme demands that it should, and this breakdown, achieved with immense artistic skill, this sudden halt, this alternation of austerity and vehement shock, of measure and violence, was the 'new tremor' that convulsed the language of French lyric poetry. One of the chief features of Romanticism was that it smashed the ordered structure of classical language and introduced new and startling ways of combining words and groups of words. But purely in terms of language it was not until Rimbaud that French poetry attained the wild originality that Blake in England and Hölderlin and Kleist in Germany had already achieved towards the beginning of the nineteenth century.

The second verse of *Le Voyage* is so clearly and austerely constructed that it might have been the work of a classical author: yet within that construction, what a riot of subjectivity, what a tumult of antitheses, what a triumph of rhythm over metre!

> *Un matin nous partons, le cerveau plein de flamme,*
> *Le cœur gros de rancune et de désirs amers,*
> *Et nous allons, suivant le rythme de la lame,*
> *Berçant notre infini sur le fini des mers. . . .*

One morning we depart, our minds full of passion, our hearts heavy with resentment and bitter desires, and we sail forth, swinging with the rhythm of the waves, cradling our infinity in the finiteness of the seas.

The last line, like a rainbow over the oceans, arches towards the final verses – that great elegy of longing and disenchantment, the flight into the unknown and the return to a world that never changes, of ennui swallowing up all passion with death looming at the end of everything as the only hope. The longing for infinity – that greatest longing of Romanticism – remains unsatisfied, the finite world is condemned and dismissed as *une oasis d'horreur dans un désert d'ennui*. *Le Voyage* resembles a lyrical summing-up of the whole of Romanticism, from Goethe's *Faust* and Byron's *Childe Harold* to the voluptuous death dreams of Novalis, Kleist, Nerval, Coleridge, and Shelley. But the death-wish in Baudelaire acquires a new tone of reckless defiance. It is no longer a passive return to the womb, as in Novalis's *Hymns to the Night*:

> *Hinüber wall' ich*
> *Und jede Pein*
> *Wird einst ein Stachel*
> *Der Wollust sein.*
> *Noch wenig Zeiten*
> *So bin ich los*

Und liege trunken
Der Lieb' im Schoss. . . .
Ich fühle des Todes
Verjüngende Flut. . . .

I wander across, and one day all pain will be a sting of voluptuousness. A little time more and I am free, and lie drunken in the lap of love. . . . I feel the rejuvenating tide of death. . . .

The longing for nothingness which is such a feature of death-drunk Romanticism is transformed by Baudelaire into a longing for something new, not for eternal peace but for endless unrest; and the work of this 'decadent' poet is permeated with a Lucifer-like joy in invention, discovery, and the conquest of new horizons and new realities. Death assumes the figure of the 'old captain': but this Ahasuerus of the seas, this Ancient Mariner, this Flying Dutchman is no longer yearning for release and redemption – on the contrary, he is a symbol of departure into the unknown. The old captain, awaited with so much impatience (one senses the atmosphere of the quayside, the jostling mass of men, masts, and sails, then suddenly the stillness and the blue distance from which the old man approaches), is passionately welcomed like a familiar friend:

O Mort, vieux capitaine, il est temps! levons l'ancre!
Ce pays nous ennuie, O Mort! Appareillons!

O Death, old captain, it is time! let us weigh anchor! This country bores us, Death! Let us get under way!

Rarely has the desire to escape from the here-and-now, from the unspeakable emptiness and boredom of the present, been more tellingly expressed. Death seems to hesitate: he is not the seducer, as in so many Romantic works; it is the poet, eager to be gone, who is anxious to court death:

Si le ciel et la mer sont noirs comme de l'encre
Nos cœurs que tu connais sont remplis de rayons!
Verse-nous ton poison pour qu'il nous réconforte!

Let the sky and the sea be black as ink, our hearts, which you know, are radiant. Pour us out your poison so that it may comfort us!

And then comes the climax of pleading, the Romantic 'I', the fearless brain that feels itself to be indestructible, more powerful than the universe outside, anticipating immortality because it is insatiable, more ardent even than the heart:

> *Nous voulons, tant ce feu nous brûle le cerveau,*
> *Plonger au fond du gouffre, Enfer ou Ciel, qu'importe?*
> *Au fond de l'Inconnu pour trouver du nouveau!*

This fire burns so fiercely in our brains that we want to plunge to the bottom of the abyss, heaven or hell, what matter? to the bottom of the Unknown to find the New!

Many poems by Romantic poets, imbued with a spirit of resignation, end with a melodious cadence. Thus Coleridge's *Dejection*:

> O simple spirit, guided from above,
> Dear Lady! friend devoutest of my choice,
> Thus mayest thou ever, evermore rejoice.

Or Mörike's *Orplid*:

> *Vor deiner Gottheit beugen*
> *Sich Könige, die deine Wärter sind.*

Kings, who are thy gaolers, bow before thy divinity.

Baudelaire's way of making the last line a shattering climax is more than mere rhetoric. Few lines in world literature equal the vehement power of this '*Au fond de l'Inconnu pour trouver du nouveau!*' The '*nouveau*' comes thrusting out of the abyss of the unknown like a vast, steep rock, like the tremendous capital of a solitary column soaring out of a bottomless waste, shouldering the firmament at sunrise. The 'pure passion' of Romanticism, recognizing neither law nor morality – '*Enfer ou Ciel, qu'importe?*' – speaks in these lines.

Baudelaire's state of flux between passion and boredom, adventure and decay, reflects the very contradiction of the bourgeois era.

Constant revolutionizing of production [we read in *The Communist Manifesto**], uninterrupted disturbance of all social conditions, everlasting uncertainty and agitation distinguish the bourgeois epoch

* Centenary Edition, Lawrence & Wishart, 1948.

from earlier ones. All fixed, fast-frozen relations, with their train of ancient and venerable prejudices and opinions, are swept away, all new-formed ones become antiquated before they can ossify. All that is privileged and established melts into air, all that is holy is profaned. . . .

'*Enfer ou Ciel, qu'importe!*' The voyage into the New has begun, and may Death be the captain!

In content, form, and language, *Le Voyage* is the poem of a social turning-point. A breath of decay blows through the bourgeois world. Emptiness gapes through wealth, boredom through passion. What to do? Remain where one is, or depart for the unknown? Stand still, or falter forwards? Baudelaire, the Romantic, calls for death. Baudelaire, the Rebel, orders the victory of the New over nothingness. Through the theme, the form, and the language of his poetry, Baudelaire reacts subjectively to an actual social situation.

Music

The problem of form and content in music – the most abstract and formal of all the arts – presents many difficulties. The content of music is conveyed in so many ways and the dividing line between content and form is so blurred that resistance against sociological interpretation has always been strongest in this sphere. The late bourgeois world has a profound distaste for any application of sociology to the arts: but where music is concerned this distaste is reinforced by what are thought to be powerful arguments.

I should like to quote as typical some remarks of Igor Stravinsky's on Beethoven:

It is the instrument that inspires him and determines the manner of his musical thought. . . . But is it really Beethoven's music with which the numerous works devoted to him by philosophers, moralists, and even sociologists are concerned? How immaterial it is whether the Third Symphony was arrived at by way of the Republican Bonaparte or of the Emperor Napoleon! Only the music matters. . . . Men of letters have made a monopoly of their explanations of Beethoven. This monopoly must be taken away from them. It does not belong to them but to those who are used to hearing nothing but music in music. . . . In his piano works Beethoven's point of departure is the piano, in his symphonies, his overtures, and his chamber music it is the instrumental score. . . . I do not think I am mistaken when I say that the monumental creations to which he owes his fame are the logical outcome of the way in which he exploits the *sound* of instruments.

Being a mere 'man of letters', I should never set myself up to explain Beethoven. Stravinsky is surely right when he says that Beethoven's works should not be examined from a purely sociological viewpoint but must be understood *as music*. But what is music? Is it only a system of sounds – or something else besides? Beethoven's point of departure is the musical instrument, not the French Revolution. What a curious antithesis! Does a musician know only about pianos and not revolutions? Does one exclude the other? Foolish as it would be to explain Beethoven's music by his sympathy for the Jacobins (for one may be a good Jacobin and a useless musician), it would be still more absurd to claim that his music had its source solely in his knowledge of musical instruments and not in the events and ideas of his age.

To say that music consists of tones arranged in a vast variety of combinations – that it is an abstract and formal art – is thought to be incontrovertibly true. But is it no more than that? Is music devoid of content because it is non-objective? Hegel in his *Philosophy of Art** provides a significant answer:

This ideality of content and mode of expression in the sense that it is devoid of all external object defines the purely *formal* aspect of music. It has no doubt a content, but it is not a content such as we mean when referring either to the plastic arts or poetry. What it lacks is just this configuration of an objective other-to-itself, whether we mean by such actual external phenomena, or the objectivity of intellectual ideas and images.

And Hegel points out further:

It is only when that which is of spiritual import is adequately expressed in the sensuous medium of tones and their varied configuration that music attains entirely to its position as a true art, and

* Routledge, 1892.

irrespective of the fact whether this content receives an independent and more direct definition by means of words, or is perforce emotionally realized from the tone music itself and its harmonic relations and melodic animation.

The continual changes in the forms and manner of expression of music through the centuries, the development of music throughout history, cannot be explained solely by the appearance of new instruments and the increasing subtlety and technical skill of musicians. Unless we also take into account the changing course of history, we are faced with an inexplicable phenomenon. (Even the use or rejection of certain instruments is in part connected with social circumstances and 'ideological' considerations: for example, Sparta's refusal to accept the more richly stringed Athenian lyre, or the rejection of Oriental percussion instruments by Alexandrine Christianity, which only allowed the use of classical string instruments in the third and fourth centuries.) Beethoven certainly 'exploited the sound of instruments' in order to achieve musical effects. But to what purpose? It is the nature of music, says Hegel, 'to put soul . . . into sounds arranged in particular tone relations and, to that extent, to elevate expression into an element made only by art and for art alone'. This element 'elevated' into organized sound, that is to say the 'content' of music, is the experience which the composer wants to communicate: and a composer's experience is not purely musical but also personal and social, conditioned by the historical period in which he lives and which affects him in many ways. We should not oversimplify this effect of historical environment on the composer and his works; on the contrary, we should try to discover, conscientiously and without pedantry, the manifold ways in which the content and the musical form of a particular work correspond to a social situation. But to hear 'nothing but music in music', to dismiss what the composer has 'elevated' into music as unimportant, is of a banality even more crass than to analyse a work in purely sociological terms without regard for its quality or form.

What is the meaning of Stravinsky's rhetorical declaration that it does not matter whether Beethoven, in composing the *Eroica*, was inspired by the Republican Bonaparte or the Emperor Napoleon? If Stravinsky means to say that the Emperor Napoleon (or any other phenomenon or event acting against the Revolution) could equally well have inspired a great composer to produce a great work, the statement is obvious and no one would dream of contradicting it. No one claims that revolution alone can be a source of inspiration for great works. But the fact that the decisive experience *for Beethoven* was the French Revolution – not the Empire nor, say, Metternich's system – certainly does matter to an understanding of Beethoven's work and personality. However great the content, it will not help a bad musician to compose great music. But what we admire in Beethoven is not only his mastery of form but also the tremendous content of a revolutionary age.

The content of music is not so clear-cut as that of literature or the visual arts: that is why music lends itself so freely to abuse as a means of blunting the edge of consciousness. And yet the content of great music is not so utterly indefinite that it does not matter whether – to keep to Stravinsky's example – that content is determined by the Revolution or by its betrayal. We find a similar view – the view that music expresses only general and unmotivated emotions – in Schopenhauer:*

Music does not, therefore, express this or that particular and definite joy, this or that sorrow, or pain, or horror, or delight, or merriment, or peace of mind; but joy, sorrow, pain, horror, delight, merriment, peace of mind *themselves*, to a certain extent in the abstract, their essential nature, without accessories, and therefore without their motives.

Accordingly it should be immaterial whether the 'joy' implicit in a piece of music arises out of a speculator's delight at having made some money on the stock exchange, a child's pleasure at seeing a Christmas tree, the satisfaction that a fresh bottle of champagne gives to a drinker, or the joy of the fighter when his cause has triumphed. The motive and the specific nature of 'joy' are supposed to be irrelevant; only joy in the abstract can

* *The World as Will and Idea*, Routledge, 1883.

be expressed in music – so that, presumably, the difference between the joy of Beethoven and that of Lehar is only one of quality, not of fundamental principle. Hegel judges differently when he writes:

The purely emotional grasp by the soul of its intrinsic nature, and the play in musical sound of this apprehension is regarded as the mere attunement of mood, . . . too general and abstract . . . [and runs the risk of] becoming generally empty and trivial. . . . If, for example, a song arouses the emotion of mourning, the lament at a loss, we inevitably ask ourselves, what is the nature of that loss ? . . . Music, in short, is not primarily concerned with the bare form of the inward soul, but with *that innermost life as replenished*, the specific content of which is most closely related to the particular character of the emotion roused, so that the mode of the expression will, or should, inevitably assert itself with essential differences, according to the varied nature of the content.

Stravinsky would have us judge Beethoven's music only by its form, by the totality of its effect *as sound*. Schopenhauer's attitude is similar, if rather more profound:

If we now cast a glance at purely instrumental music, a symphony of Beethoven's presents to us the greatest confusion, which yet has the most perfect order as its foundation, the most vehement conflict, which is transformed the next moment into the most beautiful concord. . . . In this symphony all human passions and emotions also find utterance; joy, sorrow, love, hatred, terror, hope, etc., in innumerable degrees, yet all, as it were, only *in abstracto*, and without any particularization; it is their mere form without the substance, like a spirit world without matter.

Here, too, the 'innermost life as replenished' is turned into a cold and bleak abstraction. Yet this innermost life is not a matter of pure form or pure spirit: it arises out of the very definite and specific manner in which Beethoven reacted to his times; it belongs to the *real* world in which there is no joy or sorrow *in abstracto* but only motivated sorrow and motivated joy.

The funeral march in the *Eroica* is not mourning *in abstracto*, devoid of any specific meaning: it is heroic mourning charged with revolutionary emotion. That is not the way a man mourns for a dead beloved, nor would such passion befit a Christian sorrowing for Jesus crucified: the mourning that is expressed in Beethoven's symphony is revolutionary and Jacobin. Hegel's question: 'What is the nature of that loss?' is unambiguously answered by Beethoven's music. And similarly, in the Ninth Symphony, the joy that bursts out in the choral movement is not *any* joy, not joy *in abstracto*, but a joy born of immense contradictions, despite and in defiance of dejection and despair, a negation of that despair given infinitely conscious form: and a joy, moreover, that presupposes the urban masses, that has nothing to do with rustic gaiety, harvests, and peasant dances. Or again, if we examine the 'content' of Beethoven's late chamber music, we are bound to find that it expresses a ghastly loneliness – but not loneliness *in abstracto*, and very different from the loneliness of a pious hermit or of a peasant snowed up in his mountain hut; it is the new, urban loneliness that came into being together with the masses of the modern bourgeois–capitalist age and found its first musical expression in Beethoven. In other words, if we give Beethoven's work more than one cursory glance, we do not discover in it all the human passions and emotions '*in abstracto* and without any particularization': instead, we find certain highly specific passions and emotions unknown, in that particular form of expression, to earlier times.

To turn now to a modern example: let us consider Hanns Eisler's *Cantata on the Thirteenth Anniversary of Lenin's Death*. The new and original manner in which mourning is expressed here illustrates again the importance of concrete, socially determined elements in music despite its abstract, formal character. True, Eisler had a text to work on – a text by Brecht, which rejects any trace of traditional pathos. Nevertheless the composer's task was difficult. How do we mourn Lenin? To answer this question in musical form required not only talent but also a high degree of political consciousness and vast artistic experience. As a first step, the composer had to be clear in his own mind about the elements to be eschewed. Mourning for Lenin must have nothing to do with sacramental emotion; it must recall neither a religious requiem nor a Baroque oratorio. But neither is the pathos of the Eroica – that of the bourgeois–democratic revolution – suitable to the nature of the proletarian–socialist revolution and its dead leader; and romantic extravagance or emotional fulsomeness of any kind were still more to be excluded. The composer had to find a completely new style: simplicity, precision, economy, austerity of musical gesture pointing far into the future – not into a mysterious beyond but into a brighter material world; not 'Death and Transfiguration', not resurrection and ascension, but the effect of Lenin living on within the working class whose teacher he had been. This problem of content led on to that of form: the interaction of the slender solo voices and their tremendous and overpowering echo takes place within the strict order of the twelve-tone system. In its formal construction, the *Lenin Cantata* is entirely new: but this is not form for form's sake, but form determined by a new content.

I am trying to illustrate the problem of content and form in music, but I do not wish to gloss over its difficulty. In music intended as an accompaniment to words, the 'content' is more or less given by the text – although even music of this kind may divorce itself from the text or may dominate it, and indeed it may achieve a specially powerful effect by contradicting the text rather than underwriting it. But how to define the 'content' of instrumental music? The metaphysicians have a relatively easy time of it: for Schopenhauer, music is 'entirely independent of the phenomenal world'; it is the 'copy of the will itself'; and that is precisely why 'the effect of music is so much more powerful and penetrating than that of the other arts', for these speak only of the shadow, but music speaks of the essence. For Hegel, music has 'the innermost subjective free life of the soul for content' – although Hegel, the master of dialectic, has much more than Schopenhauer to say about the concrete and specific elements in music. A dialectical materialist cannot easily say what is to be regarded as the 'content' of music; above all he cannot define it with a general formula; he is forced to examine each work in many concrete ways and to concern himself in detail with the historical development of music, the changing functions of music as a whole, and those of individual musical forms. This work still remains to be done. I am not a musical theoretician, and can only throw out a few hints. Any correction will be welcome.

It was the purpose of music from the start to evoke collective emotions, to act as a stimulus for work, orgiastic gratification, or war. Music was a means of stunning or exciting the senses, of spell-binding or spurring to action; it served to put human beings into a different state, not to reflect the phenomena of the outward world. We cannot therefore ask what was the 'content' of early music. False questions breed senseless answers. The thud of the drum, the rattle of pieces of wood, the jangle of metal is without content: the effect of organized sound upon human beings is its sole meaning. The social function of music was to exercise this effect, not to represent a reality. As Hanns Eisler points out, 'automatic associations' arose out of certain definite rhythms, tone sequences, and sound images. To this day much of the effect of music is achieved through 'automatic associations' of this kind (military marches, funeral marches, dance rhythms, etc.), which give a possibility of direct participation even to an unschooled listener. This power of music to produce collective emotions, to make people *emotionally equal* for a certain time, has been particularly useful to military and religious organizations. Of all the arts, music is the most apt to cloud the intelligence, to intoxicate, to create ecstatic obedience, or, indeed, a willingness to die.

All religious institutions – and the Roman Catholic Church more than any other – have systematically exploited this peculiar power of music. The Catholic Church in the early Middle Ages did not demand of music that it should be 'beautiful', but rather the contrary. The function of music at that time was to transport the believers into a state of abject contrition and utter humility, to crush every trace of individuality and weld them into a submissive collective. True, each man was reminded of his individual sins, but music allowed him to sink back into a sense of universal sinfulness and a universal desire for redemption. The 'content' of such music was always the same: you are a worthless, helpless, sinful creature; identify yourself with the sufferings of Christ, and you will be saved. Hegel wrote of this function of old church music:

> In old church music, take the moment of the *crucifixus est* for example, we find that the profound meanings unfolded in the central idea of the Passion regarded as Christ's suffering, death, and burial are severally so conceived that it is not simply one's merely *personal* feeling of sympathy or individual pain over these facts that is expressed, but along with this the very facts themselves, or in other words the depth of their significance is motived by the harmony of the music and its melodic progression. It is, of course, true that even here the impression is one which acts upon the emotion of those who hear it. We do not actually *perceive* the pain of the crucified, we do not merely receive a general *idea* of it: the aim is throughout that we experience in the depths of our being the ideal substance of this death and this divine suffering, that we absorb with heart and soul its reality, so that it becomes as it were a part of ourselves, permeating our entire conscious life to the exclusion of everything else.

In other words, this powerful church music does not arouse an *indefinite* feeling that allows of many different associations within the individual mind (as for instance modern symphony music): on the contrary, it forces upon the listener a *definite* reaction that tolerates no subjectivity.

The 'content' of church music of this kind is, then, determined by the liturgical text and the associations produced by it – divine suffering, human sinfulness, and so forth. But there is another important element: the congregation themselves, who are by no means a mere 'audience' but a genuine community. The sensibility of these listeners is 'acted upon', as Hegel says, not to produce an indefinite subjective feeling but a uniform, collective emotion. The purpose of such music is to create a definite and intended state of mind, to work consistently towards that state of mind; its function is not so much to 'express' a feeling as to produce it. It might be said (with some caution) that the 'content' of such music is not only within it but also outside it; it is the sum of expression and effect, of moving sounds and moved listeners. The same is true of profane dance and march music. Dance music in itself is without content; its function is to stimulate the desire to dance, and it acquires a content through the movement and excitement of the dancers. The specific nature of the dance, be it ritual dance or minuet, Viennese waltz or rock-'n'-roll, is socially determined, the curious fact being that the social element finds expression in the musical form alone – i.e. that social 'content' is conveyed purely through form – whilst any other kind of content is only rarely present. The same applies to military marches, whose form is socially determined but whose 'content' is contributed by the marching soldiers. But when musical forms of this kind are absorbed into a symphony or concert piece, they appear – because of their 'automatic associations' – to have 'content' in themselves, to have acquired a life of their own. And so we find that in music, that most perplexing of the arts, content is always transforming itself into form and form into content. Social content may manifest itself in the musical structure alone, or again, new content may make use of old forms by bestowing new functions upon them.

It is essential to distinguish between music the sole purpose of which is to produce a uniform and deliberate effect, thus stimulating an assembly of people to collective action of an intended kind, and music whose meaning is, in itself, expressing feelings, ideas, sensations, or experiences, and which, far from welding people into a homogeneous mass with identical reactions, allows free play to individual, subjective associations. Sacred music in the early Middle Ages fell into the first category, so that we may say it had an 'objective' character, in contrast to the 'subjective', expressive character of secular music whose rise coincided with that of the bourgeoisie. If we examine the long and contradictory process of the secularization of music we are bound to admit that music is an eminently social phenomenon: that, although it consists of organized sounds, the very organization of those sounds corresponds to the organization of society at a particular time. The secularization of music, starting with the troubadours and the great heretical movements – i.e., with the incipient opposition of the knights and burghers – spread gradually to sacred music itself, so that even religious music eventually became worldly. Old church music had been inseparably tied to the church; it received its 'content' from the liturgy and served, with severe and impersonal magnificence, not the listener's pleasure but his subjugation, forcing him to identify himself, kneeling, with the divine cause. But consider the *Stabat Mater* of Pergolesi: its graceful, pleasurable worldliness is all the more striking by contrast to earlier church music; this work is no longer tied to the church; it can be performed in any hall and has almost assumed the character of an opera. The 'content' is still given by the religious text, but now the music begins to play with the text, to transpose its meaning into the human and subjective, to stimulate many varied associations. Still later, the great oratorios of Bach and Handel – emigrants, and not by chance, from the church to the concert hall – represent a tremendous humanization of religious content, and, instead of swamping the hearer's subjectivity, strengthen and confirm it. What a difference between the worldly amiability of a Haydn mass and the crushing, inexorable power of the old church music! The secularization of sacred music is finally completed in Beethoven's *Missa Solemnis*, too vast for any church. To perform this work in a church would be against reason; its expressive subjectivity makes nonsense of the rigid framework of any religious rite. There is not the merest breath of incense in this work, not the faintest cloud of the beyond; in defiance of the very text it uses, it does not speak of God, of sinfulness, or contrition, of genuflection or humility, but only of man standing upright and proclaiming his pain and joy, his greatness and his triumph. The 'content' of this mass is not God but man in a revolutionary age.

The progressive secularization of music can also be seen in changing musical forms. Broadly speaking, polyphony may be defined as the music of a feudal age, of an order in which every voice has its apportioned place, one following the other without competition, in strict contrapuntal regularity; while homophony is the music of the rising bourgeoisie, of an age of social change in which first the principle of competition (the Mannheim School) and later that of the class struggle demanded that music should express a growing antagonism between themes. The character of music was now no longer shaped by a single theme polyphonically treated, but by a struggle between themes, by hitherto unknown tensions and contrasts, by expressiveness and sensibility. Music was no longer addressed to a homogeneous community but to a heterogeneous 'audience.' This did not happen all at once but ripened in the lap of the old music, just as the bourgeoisie had ripened in the lap of the old feudal system. The principle of harmony crept into the still existing polyphony, so that – for instance – Bach still appears to obey the law of polyphony, whereas in fact he was the first great exponent of harmony. Indeed it might be said that wherever harmony and expressiveness make an appearance in music, the bourgeoisie is knocking at the gate, sublimating mercantile competition in the competition of musical themes.

The secularization of music meant domination by the bourgeoisie; it was as though the merchant had displaced the priest. Music was no longer the expression of a stable religious order but of secular conflicts. The symphony developed out of monothematic Baroque music as a new form of contradiction; the unity of earlier epochs gave place to competition, to struggle between contrasts. A revolutionary element had penetrated music.

The new content was very clearly present in some works, but remained ambiguous and indistinct in many others, expressing itself rather as a general attitude, as one or another of the tendencies of its time, as an underlying mood, sometimes social, at other times individual (confident humanism, heroic optimism, disillusionment, loneliness, melancholy, etc.), as wilful subjectivity in the mastering of a formal task. One of the distinguishing features of this secularized music was that it addressed itself more and more to the connoisseur, in contrast to sacred music which presupposed, not the educated music-lover, but a multitude of believers eager for religious rather than aesthetic satisfaction. At first glance this would seem inconsistent with the nature of a music rooted in the real world of men, often incorporating popular dances and folk songs. This popular element (which we are sometimes apt to over-estimate) and the wealth of automatic associations that

come to the listener's aid, together with the expressiveness and
sensibility of the new music, made it possible even for works with
a formal structure too complex to be grasped by an untrained ear
to exercise a direct effect on large audiences. For example, the
last movement of the *Eroica*, with its direct appeal to the
plebeian masses, is one of Beethoven's formally most difficult
works. The way in which the baroque form of the *passacaglia*
is here incorporated into a symphony that bursts the confines of
Baroque tradition must inevitably escape the understanding of
an average audience; only the connoisseur can appreciate it.
Hegel was the first to note this peculiarity of the instrumental
music of his times.

The ordinary person [he wrote] likes best in music an expression of
emotion and ideas that is at once intelligible, that whereof the
content is obvious; his predilection is consequently for music under
the mode of an accompaniment. The connoisseur, on the contrary,
who is able to follow the relation of musical sounds and instruments
as composition, enjoys the artistic result of harmonious modulation,
and its interwoven melodies and transitions, on its own merits. . . .
The composer is able, it is true, on his part to associate with his work
a definite significance, a content of specific ideas and emotions, which
are expressed articulately in movement that excludes all else; conversely he can, in complete indifference to such a scheme, devote
himself to musical structure simply. . . . More penetration of character may be assumed where the composer even in instrumental
music is equally attentive to both aspects of composition: in other
words, the expression of a content, if necessarily less defined than
in our previous mode, no less than its musical structure, by which
means it will be in his power at one time to emphasize the melody,
at another the depth and colour of the harmony, or finally to fuse
each with the other.

The abstract and formal character of music that was no
longer sacred, no longer bound up with religion, demanded
virtuosity, originality, and subtle invention. There were
dangers inherent in this. Much instrumental music has become
exclusive, capable of enjoyment by the connoisseur only. As a
result, two kinds of music have developed: 'highbrow' music
alienated from the people and 'lowbrow' entertainment music,

generally of little value. Although the gap between the two has become a serious problem in the late bourgeois world, this development should not be sociologically over-simplified. We must not forget that many important works by Bach, Mozart, Beethoven, and Brahms were never 'popular' and are enjoyed to this day by only a small section of society. (To enlarge this section is one of the aims of systematic musical education.) In order to do justice to musical experimentation and to recognize its artistic necessity, we must bear in mind two things. A composer, as much as any other artist, ultimately serves a *social* need. But there is also his own individual need as an artist to take pleasure in what he is doing. In sacred music this pleasure was excluded or forced to conceal and disguise itself; in secular music, released from bondage, it insists upon its rights. When Hegel says that the composer may be concerned, quite apart from the content, 'with the purely musical structure of his work and with the wit and grace of such architecture', he recognizes the sheer pleasure that any artist takes in exploiting the complex and manifold possibilities of his art. (As an example, I have already quoted the last movement of the *Eroica*, where Beethoven, putting aside the emotionally charged, revolutionary character of the symphony, plays with formal possibilities and abandons himself to the pleasure of exercising his supreme artistic skill.)

The apparently carefree pleasure that the artist finds in mastering intensely difficult problems of form contains a deeply serious moral element which we must not overlook when we speak of the nature and essence of art. In mathematics, it is possible to solve a problem and yet to dismiss the solution as unsatisfactory if it has been clumsily achieved. Mathematicians speak of 'elegant' solutions and formulas, elegant because they are not only correct but also aesthetically pleasing by their formal perfection. The same is true, to the highest degree, of art: an 'elegant' solution of formal difficulties is in itself a major quality. The form of a work of art is more than just a suitable vehicle for its content: it is an original, 'elegant' solution of difficulties arising not only out of the content but also out of the artist's sheer pleasure in mastering them. Form is always a kind of triumph because it is the solution of a problem. Thus an aesthetic quality is transformed into a moral one. A composer cannot work for the layman alone, for this would lead to impoverishment and stagnation, above all in instrumental music. He must always tackle formal problems whose solutions can only be appreciated by specially schooled listeners, who must, however, in order to achieve maximum enjoyment, pay as much attention to the content – however elusive – as to the formal structure of the music. Subtle formal discoveries and solutions may escape the layman, indeed they may strike him as strange and disagreeable: yet they are essential for the richness of the work and for the development of music (or any other art). And it is precisely this formal inventiveness, this very serious 'playing' with means of expression, that may sometimes constitute the quality of a work of art. In his essay on *How to Make Poetry*, Mayakovsky refers to a 'rhymed street song' which he wrote for Red Army men defending Petrograd, and remarks: 'The novelty that justifies the making of this song is in the rhyme . . . [he then quotes a particular rhyme]. This novelty makes the whole thing necessary, poetic, typical.' We may assume that the Red Army men can scarcely have been aware of this formal innovation: and yet the great poet of the proletarian revolution tells us that it was precisely this that made his Red Army song into poetry and gave it a quality of its own. The same is still more true of music, where form and content interpenetrate each other in so many ways that they can hardly be separated.

Because the formal element in music is so strong, 'formalism' is liable to occur. But just because music is the most formal and most abstract of the arts, we must beware of dismissing particular works or trends as 'formalist' without sufficient grounds: otherwise we may find ourselves detecting traces of formalism in polyphonic Baroque music, in Bach's piano works, and even in some works by Mozart, Beethoven, and Brahms. I believe that the following may, in good conscience, be defined as formalism in music:

First: self-complacent virtuosity which exists for its own sake, that is to say virtuosity not concerned with solving structural problems in music but only with technical brilliance, with bravura, with stunning the audience. Formalistic virtuosity of this kind, far from setting itself at a distance from the listener, is actually dependent on his admiration; hence the charge against it is not artistic arrogance but applause-seeking vanity.

Second: crass imitation, slavish repetition of old canons, cloying harmony and sweetness in a world of dissonances, romantic pastoral tunes designed to muffle the roar of jet bombers overhead. This kind of 'modern' music lives idly on interest from the capital of the European musical tradition. Its formalism is the formalism of lies: a banquet of bankrupts, opened by the 'Marseillaise' (played not as a parody by Offenbach but to make the gluttons rise to their feet for an instant and pay homage to a debased and dishonoured past). This kind of music lives off a content that has been lost, off forms that have no strength or meaning left, off the emptiness of what had once been full of life and vigour. It goes on serving up its pretty airs as if nothing of significance had happened in the last hundred years, as if the composer's function in the mid twentieth century is to keep chewing over the classical and romantic music of the bourgeoisie. It was great music once: to imitate it under changed conditions, instead of learning from it in a creative way, is formalism of the dullest and most wretched kind.

Third: the forcible removal of all warmth and feeling. Necessary as it was after a period of hysterical effusiveness in music to carry out a cold-water cure, to get rid, as it were, of the surplus fat of music so as to reintroduce lost discipline and dignity, we cannot accept the principle that music has nothing to do with the expression of feeling but is only the embodiment of pure form. Even if we assume that it is possible, by eliminating all feeling, to capture the 'music of the cosmos', the language of stars and crystals, atoms and electrons, the principle would still be unconvincing. Let us not exclude the possibility that the laws of inorganic matter can be expressed in musical form; by no means let us reject experiments in this direction. But neither should we be prepared to abandon the *human* character of music as an expression of feelings, sensations, and ideas. Sacred music, which recognized no subjectivism and claimed a socially conditioned 'objectivity', was splendid music: but the deep-frozen, intellectualized pseudo-religious quality of some modern music, its artificial, laboured, contrived return to a 'sacred' element profoundly incompatible with the content of our age, can only be interpreted as a symptom of extreme alienation. This is conscious, demonstrative formalism, trying to deceive us in vain with a hidden 'cosmic' content.

In trying to explain, very briefly, the problem of form and content in music, I am well aware of the inadequacy of my attempts. Simplification is extremely dangerous here. The content of music is manifold and, unlike that of the other arts, extremely elusive. But just because this is so, the future development of music will be determined by the degree to which it expresses a new attitude, a new sense of life, a new intelligence, a new collective: the attitude, the sense of life, the intelligence, and the collective of the working class.

CHAPTER FIVE

THE LOSS AND DISCOVERY OF REALITY

LUDWIG TIECK, the German Romantic, first spoke of the 'loss of reality' in the preface to his edition of Heinrich von Kleist's works. This 'loss of reality', only dimly sensed in the Romantic age, has grown into a central problem in the highly industrialized late capitalist world.

The industrialized, commercialized capitalist world has become an *outside world* of impenetrable material connexions and relationships. The man living in the midst of that world is alienated from it and from himself. Modern art and literature are often reproached with 'destroying reality'. Such tendencies exist; but really it is not the writers or the painters who have abolished reality. A reality belonging to the day before yesterday, a reality that long ago became its own ghost, is being conserved in a rigid framework of phrases, prejudices, and hypocrisy. The end-product of a vast machinery of research, investigations, analyses, statistics, conferences, reports, and headlines is the comic strip, the embodiment of an illusory world of Everyman and No-man. Illusion displaces contradiction. The outcome of a multitude of 'points of view' is a hideous uniformity of minds. The answer precedes the question. A few dozen clichés, some of which were once reflections of reality, are served up again and again. Today they are as much like reality as an oil king is like a holy picture.

'I am convinced,' wrote the Austrian satirist Karl Kraus, 'that happenings no longer happen; instead, the clichés operate spontaneously.' Things have become too much for people, the means too much for the ends, the tools too much for their producers.

Once again [Karl Kraus wrote about the Press] a tool has got out of our control. We have set the man who is meant to report the fire – a man who should surely play the most subordinate part in the whole

State – above the State, above the fire and the burning house, above fact and above our imagination.

That was written half a century ago. Since then the process of 'destroying reality' has made alarming advances.

Many of the sincerest and most gifted artists and writers in the capitalist world are conscious of this loss of reality. They refuse to be led astray by outdated formulas and catchpenny phrases. They refuse to accept the system forced upon them by the ruling 'public opinion' as reality; they insist on seeing things 'as they are'. They detest all forms of propaganda, distrust all ideologies, they go out in search of reality beyond the illusory world of pseudo-facts, phrases, and conventions. They are determined to speak only of what they can see, hear, touch, or directly perceive. They cling to the smallest detail, the visible, audible, unchallengeably 'real' detail. Anything that goes beyond such details is suspect to them. Out of them they try, cautiously and without comment, to reconstruct reality. The widespread movement of neo-positivism is not wholly negative: it corresponds in part to a wish for unprejudiced sincerity.

In his fight against the fulsomeness of the late bourgeois novel and in his search for economy, purity, and lightness of form, Franz Kafka developed a narrative method whereby tiny details are linked together to make faint contours that hint at reality. Kafka once wrote of a woman he loved: 'Outwardly – at least sometimes – all I can see of F. are a few small details, so few that they could easily be counted. That is what makes her image so clear, pure, spontaneous, defined yet airy at the same time.' That is the principle according to which he drew his characters and situations.

This principle of allowing the status of reality only to the 'small true fact, the true detail', as Nathalie Sarraute never tires of repeating, has been carried to an extreme in the French 'anti-novel'. Detail follows detail, two-dimensionally, without perspective, without ever going beyond the Here and Now. Consider this passage from Camus's *L'Étranger*:

In the evening Marie came to fetch me and asked whether I wanted to marry her. I said I didn't mind and we could do it if she wanted. Then she wanted to know whether I loved her. I replied, as always, that this meant nothing, but that probably I didn't love her. Why marry me then? she asked. I explained that this was of no significance and that we could marry if she wished. Anyway she was the one who was asking; all I was doing was saying yes. She then remarked that marriage was a serious thing. I answered: no. She was silent for a moment and looked at me.

This emphasized detachment and coldness are a refusal to recognize any priority among objects, feelings, or events. The consequence of such understatement is, however, that material relationships acquire exaggerated power (almost as in the Romantic 'tragedies of fate' where human destinies were governed by mysterious objects). The world is neither meaningful nor absurd, says Robbe-Grillet, it is just *there*. 'All around us and in spite of all our adjectives meant to endow them with soul and purpose, things are *there*. Their surface is clean and smooth, it is intact, but without ambiguous brilliance or transparence.'

This principle leads to a state of torpor, a series of images jerkily strung together, not a continuum but a fragmentary discontinuity: the passing moment is unreal, and only in recollection do situations freeze into reality. Nathalie Sarraute wrote of Proust that he had 'observed psychological processes from a great distance when they were already completed: frozen in tranquillity and, as it were, in the memory'. Robbe-Grillet's novel *Le Voyeur* represents the quintessence of this method: people are merely objects among objects, a murder means no more than the sale of a watch, crime no more than the screech of a seagull; an event is no more than a confusing dream or a witness's false evidence: reality without perspective, value, or measure.

In several respects, the method of the 'anti-novel' seems to be connected with the rise of cybernetics, the study of self-regulating dynamic systems. The existence of 'learning', 'thinking', self-improving machines has given encouragement to behaviourism and neo-positivism. The difference between human beings and these dialectical machines must now be formulated, the *nature* of man must now be grasped afresh, and dialectical materialism must now be expanded and made more precise. Machines which, it has been calculated by cybernetics, are possible and which, in part, have already been made, frequently behave as though they had consciousness, although in fact conscious machines cannot and do not exist. Leading cyberneticists therefore consider consciousness to be irrelevant or even fictitious; what they describe is solely the *behaviour* of a system. W. Ross Ashby, who with Norbert Wiener is the leader of modern cybernetics, writes in *Design for a Brain*:*

Throughout the book, consciousness and its related subjective elements are not used, for the simple reason that at no point have I found their introduction necessary. . . . Vivid though consciousness may be to its possessor, there is as yet no method known by which he can demonstrate his experience to another.

I do not wish to recapitulate here all the argument between neo-positivism and dialectical materialism, but only to point out how closely the 'anti-novel' corresponds to these neo-positivistic ideas and to what a striking extent the people in these novels are reduced to the 'black box' of cybernetics, where only the relations of input and output matter and never the nature and essence of man. False philosophical conclusions from the revolutionary discoveries of cybernetics have linked up with a literary method which, in certain individual instances, may be as useful as behaviourism is in science but which, as a whole, not only describes the dehumanization of man but actually invests this dehumanization with the character of inescapable finality.

The method of the 'anti-novel' does not regain lost reality. In place of empty phrases and prefabricated conventional associations it puts forward details drained of all meaning and entirely disconnected sensory impressions. In rejecting the pseudo-facts of newspaper headlines, this literature has discarded facts altogether. All that is concrete dissolves; figures grope in a chaotic primeval fog, and there is for them no forwards nor backwards but only a timeless, directionless 'existence'. The

* Chapman & Hall, 1960.

official illusory world has been replaced by a private yet no less ghostly one. The intention is to represent uncomprehended being, the 'timeless' being of man in a timeless darkness. But 'being in itself is not yet real', wrote Hegel; 'only what has been comprehended is real'. And Marx: 'Only the comprehended world as such is reality.' *A literature which deliberately rejects comprehension lacks the decisive edge of reality.* The unreality that is its content may have come out of protest against the standardized illusory world: but in fact it is only the shadow of that world.

Some writers who also set out from the precisely observed detail nevertheless go beyond a world where everything has been frozen into an object or a fixed state. J. D. Salinger is such a writer. He too uses the behaviourist method, portraying the behaviour of people through a sequence of petty details. Here is a passage taken at random from *Franny and Zooey*:*

Ten-thirty on a Monday morning in November 1955, Zooey Glass, a young man of twenty-five, was seated in a very full bath, reading a four-year-old letter. It was an almost endless-looking letter, type-written on several pages of second-sheet yellow paper, and he was having some little trouble keeping it propped up against the two dry islands of his knees. At his right, a dampish-looking cigarette was balanced on the edge of the built-in enamel soap-catch, and evidently it was burning well enough, for every now and then he picked it off and took a drag or two, without quite having to look up from his letter. His ashes invariably fell into the tub water, either straightway or down one of the letter pages. He seemed unaware of the messiness of the arrangement. He did seem aware, though, if only just, that the heat of the water was beginning to have a dehydrating effect on him. The longer he sat reading – or re-reading – the more often and the less absently he used the back of his wrist to blot his forehead and upper lip. . . .

Yet out of such a mosaic of details, gestures, snatches of conversation, faintly outlined situations, Salinger creates a maximum of atmosphere and discovers fresh aspects of psychological and social reality. His stories are without comment and without propaganda, yet they are exciting and

* Hamish Hamilton, 1962.

gripping in an unusual way, perhaps for that very reason. In Salinger reality is newly discovered through the medium of young people sickened by the world that surrounds them and engaged, in one way and another, in a search for the meaning of life. It is this new and extraordinarily subtle form of social criticism, going far outside and beyond the behaviourism of the 'anti-novel', that makes Salinger's work so valuable and attractive. The world is seen through the eyes of children or very young people: that is why it appears, not as a conventional system to be circumscribed by ready-made phrases, but as an unexpected and shocking reality. A similar example is the film *Zazie dans le Métro* (based on Raymond Queneau's novel), where a little girl from the provinces discovers the grown-up world of Paris, the ghastly reality of a system where a toy turns into a bomb, a match can blast the ground sky-high, house-fronts collapse, and Fascist terror, murder, and fear creep out of the ruins. And when, at the end, the mother returning from a rendezvous with her lover asks the little girl how she has spent the day, Zazie replies with bitter scorn: '*J'ai vieilli.*' The positive, unforgettably beautiful counterpart to this bitter film showing a child's discovery of the capitalist world with all its fantastic antagonisms is the Soviet film *A Man Goes Towards the Sun*, in which another child discovers the world of growing socialism. These two films should be shown together all over the world. They would provide the strongest possible proof of two things: of the colossal contrast between the two worlds, seen unconventionally, without propaganda or false pathos; and of the overwhelming possibility of presenting both worlds with similar methods of modern art.

Many modern artists and writers share the belief that modern reality has nothing whatever to do with the available range of cliché images: that it is necessary to discover new situations characteristic of our time, and to build up a supply of new, powerful, unhackneyed images. Eisenstein, Mayakovsky, Chaplin, Kafka, Brecht, Joyce, O'Casey, Makarenko, Faulkner, Léger, Picasso, all those are among the outstanding researchers. I have deliberately mingled the names of socialist and non-socialist artists and writers because the rejection of clichés and the search for a new 'world picturebook' is common to them all. Where they differ is not in their method but in their perspective.

Walter Benjamin's *Theses on the Philosophy of History* includes the following passage:

There is a picture by Klee called *Angelus Novus*. It shows an angel looking as though it were recoiling from something it is staring at. Its eyes are wide open, its mouth agape, its wings outstretched. The angel of history must look like that. It has turned its face towards the past. Where we distinguish a chain of events, it sees a single catastrophe incessantly piling ruins upon ruins and hurling them down at its feet. It would surely like to stay there, awaken the dead and make the murdered ones whole again. But a storm is blowing from paradise, a storm that has caught the angel's wings and is so strong that the angel can no longer fold them. This storm drives it inexorably towards the future, to which it turns its back, whilst the heap of ruins before it grows sky-high. That storm is what we call progress.

The same angel inspired Proust and Joyce, Kafka and Eliot: the shattered fragments of the past, the past as reality, grew vast before the eyes of their creative imagination. In the film *L'Année dernière à Marienbad*, for which Robbe-Grillet wrote the script, the present is composed of masks, ghosts, and the sound of footsteps in the sand, the future is shrouded in complete darkness, and only the stony images of memory are real. The angel of Mayakovsky and Brecht is different. It has a second face, turned forward. This different 'Angelus Novus' sees not only what lies in ruins but also what is as yet incomplete, sometimes scarcely discernible, sometimes obscure, sometimes strange. This other, different angel's range of reality is not only what has already become fact but whatever is possible. The realities and the essential situations it discovers are not idyllic but they are encouraging; they are not soothing, but they show the way forward.

Kafka dreamed of an angel that suddenly turned into a dead thing, 'not a live angel but only a painted wooden figure from the bow of a ship such as you see hanging from the ceiling in sailors' taverns. Nothing further . . .'. It was a ghastly dream about all living things turning into objects. Eisenstein, in *The Battleship Potemkin*, discovered the opposite situation. When the guns that are pointed at the rebel ship unexpectedly change aim, the victory of men over the power of these lifeless things overwhelms the onlooker. The free decision of men communicates itself to objects. One of the great functions of art in an age of immense mechanical power is to show that free decision exists and that man is capable of creating the situations he wants and needs. Chaplin, too, in his grotesque parodies of everyday life, hints at this victory: not a revolutionary event like Eisenstein's but a victory all the same, the victory of man enslaved by the machine over the machine itself. Picasso, using the painter's means, showed a world blown into a million pieces, not as an expression of anonymous fate or as a cosmic event, but as *Guernica*, as human existence threatened by Fascist dictatorship. This magnificent painting does not merely represent reality in its most concentrated form: it sides with tortured humanity, writing its accusation in the light. If these were a case of so-called 'formalism', Picasso would not have called his work *Guernica* but *Explosion*, *Destruction*, *Under the Sign of the Bull*, or something of that kind. No anti-Fascist should ask, 'What is there to understand in this picture?' The question is better left to Fascists as they guiltily look away. When hundreds of genre paintings and academic historical canvases that hope to pass as realistic have long been forgotten, our great-grandchildren will recognize a chronicle of our times in the bitter, extreme realism of this tremendous work.

And then Brecht. In his work, the new situation is often the very reverse of the old, familiar one. In *The Caucasian Chalk Circle*, for instance, the judgement of Solomon that belonged to a patriarchal age is changed into a more humane one: the child is not awarded to its mother but to the woman who is truly motherly. Or the situation in *Galileo*: the man who knows yet who refuses to be a hero, the opponent of intolerant superstition who is willing to cower in the dirt in order that his work may outlive him. These portrayals of new, essential situations will increasingly create a total image of the new reality as it struggles against clichés, dogmas, phrases, the illusory world of files and pseudo-facts, prejudices, conventions, and everything officially celebrated as 'reality'.

This total image cannot be attained without the dialectical philosophy of Marxism. But non-Marxist artists and writers are also taking part in the discovery of the world in which we live and in the artistic expression of many of its aspects. Every effort to present reality without prejudice – that is to say, with all sincerity – helps us all to advance. Not that sincerity alone can represent the complex reality of our age in anything but a fragmentary way. But without it nothing can be done at all.

Art and the masses

The efforts of socialist literature and art to discover new social realities were temporarily inhibited by bureaucracy, and even today these efforts are liable to run into bureaucratic opposition from time to time. The problematic nature of the transitional stage through which we are living today has deeper causes, however, than simple bureaucratic interference. The decisive task of contemporary socialist literature and art – that of representing the new reality through the means of expression appropriate to it – is intimately linked with another contemporary problem: the entry of millions of people into cultural life.

When Goethe wrote *Faust*, ninety per cent of the inhabitants of the Grand Duchy of Weimar were illiterate. Art and literature were the privilege of a narrow élite. Industrialized society, however, needs people who are able to read and write. Knowledge, and with it the need for further knowledge, grew together with industry. 'It has always been one of the most important functions of art,' wrote Walter Benjamin, 'to create a demand for the complete satisfaction of which the hour has not yet struck.' And André Breton has written: 'A work of art has value only if tremors from the future run through it.' But apart from this anticipation of future needs by the *avant-garde*, there also exists a present need to cover lost ground, and this chiefly takes the form of a demand for entertainment. The deriving of profit from this demand is the main object of the producers and distributors of 'mass art' in the capitalist world. The immense possibilities of mechanical reproduction allow good books to be distributed on a mass scale, good pictures to be printed in large quantities, good works of music to be 'canned', and good films to be shown to millions of people. But on the other hand, the capitalist world has discovered rich possibilities of profit through the production of artistic opiates. The producer of these opiates starts with the assumption that most consumers are troglodytes whose barbarian instincts he must satisfy. And on this assumption he actually arouses those instincts, keeps them awake, and systematically stimulates them. The dream-image is commercialized: the poor girl marries the millionaire; the simple boy overcomes, through sheer brute strength, all the obstacles and opponents of a hostile, sophisticated world. The fairy-tale motif is brought up to date and mass-manufactured. And all this at a time when artists and writers are struggling against the cliché and painfully experimenting for means of reproducing a new reality!

The discrepancy is alarming: on the one hand, the necessary search for new means of expressing new realities, an awareness that 'our artistic means are worn out and exhausted; we are bored with them and we probe for new ways' (Thomas Mann); on the other hand, masses of human beings for whom even old art is something wholly new, who have yet to learn to distinguish between good and bad, whose taste must still be formed, and whose capacity to enjoy quality must still be developed. The composer Adrian Leverkühn in Thomas Mann's *Doctor Faustus* believes that all art needs to be set free 'from being alone with an educated élite, called "the public", for this élite will soon no longer exist, indeed it already no longer exists, and then art will be completely alone, alone unto death, unless it finds a way to "the people", or, to put it less romantically, to human beings'. If that happened, art would 'once more see itself as the servant of a community, a community welded together by far more than education, a community that would not *have* culture but which would perhaps *be* one . . . an art on intimate terms with mankind'.

In the Soviet Union there is an intensive striving to achieve this. In the late bourgeois world, art is regarded as a kind of hobby, a distraction, unworthy of the attention of people occupied with matters as grave as business and politics. The socialist world takes art seriously. I have discussed Yessenin, Blok, Mayakovsky, Yevtushenko, and Voznessensky with young workers in Moscow, and have admired their intelligence and understanding. New books, films, plays, and musical works are not only consumed by hundreds of thousands, by millions of people, they also stimulate them to passionate discussion. The social, educational, formative force of words and images is taken for granted. A work of art is regarded, not as an ephemeral event, but as an action with far-reaching consequences. Born of reality, it acts back upon reality. Young people will argue a whole night long over a poem. Poetry has come out into the streets. A discussion about the characters and situation in a novel stirs up decisive problems of social life and philosophy. Art and the discussion of art are a forward-thrusting part of life in the socialist world.

This 'taking art seriously', splendid as it is, has also led to various mistakes and excesses. The way from art to man – 'putting art on intimate terms with mankind' – is not the shortest distance between a Party Secretary's office and an organization. It is bound to be a long road, not a short one, leading through many and varied experiments by artists and through the large-scale, generous education of the masses. What is alarming in the capitalist world is not 'formalism', not abstract paintings or poems, not serial music or the anti-novel. The real and terrible danger lies in the highly concrete, down-to-earth, 'realistic' if you will, productions of idiotic films and comics, commodities for the promotion of stupidity, viciousness, and crime. Anti-Communism does not use 'abstract' methods. War is not prepared by subtle works of art but by a very coarse diet indeed. In the Soviet Union one finds boring plays, boring books, and boring films side by side with excellent ones, tastelessness side by side with art, sticky sentimentality side by side with passionate truthfulness; but not the corrupting, evil filth of capitalist 'pulp' art. This great difference cannot be valued too highly. The negative element in the Soviet Union – the conservative clinging to forms of expression no longer appropriate to the times – is only a problem of transition.

The first motor-cars were designed like horse-drawn carriages. But the new core – the engine – was stronger than the old shell; new forms developed out of the demands of increasing speed; technology became the midwife to a new kind of beauty. The taste of every victorious class usually starts where that of the fallen class has left off, and tends to build a new life behind an old façade. The rise of the English bourgeoisie in the eighteenth century meant that Gothic architecture suddenly became 'modern' and ruins a sought-after attraction. The bourgeois wanted to disguise his capital in fancy dress, to own a castle – more than that, the ruin of a castle – as a symbol of a noble past. In 1760 a merchant by the name of Sterling had a ruin renovated with such consummate art that 'you believed it was going to collapse over your head'. A hundred years later, the rise of the German and Austrian bourgeoisie led to similar phenomena. An architecture of triumphant hypocrisy, a pastrycook's Neo-Gothic, came into existence. Banks postured as castles, railway stations as cathedrals. Adolf Loos, one of the pioneers of modern architecture, called such ornamentation a 'crime' and saw in the pretentious stuccoed house-fronts of gloomy offices and dwellings the architectural expression of the bourgeoisie's inherent hypocrisy.

Similarly, many workers, having achieved political victory, begin by adopting the taste of the petty bourgeoisie. As a result there is at first a discrepancy between the artistic ideas of many progressive intellectuals and those of most of the working class. It can even happen that the gap between what is socially progressive and that which is modern in the arts becomes so absurdly large that the very word 'modern' becomes a term of abuse on the lips of certain officials. The younger generation gradually overcomes this curious contradiction; it wants to be not only progressive but also truly modern; it looks for a modern style of living – that is to say a style appropriate to the times – and watches out for innovations

of all kinds. A struggle between the old and the new thus
begins in the sphere of culture, and apologists of the old may
frequently invoke the 'healthy instincts of the simple man'.
I must confess that such talk makes me thoroughly uncomfort-
able; I cannot help hearing overtones of condescension in it.
Does he still exist, this much-praised 'simple' man, this
ordinary, unsophisticated reader, listener, or gallery visitor?
And if he does, is he really the highest court of appeal, the full
and many-sided personality that Communism sets out to
form? The 'simple man' belonged to primitive social conditions which produced works of art compounded of instinct,
intuition, and tradition. Such people are becoming increasingly
rare in our industrialized, town-dominated civilization. The
combination of spontaneity and custom characteristic of the
bards of feudal times has been lost; industry and the town have
had a disintegrating effect. Man in industrial society is exposed
to many different stimuli and sensations. His taste is not
tabula rasa – it has been affected by all the mass-produced
commodities that have flooded his life since childhood. His
artistic judgement is in most cases a prejudice. The Viennese
operetta would triumph over Mozart in almost any plebiscite.

The 'simple man' belongs to an illusory world of clichés. He
exists as little as 'the worker' or 'the intellectual'. Even in the
capitalist world with its commercial tendency to level out all
cultural differences, the differences are in fact infinitely greater
than simplifiers allow. The effect of inferior mass-produced
commodities is great, but spontaneous opposition is by no
means lacking. An exhibition of drawings and paintings by
Austrian railway workers was held in Vienna recently. Contrary to all expectation, only about a third of the items shown
were the familiar mixture of naturalism and false sweetness;
two-thirds showed the influence of van Gogh, Gauguin,
Cézanne, Picasso, and modern Austrian artists. It would be
quite wrong to assume that 'the workers' or 'simple people'
instinctively reject modern art; the percentage of workers who
prefer conventional art is probably no higher than that of
businessmen, company directors, or politicians.

The major task of a socialist society, where the 'art market' is no longer supplied with commodities mass-produced by capitalist speculators, is therefore twofold: to lead the public towards a proper enjoyment of art, that is to say, to arouse and stimulate their understanding; and to emphasize the social responsibility of the artist. That responsibility cannot mean that the artist accepts the dictates of the dominant taste, that he writes, paints, or composes as so-and-so decrees: but it does mean that, instead of working in a vacuum, he recognizes that he is ultimately commissioned by society. There are many cases, as Mayakovsky pointed out long ago, when this general social commission does not coincide with the explicit commission of any particular social institution. A work of art does not have to be understood and approved by everyone from the start. It is not the function of art to break down open doors but rather to open locked ones. But when the artist discovers new realities, he does not do so for himself alone; he does it also for others, for all those who want to know what sort of a world they live in, where they come from, and where they are going. He produces for a community. This fact has been lost sight of in the capitalist world, but it was taken for granted in ancient Athens and in the age of Gothic art. The desirable synthesis – freedom of the artist's personality in harmony with the collective – cannot be achieved all at once; it requires much undogmatic thought and experimentation. Every great revolution is an explosive synthesis; but disturbances in the dynamic equilibrium always occur again and again, and new syntheses have to be re-established under changing conditions. The romantic and individualistic revolt of the young Mayakovsky drew its great content from the Revolution; personal and collective experiences were merged into one. Such unity is not static and cannot be preserved, least of all by decree. But socialist art must always draw strength from this very task of re-establishing unity, so that finally, through a slow and painstaking process, all the symptoms of alienation are eradicated.

All kinds of misunderstanding are liable to arise. The demand for art in the Soviet Union and the People's Democracies cannot be fully satisfied either by enormous editions of the classics or simply by the works of outstanding socialist artists and writers. The desire for an art that simply 'entertains' is legitimate, and side by side with the more original innovators there is bound to be a large number of 'average' artists. The boundary between entertainment and serious art cannot be clearly drawn, nor is it unalterable, least of all in a society that deliberately sets out to educate the entire people towards knowledge and culture. Entertainment should not mean silliness any more than serious art should mean boredom; both the public's education and the artist's social consciousness should prevent this. A society moving towards Communism needs many books, plays, and musical works that are entertaining and easy to grasp, yet at the same time also serve to educate both emotionally and intellectually. But this need carries with it the danger of hackneyed over-simplification and crude propaganda disguised under a high moral tone. Stendhal wrote as a young man: 'Any moral intention, that is to say any self-interested intention of the artist's, kills the work of art.' No socialist artist can work without moral intention, but he should always endeavour not to allow it to become 'self-interested', not to over-simplify it in terms of propaganda, but to elevate and purify it in terms of art. This should be the motto, too, of artists producing 'entertainment', i.e. working purely for the needs of the day. In a socialist world, works of entertainment, like all other art, are addressed to mature human beings. They are entirely failing in their purpose if they patronize their public.

It would be foolish to denigrate those who produce decent, unobjectionable literary or musical works by the dozen. But it would be a much more serious error to set them up as an example to those who are trying to express new realities with new artistic means. We can understand why many socialist artists cling to old styles during difficult transitional periods; even a socialist society, whose very essence is novelty, has need of certain conservative tendencies, if only so that, in the struggle against them, the new should grow stronger and more resolute. But it is the original artists who create new styles – artists like Mayakovsky, Eisenstein, Brecht, or Eisler – and it is they who will live on in the future. Even today, and not only in the socialist but also in the capitalist world, the new proves itself more effective than imitations of the old. For although the two economic systems are fundamentally antagonistic to each other, and although the struggle and competition between them is one of the central problems of the new social reality, nevertheless many elements of modern life are common to both systems: industrialization, technology, science, large cities, speed, rhythm, many modern experiences, sensations, and stimuli. Life in a large city demands to be expressed in a different way from life in a sleepy provincial town. A skier's or motor-cyclist's experience of nature is different from a peasant's or a rambler's. The content and style of life of the modern working class and its intelligentsia are no longer directly related to the poetic methods of the last century. We see, hear, and associate differently from our ancestors. The things that shocked them in art – the Impressionists' use of colour or the dissonances of Wagner – no longer worry us in the least. The average public today is thoroughly familiar with such things and no longer thinks of them as 'modern'.

Cybernetics envisages the possibility of machines giving theoretical answers to questions concerning as yet unexplored areas of reality, these answers being beyond the powers of comprehension of the human brain. Science does not capitulate before such a staggering possibility, nor will it scornfully reject the answers supplied by such computers because the human brain cannot yet cope with them. On the contrary, cyberneticists say that it may become necessary to design 'brain amplifiers' in order to equip the brain with the means for coping with the new concepts. Science and art are two very different forms of mastering reality, and any direct comparison would be misleading. Yet it is equally true of art that it also discovers new areas of reality, making visible and audible what had been invisible and inaudible before. Artistic comprehension, too, is not a constant; it too can be expended and more finely adjusted by means of 'amplifiers'. Socialism, convinced of man's infinite capacity for development, should therefore not reject the new in any field just because it is new: instead, it should use 'amplifiers' in order to grasp what at first seems incomprehensible, and, having grasped it, submit it to close examination and analysis.

Often all the artistic means of expression discovered since the middle of the last century are lumped together and dismissed as 'decadent'. It is certainly true that the late bourgeois world is a declining world and therefore by its very nature decadent. But it is by no means homogeneous – on the contrary, it is exceedingly rich in contradictions, not only between the bourgeoisie and the working class but also within each social stratum; the struggle between the new and the old rages with particular violence among the intelligentsia. What is new is not of course *ipso facto* on the side of the working class. It is more complicated than that. On the one hand, many workers have been infected by the decadence of the bourgeoisie; on the other hand, the capitalist world is incessantly influenced by the existence of the socialist world, and this influence itself is full of contradictions in that it not only provokes anti-Communism but also stimulates intellectual inquiry. The protests of artists against the capitalist world, their direct or indirect reactions to the fact of Communism, their discovery of a highly complex reality, all give rise to new forms and means of expression in which the decay of what is old is inseparable from the fermentation of what is new. In many cases it is impossible for us to distinguish between what is useless and what may be of future value. But to dismiss all modern elements in the literature and arts of the capitalist world as 'rotten' is like Lassalle's idea, condemned by Marx, that the working class confronts a uniformly reactionary mass. Such compact uniformity does not exist in politics – still less in the arts of any period, let alone ours.

The insistence of conservative elements in the socialist world on the idealized figure of the 'simple' man as the final arbiter in all artistic matters is a retrograde tendency. It is part of the irresistible advance of socialism that the 'simple' man gradually turns into a subtle and highly differentiated man. The structure of a people can change more quickly than the minds of certain administrators. Already the dividing line between the qualified worker and the intellectual technologist is beginning to blur; the working class and the intelligentsia are beginning to overlap; the highly educated sons and daughters of the working class are acquiring a taste for intellectual adventure, for daring artistic experiment. They smile when their fathers shudder at the names of Moore, Léger, Picasso, or when they dismiss Rimbaud, Yeats, and Rilke as 'obscure', or say that twelve-tone music is the work of the devil. The younger generation in the socialist world will not be deprived of their right to know these things. Nor will they stop there. There are new Soviet films and the works of certain young writers, sculptors, and painters which justify the belief that we are about to see a flowering of Soviet art in which socialist content will be triumphantly expressed in a truly modern form.

Between rise and decline

The late bourgeois world is still capable of producing art of importance (and the existence and challenge of the socialist world, the moral and intellectual issues which it poses, are of considerable help here). But in the long-term view socialist art has the advantage over late bourgeois art. The latter, although it has much to offer, lacks one thing: a large vision of the future, a hopeful historical perspective. Despite disappointments, this vision still belongs to the socialist world. It is far more than a question of bread and space rockets, prosperity and technical perfection: it is a matter of the 'meaning of life', a meaning that is not metaphysical but humanist.

Despite all the conflicts it has undergone, socialism remains convinced of the unlimited possibilities that exist for man. The vision of the future expressed by many of the most gifted and sincere artists and writers in the late bourgeois world is negative, indeed apocalyptic. Superficial optimism cannot provide a counterweight to these gloomy views, for it is true that, for the first time in history, the suicide of the human race has become a possibility. Many years ago, one of Karl Kraus's aphorisms anticipated this: 'The modern end of the world will come about when machines become perfect and, at the same time, man's inability to function reveals itself.' Human consciousness has lagged far behind technical progress. Socialist artists and writers cannot, therefore, argue lightly against the grim vision of the future depicted in bourgeois art and literature. Even if there were life left after an atomic war, this life, the infected air of a moon landscape, would have nothing whatever to do with the vision of a socialist world.

To prevent war is therefore the duty of all reasonable men under all social systems. Those who despair of the power of reason believe the catastrophe to be unavoidable; and the pale shadow of destruction falls on their work. Against this *possibility* of the end of the world, the socialist artist sets another *possibility*, that of a rational and therefore humane world. The second possibility is not predetermined any more than the first is inescapable. The choice, as never before, lies with the individual, and Hebbel's lines are truer than ever:

> *Du hast vielleicht*
> *gerade jetzt dein Schicksal in den Händen*
> *und kannst es wenden, wie es dir gefällt.*
> *Für jeden Menschen kommt der Augenblick*
> *in dem der Lenker seines Stern ihm selbst*
> *die Zügel übergibt. . . .*

Your fate perhaps is in your hands at this very moment, and you can turn it as it please you. For every human being comes the moment when he who guides his star passes the reins into his own hands. . . .

In a world in which the concentration of power is so great and the workings of that power so obscure, many people are inclined to think that their personal decision does not matter and, therefore, they surrender to 'fate'. In such a situation, the central problem of socialist art is to portray the men behind the nameless objects and to present the possibility of man's victory over them – without grand phrases or over-insistent optimism. William Faulkner's tremendous novel *Sanctuary* – a tragedy about the impotence of human beings who, when they try to break out of their allotted social situation, are destroyed in the attempt or driven back into the past – has not yet found its socialist counterpart. Alexey Tolstoy's *Road to Calvary* deals with a corresponding theme, but it is set in the special emergency situation of a revolution. A writer tackling the same theme today would need to have, apart from a talent comparable with Faulkner's, unerring sincerity and the determination to ignore all tactical considerations, however worthy. The theory (originating in Stalin's time) which ordered the 'conflict-free' novel, which claimed the existence of non-tragic solutions to all problems that could arise in a socialist society, and which consequently demanded a happy ending to every story, has fortunately been cast aside – along with the equally false theory of increasing class differences under socialism. But there is still a tendency to sidestep the portrayal of conflicts and to substitute wish-fulfilments for reality.

The less socialist art confuses its vision of the future with idealization of the present, the more it gains in authority and conviction. The genuine despair of serious artists and writers in the late bourgeois world cannot be dismissed by being labelled 'decadent', nor by the argument that, in the grand scheme of world history, everything is really going according to plan. The apocalyptic contingency must be recognized as *conceivable*, yet shown to be *avoidable*. This does not mean that the struggle for peace must now be the exclusive theme of all socialist art. What it does mean is that the argument of 'inevitable' disaster so common in late bourgeois art must be answered by works which show how it is possible to avoid disaster; but these works must be real, they must not be trimmed to propagandist aims.

If saving peace is the one great common task – and everything suggests that it is – then socialist art should not concentrate its attention wholly on internal problems of the socialist countries, but should speak to the world at large as an essential contribution to world art. The works of Gorky, Mayakovsky, Isaak Babel, Alexey Tolstoy, Eisenstein, and Pudovkin have meant a great deal to a vast non-Socialist public; conversely, Chaplin, de Sica, Faulkner, Hemingway, Lorca, and Yeats have a large following in the Socialist countries. Though we belong to

different social systems and pursue different aims and ideas, we
live, after all, in one world. And our world needs Russian as
well as American literature, Russian as well as French and
Austrian music, Japanese as well as Italian, British, and Soviet
films. It needs the modern Mexican painters as well as Henry
Moore, Brecht as well as O'Casey, Chagall as well as Picasso.
The political struggle between the two social systems will
continue. That it should take place in peace, not war, is a
condition of the existence of us all. And that men on both sides
should not speak in a vacuum but should understand each
other's problems, aims, and desires has become one of the
greatest functions of contemporary literature and art.

The dream of the day after tomorrow

An opposite line of argument might go something like this:
'What confidence! What makes you so certain of the necessity
of art? Art is on its last legs. It has been driven out by science
and technology. When the human race can fly to the moon, is
there any real need of moonstruck poets? The aeroplane is
swifter than the gods, the car more efficient than Pegasus. The
astronaut can see what the poet merely dreamed of. Remember
Byron's Cain flying through space with Lucifer:

> 'CAIN: Oh god, or demon, or whate'er thou art,
> Is yon our earth?
> LUCIFER: Dost thou not recognize
> The dust which form'd your father?
> CAIN   Can it be?
> Yon small blue circle, swinging in far ether
> With an inferior circlet near it still,
> Which looks like that, which lit our earthly night? . . .
>   As we move
> Like sunbeams onward, it grows small and smaller
> And as it waxes little, and then less,
> Gathers a halo round it, like the light
> Which shone the roundest of the stars, when I
> Beheld them from the skirts of Paradise. . . .

'Are not Gagarin's, Titov's, or Glenn's prose reports even

more overwhelming than this vision in verse? Is art not something that belonged to the childhood and puberty of mankind? Can it not be dispensed with now that we have reached maturity?

'It is clear that capitalism is no longer capable of producing a new renaissance of the arts. But socialism? Is it conceivable that another Homer or Shakespeare, Mozart or Goethe will be born? And if he is, will society need him? Is art not an enchanting substitute, a magic invocation of reality by men and for men who cannot cope with it? Does it not presuppose a mental passivity that is prepared to accept the dream for the deed, shadow for existence, and a cloud for Juno? Within the foreseeable future we shall have perfect cybernetic machines capable of handling reality with mathematical precision. No feeling will lead them astray, no passion will tempt them into error. What use is art, what use is Helen's ghostly veil in an age of total automation, unlimited productive forces, and unlimited consumption?'

In future, machines will eventually relieve men of all mechanical labour, which will come to be regarded as unworthy of human effort. But as machines become more and more efficient and perfect, so it will become clear that *imperfection is the greatness of man*. Like cybernetic machines, man is a dynamic, self-perfecting system – but never sufficient unto himself, always open towards infinity, never capable of becoming a creature of pure reason obeying only the laws of logic. '*Quod nunc ratio est, impetus ante fuit*,' wrote Ovid. This passion, this *impetus*, this creative imperfection will always distinguish man from the machine.

'Agreed,' my invisible opponent may say. 'The perfect machine will have no urge to express its suffering, because it will not suffer; outside joy or suffering, it will carry on with solving the mysteries of reality. But even if man will never possess the absolute infallibility of the machine, why should he need art in a Communist society? You have said that the mission of art is to help us, half-men that we are, fragmentary, wretched, lonely creatures in a divided, incomprehensible, terrifying class society, towards a fuller, richer, stronger life –

to help us, in other words, to be men. But what happens when society is itself the safeguard of a truly human life? All true art has always invoked a humanity that did not yet exist. When once we have attained it, what is the use of all the Faustian magic?'

Questions of this kind are prompted by naïve hopes – or fears – that human development will one day reach a final goal: universal happiness, the fulfilment of every dream, the accomplishment of the cycle of history. But only the pre-history of mankind will have been accomplished then; man will never be condemned to the immobility of paradise, but will always continue to develop. He will always want to be more than he can be, will always revolt against the limitations of his nature, always strive to reach beyond himself, always struggle for immortality. If ever the desire to be all-knowing, all-powerful, all-embracing vanished, man would no longer be man. And so man will always need science in order to prise every possible secret and privilege out of nature. And he will always need art in order to be at home not only in his own life but in that part of reality which his imagination knows to be still unmastered.

In the first collective period of human development art was the great auxiliary weapon in the struggle against the mysterious power of nature. Art in its origins was magic, essentially one with religion and science. In the second period of development – the period of the division of labour, of class distinction, and the beginning of every kind of social conflict – art became the chief means of understanding the nature of these conflicts, of imagining a changed reality by recognizing existing reality for what it was, of overcoming the individual's isolation by pro-viding a bridge to what all men shared. In the late bourgeois world of today, when the class struggle has become more intense, art tends to be divorced from social ideas, to drive the individual still further into his desperate alienation, to encour-age an impotent egoism, and to turn reality into a false myth surrounded by the magic rites of a bogus cult. And in the Socialist world today art tends to be subordinated to specific social requirements and to be used as a simple means of enlightenment and propaganda. But when the third, Communist, period is reached – when the individual and the collective are no longer in conflict, when classless society exists in an age of abundance – the essential function of art will consist in neither magic nor social enlightenment.

We can only dimly imagine such an art, and our visions of it may well be mistaken. Marxism rejects any ideal Utopia with all the severity of science; yet Utopia is its golden background. And so we may be allowed, as we dream of the future, to evoke a picture of a world where human beings, no longer exhausted by labour, no longer weighed down by today's cares and tomorrow's duties, have time and leisure to be 'on intimate terms' with art.

We need not fear that a prosperous and highly differentiated society will mean an impoverishment of the arts. The differentiation will be between personalities, not classes; between individuals, not social masks. Everything will encourage the interplay of the intimate and the universal, the fanciful and the problematic, reason and passion. Highly developed means of art reproduction will allow the 'public' to become individuals, each becoming familiar with art in his own home. At the same time public festivals and competitions of all kinds will encourage direct participation. It may well happen that apart from the novel, whose essential function is to analyse and criticize society, there will be a revival of the epic, for the epic is the literary form that affirms social reality. Tragedy will doubtless continue to exist, because the development of any society – even a classless one – is inconceivable without contradiction and conflict, and perhaps because man's dark desire for blood and death is ineradicable. Our own appetite today for the grotesque and scurrilous in art may not only be the consequence of the juxtaposition of the terrible and the comic in modern life; it may also be the forecast of a rebirth of comedy. Hitherto comedy has generally meant criticism – destructive laughter, or, as Marx put it, 'a merry farewell to the past'; in a distant future it may reflect the life of sovereign man, his freedom, gaiety, and spirit.

Perhaps it is more than personal taste that links the names of

Homer, Aristophanes, Villon, Giotto, Leonardo, Cervantes, Shakespeare, Brueghel, Goethe, Stendhal, Pushkin, Keller, Brecht, Picasso, and above all Mozart, always and always Mozart. The differences between these artists only emphasize one thing they all have in common: a triumphant rejection of all that is heavy, puritan, oppressive. In many of their works reality has been distilled by the imagination to such a point that it seems altogether weightless: the gravity of things vanishes, suspended between nothingness and infinity. Terror is not toned down, causes for fear are not denied, but everything is touched with grace and nothing is a stranger to gaiety. On the island of Caliban and Ariel, Prospero transforms cruelty, darkness, and blood into comedy, into clouds suffused with light. The magic of art blends *seeming* into *being* and beauty into nothingness.

> . . . These our actors
> As I foretold you, were all spirits, and
> Are melted into air, into thin air:
> And, like the baseless fabric of this vision,
> The cloud-capp'd towers, the gorgeous palaces,
> The solemn temples, the great globe itself,
> Yea, all which it inherit, shall dissolve,
> And, like this insubstantial pageant faded,
> Leave not a rack behind. We are such stuff
> As dreams are made on. . . .

Prospero's wand also wields a tragic power:

> . . . the strong-based promontory
> Have I made shake, and by the spurs pluck'd up
> The pine and cedar: graves at my command
> Have waked their sleepers, oped, and let 'em forth
> By my so potent art. But this rough magic
> I here abjure. . . .

Prospero's magic finally transforms itself into 'heavenly music', into 'airy charm' and gaiety full of wisdom. Leonardo's smile is of the same essence; so is the bright sky against which Stendhal lightly draws outlines of passion, failure, and death; so too is the blend of enlightenment and romanticism, reason and jest in Brecht. And Mozart is the epitome of such art, Mozart in whose music tension is so delicately adjusted that the slightest variation produces a *non plus ultra* of delight. The magic wand that Prospero dropped is passed on from generation to generation. The abundance of life (not only of consumer goods!) promised by Communism will affirm, gladly, without sadness, that 'we are such stuff as dreams are made on'.

The Romantic yearning for the 'universal' work of art – itself the expression of a deeper longing for man's unity with the world and with himself – may find fulfilment (in contrast to Wagner's theories) in a new kind of comedy that will make use of all the possibilities of the theatre and create a synthesis of word and image, dance and music, logic and harlequinade, sensuality and reason. Martyrdom and sacrifice, the smell of blood and incense, the tying of art to religion, all this belongs to the prehistory of mankind. And it may be that comedy will be the most apt expression of man's liberation.

In one of his dialogues entitled *On Stupidity in Art*, Hanns Eisler writes: 'The whine of the disappointed petty bourgeois, of the hard-done-by shopwalker – *that* exists in music, too. And in music under capitalism it seems to be the typical characteristic.' We can expect that music in a Communist future will free itself of all romantic whimpering and smug silliness, all hysteria and all ham-handed propaganda: that it will presuppose listeners who are neither nervously over-stimulated nor sentimentally flabby; that its effect will be to refresh rather than to stun, to illuminate the mind instead of dimming it – and that, although it will use many new means of expression and never try to imitate the past, it will nevertheless have something of Mozart's serene richness and Mozart's wise audacity.

The function of painting and sculpture will no longer be to fill museums. There will be patrons, both public and private; and halls, squares, stadiums, swimming pools, universities, airports, theatres, and blocks of flats will each have sculptures and paintings to fit their character. The visual arts will probably not conform to a uniform style as they did in previous periods of class and imperial domination: the idea of a uniform style being the distinguishing feature of a culture may well prove to be old-fashioned. It is more likely that a wide variety of styles will be the new characteristic of a culture and age in which nations will merge into one, new syntheses will destroy all that is parochial and static, and no centre, either of class or nation, will predominate. In a classless society we are likely to find a *multiplicity of styles*.

Man, being mortal and therefore imperfect, will always find himself part of, and yet struggling with, the infinite reality that surrounds him. Again and again he must face the contradiction of being a limited 'I' and at the same time part of the whole. Mystics have striven towards another state where man would be 'beside himself' and at one with a totality mysteriously called God. We are not mystics and we do not yearn for that paradoxical state where man, by maximum concentration upon himself, succeeds in blotting out that very self; where, by totally denying reality, he hopes to lose himself in the reality he destroys and so achieve communion with an infinity drained of life. Our aim is not unconsciousness but the highest form of consciousness. But even the highest attainable consciousness of the individual will not be able to reproduce the totality in the 'I' – will not be able to make one man encompass the whole human race. And so, just as language represents the accumulation of the collective experience of millennia in every individual, just as science equips every individual with the knowledge acquired by the human race as a whole, so the permanent function of art is to re-create *as every individual's experience* the fulness of *all that he is not*, the fulness of humanity at large. And it is the magic of art that by this process of re-creation it shows that reality can be transformed, mastered, turned into play.

All art has to do with this identification, with this infinite capacity of man for metamorphosis so that, like Proteus, he can assume any form and lead a thousand lives without being crushed by the multiplicity of his experience. Balzac used to imitate the gait and movements of people walking ahead of him in the street in order to absorb them, even as unknown strangers, into his own being. He was so obsessed with the characters in his novels that they were more real to him than the reality surrounding him. Those of us who simply enjoy art do not often run such a risk; but our limited 'I' is also marvellously enlarged by the experience of a work of art; a process of identification takes place within us, and we can feel, almost effortlessly, that we are not only witnesses but even fellow-creators of those works that grip us without permanently tying us down. And so it is a little true to say that what art offers us is a substitute for life. But let us try to realize how much the unsatisfied man of today, identifying his sad ego with princes, tough gangsters, and irresistible lovers, differs from the free and self-aware man of a future society. This man will no longer need primitive mass-produced ideals but, because his life will be full of content, will strive for a content that is grander and richer still. Art as the means of man's identification with his fellow-men, nature, and the world, as his means of feeling and living together with everything that is and will be, is bound to grow as man himself grows in stature. The process of identification, which originally covered only a small range of beings and natural phenomena, has already extended beyond recognition, and will eventually unite man with the whole human race, the whole world.

In his novel *Wilhelm Meister* Goethe created the marvellous and enigmatic character of Makarie, the strange woman who identifies herself with the solar system and whose magic unity with the universe is watched and verified by a matter-of-fact astronomer. Goethe wrote:

Makarie stood in a relationship to our solar system that one hardly dares to name. She does not merely contemplate and cherish it in her mind, her soul, her imagination – no, she is, as it were, a very part of it; she believes herself to be drawn along in those heavenly cycles, but in a very special way; since her childhood she has been travelling round the sun, and more precisely, as we have now discovered, in a spiral, moving further and further away from the centre and circling towards the outer regions. . . .

This property of hers, glorious though it is, was nevertheless imposed upon her from her earliest years as a heavy task. . . . The superabundance of this condition was in some degree mitigated by the fact that she, too, seemed to have her night and day, for when her inner light was dimmed she strove most faithfully to fulfil her outward duties, but when the inner light blazed afresh, she yielded to a blissful rest.

This curious description, reminiscent of the reports of certain mystics, expresses Goethe's pantheism. Makarie is a symbol for the world unity of creative man, and the astronomer at her side is a personification of science. True, the 'super-abundance of her condition' lacks a social element, that of the creative human being's unity not only with the natural world but also with the rest of mankind. Such 'superabundance' in society as we have known it until now has been the lot and the heavy burden of only very few men and women; but in a truly human society the springs of creative power will gush forth in many, many more; the artist's experience will no longer be a privilege but the normal gift of free and active man; we shall achieve, as it were, *social genius*.

Man, who became man through work, who stepped out of the animal kingdom as transformer of the natural into the artificial, who became therefore the magician, man the creator of social reality, will always stay the great magician, will always be Prometheus bringing fire from heaven to earth, will always be Orpheus enthralling nature with his music. Not until humanity itself dies will art die.

INDEX

MORE ABOUT PENGUINS
AND PELICANS

Penguinews, which appears every month, contains details of all the new books issued by Penguins as they are published. From time to time it is supplemented by *Penguins in Print,* which is our complete list of almost 5,000 titles.

A specimen copy of *Penguinews* will be sent to you free on request. Please write to Dept EP, Penguin Books Ltd, Harmondsworth, Middlesex, for your copy.

In the U.S.A.: For a complete list of books available from Penguins in the United States write to Dept CS, Penguin Books, 625 Madison Avenue, New York, New York 10022.

In Canada: For a complete list of books available from Penguins in Canada write to Penguin Books Canada Ltd, 2801 John Street, Markham, Ontario L3R 1B4.

PEREGRINE BOOKS

GEOMETRY AND THE LIBERAL ARTS
Dan Pedoe

For an architect like Vitruvius and artists like Leonardo and Dürer the fascination of geometry lay in its contribution to solving problems of order, proportion and perspective. With more recent excitement over the 'new mathematics' we have tended to neglect geometry's lasting appeal to artists, scientists and philosophers; but in this book Professor Pedoe, taking these three great practitioners as his principal examples, redresses the balance and traces the effect that geometry has had on artistic achievement.

After a refreshing look at Euclid's *Elements* (still the inspiration of modern geometry) he guides the reader through the discoveries stimulated by the theory of perspective and discusses form in architecture, projective geometry, and mathematical curves as well as the concept of space.

Professor Pedoe, whose infectious enthusiasm dominates a fascinating and informative book, also includes suggestions for practical and theoretical exercises in construction, 'curve-stitching' and making geometrical models.

PEREGRINE BOOKS

ASTRAEA

Frances A. Yates

'Frances Yates . . . is that rare thing, a truly thrilling scholar' – Michael Ratcliffe in *The Times*

With her work on Giordano Bruno, the Rosicrucians, the Art of Memory and the Elizabethan theatre, Frances Yates has astonished and delighted laymen and scholars alike. Now she turns her attention to the imagery of imperial promise which surrounded European monarchy in the sixteenth century. The accession of Charles V, with his vast dominions in both Old and New Worlds, was the occasion for a renewal of the myth of Empire in the West. The theme was echoed in the glorification of Elizabeth I and the magnificent pageants and ballets of the declining Valois in France.

In these pages, Sir Philip Sidney and Edmund Spenser mingle with Ronsard, Erasmus and Ramon Lull, John Foxe with Giordano Bruno, and Bishop Jewel with Dante and Ariosto. Frances Yates's exquisite scholarship has illuminated our understanding of the renaissance monarchies as they struggled with the dark undertow of reformation and counter-reformation.

'Miss Yates's exactness of touch, of re-experience from within, are admirable' – George Steiner in the *Sunday Times*

'Dr Yates is among our greatest discoverers. Where lesser historians are grappling with mundane matters, she soars above. This book, like all her others, is a triumph of intellect and imagination' – Henry Kamen in the *Tablet*

PEREGRINE BOOKS

ART AND ITS OBJECTS

Richard Wollheim

'To say that it is the best modern book on philosophical aesthetics is fainter praise than it deserves. In about 50,000 words it
covers a wide range of problems with great verve and originality. Professor Wollheim is a highly sophisticated man, as is
shown by the vast range of his allusions to works of art of all
kinds, by the mannered but engaging elegance of his style and by
the authority with which he handles a large number of complex
disciplines that overlap marginally in the field of his interest – the
kind of authority that consorts with high lucidity and the brisk
exclusion of inessentials. He has never written anything better,
nor, on this subject, has anyone else' – Anthony Quinton in the
Listener

'This excellent book will certainly be compulsory reading for
students of aesthetics for many years' – Peter Jones in the *British
Journal of Aesthetics*

PEREGRINE BOOKS

FICTIONS

Michel Zéraffa

'The novel is no more the work of imagination than it is a reflection of reality: its essence, its necessary quality lies in the connection between the real and the imaginary'

In this absorbing study of literary and social theory Michel Zéraffa examines the relationship between the novel as it delineates the author's view of society and as a subjective work of art. Drawing examples from the entire spectrum of Western literature, from Cervantes to Robbe-Grillet, he shows that while the novel possesses its own integral aesthetic logic, this logic is always congruent with the logic of society. Indeed, the social and historical dimension is always present, even in the work of such anti-traditional 'anti-social' writers as Virginia Woolf and Samuel Beckett. Zéraffa believes that the 'sociology of the novel should enable the history of a society to be read not *in* its literature but *through* its literature'. In this he provides a valuable counterweight to the Marxist strictures on the direction that the novel has taken in the West – into 'the luxury hotel of the absurd' – a direction which he considers both inevitable and authentic.